COMPLEX
Derivatives

COMPLEX
Derivatives

Understanding and
Managing the Risks of
**Exotic Options,
Complex Swaps,
Warrants
and Other
Synthetic Derivatives**

ERIK BANKS

PROBUS PUBLISHING COMPANY
Chicago, Illinois
Cambridge, England

First published in the United Kingdom by MACMILLAN PUBLISHERS LTD, 1993
Distributed by Globe book Services Ltd
Brunel Road, Houndmills
Basingstoke, Hants RG21 2XS, England

This publication is designed to provide accurate and authoritative information in regard to the subject matter covered. It is sold with the understanding that the author and the publisher are not engaged in rendering legal, accounting, or other professional service.

ISBN 1-55738-550-5

Typeset and printed in Great Britain

1 2 3 4 5 6 7 8 9 0

A catalogue record for this book is available from The British Library.

Probus books are available at quantity discounts when purchased for business, educational, or sales promotional use. For more information, please call the Director, Corporate/Institutional Sales at (800) 998-4644, or write:

Director, Corporate/Institutional Sales
Probus Publishing Company
1925 N. Clybourn Avenue
Chicago, IL 60614

Contents

Acknowledgements

I would like to thank the following individuals for their valuable contributions to various aspects of the text: William Lyman, Frederic Salomon, Sheila Kerins and Dr Robert Banks. Their enormous assistance during key moments in the researching, writing and editing of this text made the project flow very smoothly. I would also like to extend thanks to the excellent publishing and editing staffs at The Macmillan Press and Probus Publishing for once again helping me complete the project in a timely and efficient manner. I would particularly like to thank Andrea Hartill at Macmillan for being so supportive of these projects from the very beginning. And, of course, my great thanks, always, to Milena.

E.B.
Tokyo, Japan
August 1993

PART I

DERIVATIVES AND RISK

1: Issues in the Derivatives Market

'We've spoken with the client and we're ready to sell him a 2-year Asian-exercise 10 per cent out-of-the-money put spread collar on the Hang Seng with an embedded quanto; he'll pay us premium over time, 12-month Libor plus 50 annually.' Derivatives salesman in conversation with his sales manager.

'I do not for one moment wish to suggest that you have got it all wrong. What I do ask is, are you quite sure you have got it all right?' R Farrant, Deputy Head of Banking Supervision, Bank of England, March 1992, in an address to participants at International Swap Dealers Association (ISDA) conference.

INTRODUCTION

During the 1980s the financial markets were witness to a host of new financial instruments, products and strategies. These products were created to meet specific financial needs and to obtain certain financial results, and most are still serving their purpose in the financial markets of the 1990s. To most players, whether issuers or investors (those who ultimately benefit in some fashion from a given product) or 'originators' (the large investment and commercial banks which create and package the products), the financial instruments of the 1980s are relatively commonplace in today's business. Interest rate and currency swaps, forward rate agreements, over-the-counter options (on Treasuries, mortgage-backed securities, foreign exchange), high-yield bonds, asset-backed commercial paper and medium term notes, to name but a few, are employed by small and large corporations, investors, and financial intermediaries on a continuing basis.

As a result of widespread acceptance and active participation, many of these instruments have been 'commoditized'; that is, they can be created quickly in standard form by a given trading desk for a particular client, without the need for extensive negotiation or complex documentation. In addition, they tend to carry narrower profit spreads (as a result of extreme competition for standard structures) and can often be purchased or sold in an active secondary market. Many financial institutions rely on such 'commoditized' products for a stream of regular, albeit declining, profits.

Being ever-vigilant to both the requirements of customers and the need for new sources of revenue and profitability, major financial institutions with strong capabilities in the above products have been very quick in the 1990s to create a series of new instruments and strategies designed to provide additional (or tailor-made) types of risk protection or investment opportunity.

Many of these products have their foundation in the basic instruments mentioned above; in certain cases they represent 'derivatives' of now standard products like interest rate and currency swaps. Leveraged swaps, inverse floater swaps, differential swaps, and index principal swaps are all examples of derivatives on the standard swap structure. These, and other swap instruments, are discussed in Part IV of this book.

In certain other cases, the products are entirely new to the markets. Though they may parallel certain concepts found in existing instruments such as swaps, these products tend to be unique in most other aspects, primarily because they allow for very specific results to be attained in markets which have not previously been 'tapped'. Many of the equity derivative swap and exotic option structures discussed in Part III form this cadre of new products.

In addition to creating new products to meet new or specific needs (whether by adapting existing ones or starting anew), many financial institutions have been active in recent years in recommending alternative risk management and/or profit-making strategies which rely on use of over-the-counter (OTC) options, in linked combinations which yield very specific results: unlimited profit opportunities with unlimited downside risk; limited profit opportunities with limited downside risk; effective risk hedging with potential upside profit; and so on. Put and call spreads, straddles and strangles are all examples of such strategies. These and other option strategies are covered at length in Part II.

Regardless of whether one refers to new products, derivatives of existing products or the use of products in particular combinations, there is one clear commonality among all: such products and strategies have risks to the financial institution and the ultimate user which must be well understood prior to employing them in financial operations. Failure to understand the risks effectively may result in detrimental consequences to the originator and/or the 'end user', particularly if there is outright financial failure involved (with potentially large systemic difficulties should a major financial institution collapse, which is a prime concern of the major regulators). The current debate between many derivatives professionals and the regulatory authorities with oversight of institutions active in these instruments is explored in greater detail later in this chapter. Sample quotations from recent press articles are cited which indicate concern over the nature, type and magnitude of risks encountered when dealing with these products and strategies. Since failure accurately to identify and measure risks encountered when dealing with derivative products can lead financial institutions erroneously to attribute risk to a given transaction (which may ultimately lead to an unwise credit decision), there is a strong need to ensure that some framework exists by which such instruments can be examined and their risks analysed.

Although the number and variation of derivative products is very wide, and is growing at a very quick pace, it is possible for purposes of this discussion to encapsulate the major categories of derivatives in Figure 1.1.

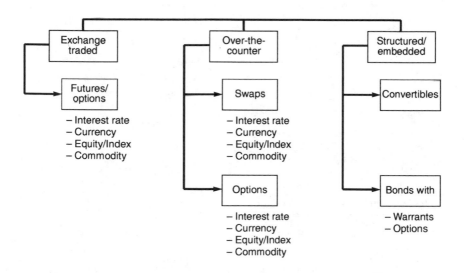

Figure 1.1   The derivatives world

All derivatives are important, but this text will focus almost exclusively on the centre category, 'over-the-counter' (OTC) derivatives. The primary reason for this focus is because the OTC market has witnessed most of the growth and innovation in the derivatives sector in recent years. In addition, it is the market where credit risk issues (i.e. the risk of credit loss should a counterparty fail to perform) are at the forefront. We shall discuss this topic at length throughout this book. When dealing with exchange-listed and traded futures and options, participants regularly post initial and/or variation margins and deal through clearing houses to mitigate the effects of credit risk. This does not imply that exchange-traded products are free from risk; ineffective use of these markets and instruments, particularly in terms of risk management and control, can lead to losses. However, credit risk is not a central concern with this sector. Likewise, in the case of structured financings with embedded warrants or options, credit risk is centred primarily with the counterparty as an issuer of the bond or convertible, which is covered by a very different risk category, so-called inventory risk. (For a further discussion see Banks, 1993.) Risks attributable to counterparty default when holding a bond with an embedded option or warrant will be greater because of the bond than the embedded derivative.

Again, although the vast number of combinations which have been created in the derivatives market has been oversimplified, some of the major over-the-counter swap and option categories are highlighted in order to give an indication of the myriad products which are available to those actively seeking risk protection, yield enhancement or market participation. Figure 1.2 highlights a sample of swap products, while Figure 1.3 highlights option products.

Interest rate swaps	Currency rate swaps	Equity swaps	Commodity swaps
Fixed/floating	Fixed/floating	Index call	Gold
Basis	Coupon	Index put/call	Energy
Forward start	Forward start	Equity/equity	Physicals
Puttable/callable	Puttable/callable	Index with embedded option	
Discount	Discount		
Premium	Premium		
Zero coupon	Zero coupon		
Amortizing	Amortizing		
Inverse floater/ yield curve	Inverse floater/ yield curve		
Leveraged	Leveraged		
Mortgage	Differential/quanto		
Arrears	Forward rate agreement		

Figure 1.2   A sampling of swap products

Interest rate options	Currency rate options	Equity derivative options
Caps	Caps	Path independent – binary
Floors	Floors	Path dependent – knock-out –knock-in – lookback
Collars	Collars	
Corridors	Corridors	
Power caps	Currency swaption	Outperformance/ basket
Swaptions	Path dependent	Preference
When-in-the-money options	Path independent	Quanto
Compound (nested) caps/floors	Preference	
Path dependent	Outperformance	
Path independent		
Preference		
Outperformance		

The above are in addition to standard puts/calls on equities, indexes, currencies, commodities, and so on

Figure 1.3   A sampling of option products

In addition to these derivative products, certain financial institutions have been pioneering other structures which have yet to make their debuts, or to be utilized in a significant and widespread fashion by market participants. Examples of these include property, tax, macroeconomic, credit, insurance and inflation derivatives. Although most of these structures are in their infancy or have yet to be introduced, it is entirely possible that they will, at some future date, be as commonplace as interest rate, currency, equity and commodity swaps are today. This developing area of derivatives is not covered in the text.

THE MOTIVATION FOR DERIVATIVES TRANSACTIONS

The need and motivation for both originators and end-users to enter into derivative transactions is relatively straightforward: to earn income (either by selling a derivative or utilizing a derivative) and to manage risk.

Institutions active as originators, structurers and market-makers of derivative products (primarily the large commercial and investment banks of the world), create derivative transactions because the volatile market environment causes end-users to demand such products. Banks are by now skilled in risk management techniques and are generally adept at managing the risks inherent in their own business. Therefore they are willing and able to transfer their knowledge of risk and investment management to client institutions in order that they too may cope with risk or generate income which is necessary and possible because of market volatility. Transferring this knowledge is not free, of course, and by creating such structures, originators earn substantial fee income. Although much of the now standard business of interest rate and currency swaps is only modestly profitable with earnings per discrete transaction down to just several basis points (given both widespread participation by an increasing number of institutions and the relative ease with which transactions can be assembled and executed), the more complex and structured business remains highly profitable, as it involves a certain amount of financial engineering and risk management expertise. Single complex transactions can earn for an institution what dozens, or even hundreds, of 'plain vanilla' transactions may earn. As long as banks are able to provide their expertise and earn handsome profits, it is entirely likely that they will continue to be active in the derivatives market.

From the standpoint of the investor or issuer using derivatives, the presence of volatility in major financial markets means they can employ derivative instruments to take advantage of this volatility by lowering funding costs (e.g. issuing an index-linked bond); by enhancing the return on certain underlying investments they may hold (e.g. writing options); by gaining upside (or downside) participation in a given market (e.g. entering into a derivative swap); or by obtaining rate protection for a liability or an asset (e.g. purchasing a cap or floor). 'End-users' may also utilize derivatives to achieve specific accounting or regulatory goals.

Figures 1.2 and 1.3 illustrate certain general categories of derivatives which might be employed by 'end-users' to solve a specific problem or fulfil a given requirement. These structures have been developed over time by major financial institutions in response to the needs of issuers and investors in meeting such requirements. Though many of the products introduced by financial institutions to meet client requirements are quite sophisticated and very profitable, they exist because of client demand. If there were no issuers or investors interested in utilizing the products, they would not endure in the marketplace. Thus, the derivative structures which are prevalent in the market prosper because supply and demand (i.e. originator and 'end-user') forces are present. Perhaps Fabozzi and Modigliani have summed it up best:

> New financial instruments are not created simply because someone on Wall Street believes that it would be 'fun' to introduce an instrument with more 'bells and whistles' than existing instruments.
>
> The demand for new instruments is driven by the needs of borrowers and investors based on their asset/liability management situation, regulatory constraints (if any), financial accounting considerations, and tax considerations (Fabozzi and Modigliani, 1992, p.xxi).

An examination of some of the recent historical activity in a number of the world's main financial markets provides at least one indication of why derivatives have become so popular and widespread. Given the tremendous volatility in interest rates, stock market indexes and currency rates, it is little wonder why so many are trying to profit, or protect, by entering into derivatives trades.

Figure 1.4 highlights some of the substantial market moves which have occurred in interest rates (US$ Libor, US Treasury rates), currency rates (sterling, and the yen, against the US dollar), and stock market indexes (US S & P 500, UK FTSE 100, Japanese Nikkei, and German DAX) over the past few years. Graphs are included for both absolute price moves for the past three years, as well as rolling historical volatilities for the past ten to one hundred days. Historical volatility is discussed at greater length in Chapter 2.

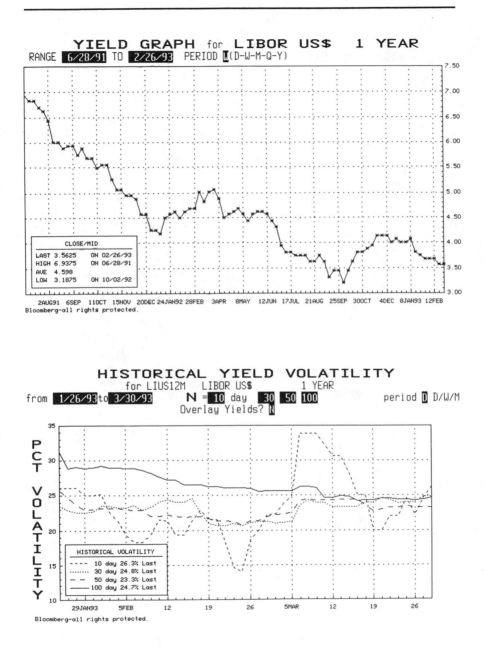

Figure 1.4(i)   US dollar Libor

Source: Bloomberg Financial Markets

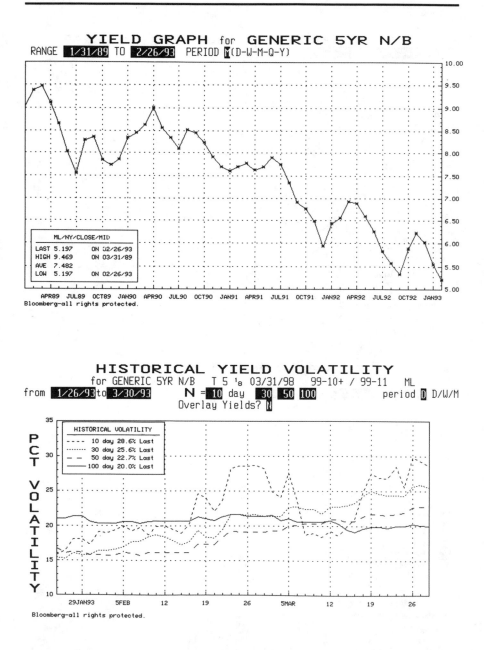

Figure 1.4(ii)   5-year US Treasury note

Source: Bloomberg Financial Markets

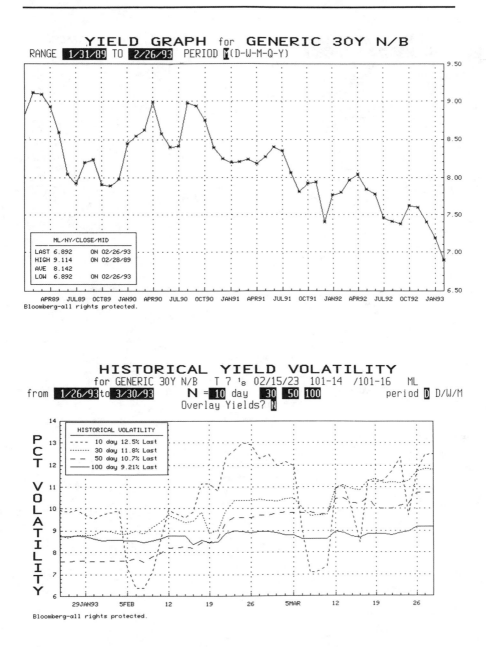

Figure 1.4(iii)   30-year US Treasury bond

Source: Bloomberg Financial Markets

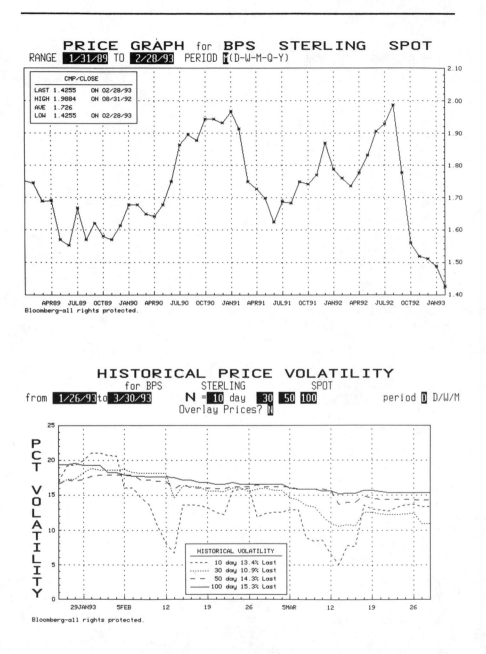

Figure 1.4(iv)   Dollar/sterling spot exchange rate

Source: Bloomberg Financial Markets

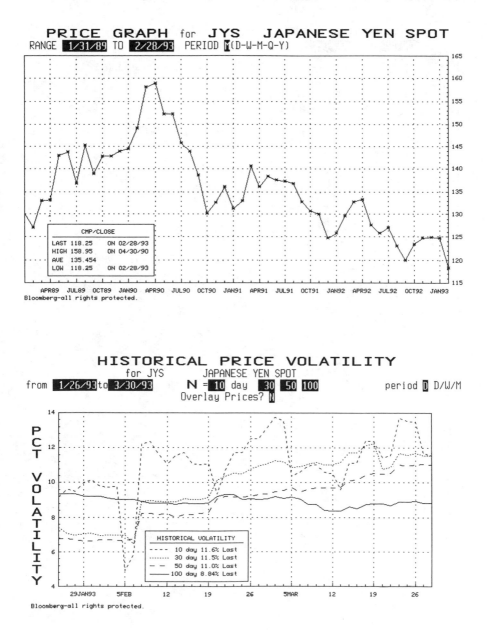

Figure 1.4(v)   Yen/dollar spot exchange rate

Source: Bloomberg Financial Markets

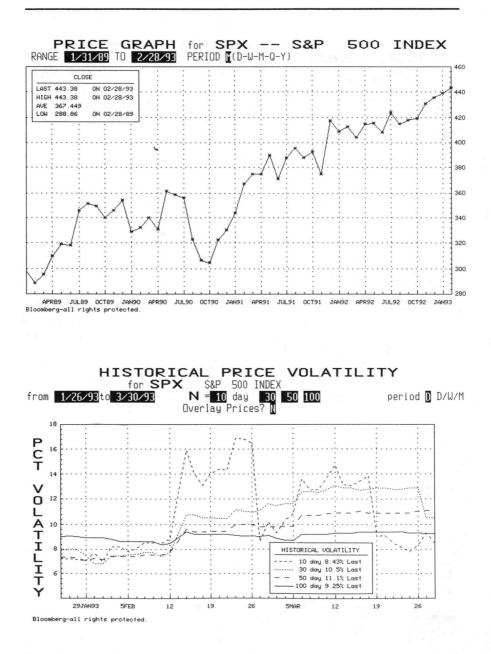

Figure 1.4(vi)   S & P500 stock market index

Source: Bloomberg Financial Markets

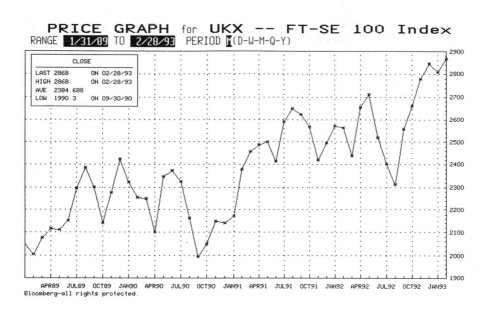

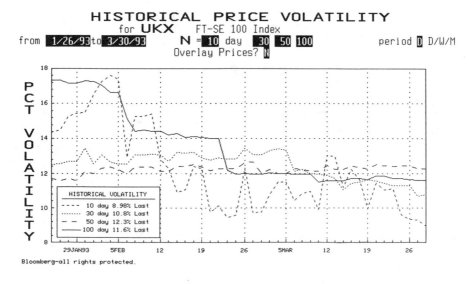

Figure 1.4(vii)   FTSE stock market index

Source: Bloomberg Financial Markets

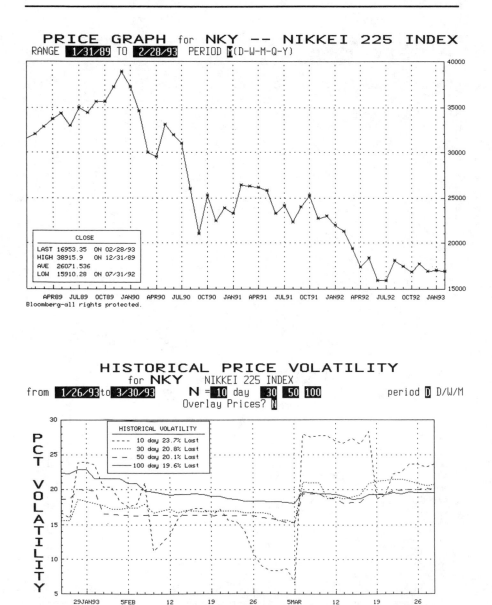

Figure 1.4(viii)   Nikkei stock market index

Source: Bloomberg Financial Markets

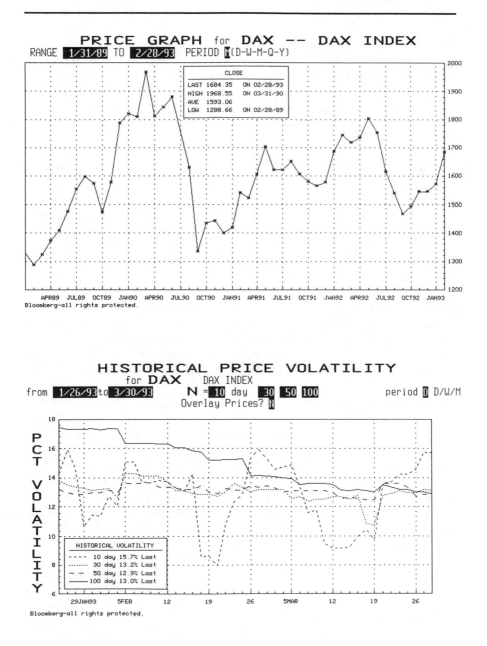

Figure 1.4(ix)   DAX stock market index

Source: Bloomberg Financial Markets

It seems logical to presume that while volatility is present in different financial markets (as shown in Figure 1.4), creators and users of derivatives will continue to develop and utilize new products. These products will protect against market movement or will allow participation in market movement. With innovation in these markets comes the need for market participants (including originators and 'end-users') and regulators to be well informed of the risks governing new or evolving product mix.

THE CONCERNS OF MARKET PARTICIPANTS AND REGULATORY AUTHORITIES

When any market is created, or when any new product within a market is designed, participants and regulators have both the need and the responsibility to ensure that all aspects and characteristics of the market or product are thoroughly examined and completely understood. Nowhere is this more true than in the market for financial derivatives, which by definition and necessity demands the review of some of the most complex structural details known to finance professionals. Given enormous and rapid growth in these markets, the need is intensified. At the end of December 1991, the International Swap Dealers Association (ISDA) estimated total interest and currency swaps, caps and floors at the notional equivalent of approximately $4.4 trillion; according to ISDA, the figures for the first six months of 1992 showed a further increase of $1.5 trillion in the total notional outstanding. Although this is not an amount which is at risk (the more relevant measure will be discussed later in this chapter and again in Chapter 7), it has drawn significant attention, considering that the market was only developed in the early 1980s.

Understanding the explicit functioning of products within these rapidly growing markets, including return, structure, flows, obligations and termination, is vital. Very often it is simply necessary to review all salient aspects of a transaction as reflected in a term sheet or flowchart. At other times a more rigorous review is required, including asking product specialists details about a given structure. Appendix III lists the '20 questions' to pose to a derivative specialist when attempting to capture the unique details of a given product or structure.

To understand fully a given derivative product it is often useful to focus on the basic elements and tradeoffs common to all financial transactions: risk and return. The return, or profit, mechanisms of a given instrument are generally the concern of a bank's trading and sales desks or origination unit. These groups design the function and parameters of the instrument and are charged with ensuring that it meets the customers needs. After all, if the customer is not interested in or satisfied with the product it will have no market and therefore no existence. When creating such instruments, the trader or originator will know generally what type of return is possible or necessary, depending on factors such as the originality of the product, competitive pressures and customer demand. The profit elements may be derived from upfront fees, an above market rate on a particular flow or greater upside potential on an index. Profits may be guaranteed or, in certain instances, may be dependent on the direction of a given market. Such profit payoffs must be well understood by the product professional, and agreed by senior bank management. What should necessarily be included in any profit mechanism is, of course, a variable which accounts for the dimensions of the second category, the risk component. It should be obvious that the riskier the product, the greater the return. If a given product carries unusually high or complex hedging, liquidity or market risk parameters, the profit structure should reflect these characteristics. A prudent pricing mechanism should also reflect the credit quality of the counterparty: the weaker the credit, the higher the profit spread, and vice versa. This is currently the subject of much discussion among banks and bankers, many of whom are seeking ways to link the return on a derivatives transaction with the credit quality of a counterparty. Though certain commercial banks have had a great deal of success in pricing traditional loan products according to credit quality, it is proving more challenging for commercial and investment banks to do the same with derivatives, particularly customized packages of derivatives. There is substantial evidence that derivatives are often underpriced from a credit perspective when compared with traditional banking products (see, for instance, Shirreff, 1985; Smith, Smithson and Wakeman, 1986; Felgran, 1987; or Smith, Smithson and Wilford, 1990). Much work remains to be done in this area.

In determining how a new product functions it is vital that the risk aspects of the instrument be focused on with a good degree of detail. Understanding risk parameters enables a finance or corporate professional to decipher the logic in executing a transaction, and also allows a specific quantification of the downside potential (i.e. credit loss) should a counterparty default. Risk, which is covered in Chapter 2, comes in many different forms. These, at any time, may include credit, market, liquidity, settlement, hedging, operational, legal, and sovereign risk. While it is true that not all types of risk will be present in every situation, one of the worst avenues to follow is either to ignore what risks may be present, or to proceed with a given transaction without fully appreciating and understanding all risk dimensions. Although there is often pressure to act and react quickly to a given structure, deal or opportunity, prudence dictates patience and thoroughness when evaluating complex structures. Not understanding all aspects of risk can prove detrimental to those involved, from the bank originating a given derivative product, to the issuer or investor active as a user, to the regulator charged with specific oversight of markets, institutions and products. The notion of risk awareness as it relates to the three groups just mentioned may be isolated, to review what are the vested interests in thoroughly understanding a given product and its risks.

The Bank
The bank, as the originator, trader, and/or market maker of derivative products, has at least two interests in ensuring a thorough understanding of derivative risks at all levels within a given institution: preventing losses on its own books, and ensuring that it will retain an active and interested clientele. In the case of the former, it seems obvious that if a given bank is unable to understand and control the risk emanating from its own derivatives book, it will eventually book losses. These losses may be the result of not

fully understanding risk elements or profiles of a given derivative or may come as a result of transacting a derivative with a counterparty who ultimately defaults (where the reason for the loss comes as a result of not directly understanding the risk parameters of a given deal, which would normally result in a specific transaction being rejected for a weaker counterparty). Either path will lead a bank to sustain losses. The responsible banking institution must ensure that all levels of management are educated about derivatives and their associated risks: senior bank managers, law and compliance professionals, credit officers, risk managers and operations managers. In short, any group which has responsibility for certain aspects of a given transaction should understand the structure and risk of the transaction. In addition to protecting its own business, the bank has a strong interest in ensuring that its client base is fully aware of the profit, loss and risk parameters of a given structure. If a bank takes a short term view with a client and simply tries to structure and sell a given instrument without spending the time to explain its benefits, risks and costs, it will only be a matter of time before a client is harmed financially. When that occurs, it is very likely that the bank's franchise and reputation will sustain some level of damage.

The Client

The client of the derivatives package is active either as issuer or investor. Clients are very often approached with new ideas from the derivative marketers of commercial and investment banks, and it is clearly in their own interests to ensure that all aspects of the transaction are thoroughly analysed. This will add comfort that it is deriving the economic gain it is expecting (e.g. either a lower funding cost or an enhanced yield, or perhaps exposure to the upside potential of a given market) and that it understands the credit, liquidity and market risks which may be imposed on it. It is important to remember that it is not only the financial institution originating the transaction which may face risks: very often the client is exposed to these or slightly variant risks as well. As in the case of the bank, it is vital that all relevant parties at the client institution are informed of these transactions and risk parameters, from senior managers to treasury officers. Although many end-users of these products (e.g. large pension fund managers and the treasury units of large multinational corporations) are very sophisticated with regard to comprehending financial engineering and taking advantage of financial opportunities, not all client institutions have the same level of knowledge and expertise. It is in their own interests to review all structures with an objective and analytical eye.

The Regulator

There has been a great deal of attention in the press in recent years regarding regulatory concerns over the pace of growth in derivatives and the increased level of sophistication and complexity involved in the derivative business. Certain regulators have a real fear that they are being 'left behind', that senior bank managers are unaware of the structures the high-powered trading desks are creating, and that clients are being sold instruments they may not understand, either partially or totally. Regulators must be aware of these transactions, so they may impose, on a reasonable and fair basis, regulation which is required to ensure orderly and secure markets and appropriate use of derivative products. Failure by regulatory authorities to understand all aspects of these transactions may result in disparate views between regulators and bank participants on the level of regulation required (if any) for these products.

A fairly extensive sampling of the recent press is instructive in reflecting the concerns and opinions of certain regulators and market professionals. A broad range of quotes from a broad range of professionals is included to illustrate the issues and the debate currently present in the market. It also helps explain the need for a clear understanding of what all participants are doing.

> The growth of trading in derivatives markets has made it impossible even for experienced financial analysts to gauge a bank's health from its published accounts. (A Lamfalussy, General Manager, Bank for International Settlements (BIS), quoted in its annual report. *Financial Times*, 25 November 1992.)

> The lack of transparency from the growth of derivatives has rendered the nature and distribution of risks in financial market operations much more opaque. (*Financial Times*, 25 November 1992.)

> While the management of market risks may have been facilitated by the growing availability of derivative instruments and related techniques, credit risk management, cash and market liquidity risks and settlement and legal risks may have become more complex. (BIS working group report. *Australian Financial Review*, 3 November 1992.)

> The availability of derivative instruments has enabled participants to take complex positions that rely on a presumption of liquidity in a number of markets. That presumption may prove illusory in times of stress. (BIS working group report. *International Herald Tribune*, 2 November 1992.)

> Bankers like the high profits which new activities bring in and thus do not want to constrict the business too much with tight internal limits. But, in many cases, senior management does not have a good handle on what risks are being taken. The fact is that sizeable losses have been incurred in such areas as mortgage derivatives by even generally well-run institutions. Yet, when it comes to deciding how to regulate financial innovations, the authorities tend to be deferential to the views of the successful innovator. (Dr H Kaufman, Economic Consultant, speech at annual meeting of International Organization of Securities Commissions (IOSCO). *International Financing Review*, 31 October 1992.)

> We feel that some directors are not wholly comfortable with derivatives, and they don't know anybody who they can trust. There is a gulf between the top and medium level that is not being wholly bridged. (Senior regulatory official speaking anonymously about bank managements. *Financial Times*, 2 December 1992).

> Bad risk management [of derivatives] could sink a firm in 24 hours. (M Carpenter, Chairman and CEO of Kidder Peabody, speech to US Securities Industry Association. *Global Custodian*, November 1992.)

The downside of a customized [derivative] package is the complete or near complete absence of a secondary or an interdealer market. (M Schapiro, SEC Commissioner. *Global Custodian*, November 1992.)

The worst-case scenario [of derivatives valuation] and the nightmare-scenario are not the same thing. Most of the disasters that have occurred have been due to traders who where literally out of control. (J Howland-Jackson, former Chairman, Nomura International, risk symposium, November 1992, commenting on the September interest rate and currency volatility. *International Financing Review*, November 1992.)

I believe some intermediaries are writing 30 year options. Quite how confident anyone can be that the premium received for such options is an adequate reward for the risks taken is a subject which falls into my personal knowledge gap. (P Kent, Director, Bank of England, risk symposium, November 1992. *International Financing Review*, November 1992.)

[There is] complacency which has crept into the institutions' perception of their ability to control market risk [in derivatives]. (V Fitt, Head of Risk Analysis, UK Securities and Futures Authority, risk symposium, November 1992. *International Financing Review*, November 1992.)

[Bankers had better] take a very, very hard look at off-balance sheet [derivative] activities. I hope this sounds like a warning, because it is. The growth and complexity of off-balance sheet activities and the nature of credit, price and settlement risk they entail should give us all cause for concern. (G Corrigan, President, New York Federal Reserve, address to NY State Bankers Association, January 1992. *Institutional Investor*, September 1992.)

26 year olds with computers are creating financial hydrogen bombs. (F Rohatyn, Senior Partner, Lazard Freres. *Institutional Investor*, July 1992.)

I do believe most major houses have very carefully controlled risk and that much of the derivatives activity entails a hedging which reduces risks. There might never be a problem. But – and it is a big but – if there were, it would be a very big problem. (A Lamfalussy, General Manager, BIS. *Institutional Investor*, September 1992.)

[The Fed's examiners had uncovered] basic internal-control weaknesses in the cash market and derivatives trading operations of domestic and non-US banks operating in its jurisdiction...sophisticated trading strategies and complex instruments by their very nature require robust risk management and controls. (C Feldberg, Head of Bank Supervision, New York Federal Reserve. *Institutional Investor*, September 1992.)

The growth of this [derivatives] market has been not only in volume but in density as well. It pricks up your ears and raises an eyebrow because it brings up the question of controls. (B Quinn, Director of Banking Supervision. *Institutional Investor*, September 1992.)

In general, those financial firms that are most heavily involved in the OTC derivatives market tend to be the most cautious. They have the most trading expertise, and they control their risks using the most advanced risk-management systems and techniques. But behind these big guns is a rapidly growing number of smaller outfits anxious not to miss the boat, who cobble together OTC derivatives capabilities in an attempt to keep up with the play and get their share of the market with limited regard to the dangers. (V Fitt, Head of Risk Analysis, UK Securities and Futures Authority. *Institutional Investor*, September 1992.)

We do not know the web of interconnections between banks that has been established through derivatives. The market is losing transparency and we do not know who is dependent on whom anymore. Now we will only know after the fact, and by then it could be too late. (A Lamfalussy, General Manger, BIS. *Institutional Investor*, September 1992.)

I was a mathematics student. I cannot believe all these derivatives people are competent. (W Heyman, Head of Market Regulation, Securities and Exchange Commission. *Institutional Investor*, September 1992.)

I am certain that people do not understand the risks of some of the transactions that they are putting on – and not just the end-users but, I suspect, some of the supposedly sophisticated dealers. (J Copenhaver, Head of Derivatives, Sumitomo Bank Capital Markets. *Euromoney*, September 1992.)

We believe that the internal capital allocation to these [derivative] businesses by most dealers is low given the potential for market disruptions, and the measurement and management challenges. For most institutions, [capital allocation] has been below Basle requirements. (C Griep, Executive Managing Director, Standard & Poors. *Euromoney*, September 1992.)

Multi-legged positions are growing rapidly, both in size and variety. Because of the increasing prevalence of these positions, a major default or disruption may not be isolated as easily as was once the case...The complexities and interdependencies inherently associated with multi-legged positions...are such that the sudden failure of a major market participant might disrupt the financial system, especially if that failure were to occur in an already unsettled market environment. (Federal Reserve, FDIC and the Office of the Comptroller of the Currency, 'Derivative product activities of commercial banks', quoted in *Risk*, February 1993.)

We wrote the report to draw greater attention to off balance sheet business on the part of executives of financial institutions and authorities, including ourselves. We have to admit that understanding of derivative trading and its effects on financial markets is relatively inadequate in Japan. (S Kimura, Chief Manager, Int'l Division, Bank of Japan, commenting on BOJ's participation in BIS's working group report on derivatives. *Nikkei Financial Weekly*, 8 March 1993.)

Regulatory institutions which are currently studying the derivatives markets, its risks and potential regulation, capital allocation and exposure measurement issues include the primary regulatory bodies of the world: the Securities and Exchange Commission, the New York Federal Reserve, and the Commodity Futures Trading Commission in the US, the BIS and IOSCO and the Bank of England. The Group of Thirty recently released its 'Derivatives: Practices and Principles' study.

In fairness, not everyone feels that derivative growth and sophistication has expanded out of control. This is particularly true of market professionals at major financial institutions who are creating these derivative packages. However, certain regulators have also expressed the same view:

> Concern over extra risks created by the growth of the derivatives markets has been overstated in some quarters. Derivatives markets have on balance reduced rather than increased risk. (P Kent, Executive Director, Bank of England. *Financial Times*, 2 December 1992.)

> We've seen 2500 banks fail because of credit risk. We have a long way to go before the derivatives market is as threatening. (R Breeden, Chairman, Securities and Exchange Commission. *Institutional Investor*, September 1992.)

> Somebody may have expected that we were going to say derivatives are bad, but when you look around, there aren't any bank failures caused by derivatives. Banks fail because of bank loan credit risk. (W Stark, Assistant Director of Capital Markets, Federal Deposit Insurance Corp. *Risk*, February 1993.)

> In my view, however, cultural differences within banks and the regulatory community have magnified concerns about banks' participation in OTC derivatives and threaten to produce an overreaction to the risks these instruments actually entail. (S Phillips, member of the Board of Governors, Federal Reserve System. *Risk*, January 1993.)

> The specter of trillions of dollars in notional amounts [of derivatives] has scared many people and resulted in hyperventilating rhetoric over the past couple of years...Swaps and derivatives are not the last new financial instruments; markets will continue to evolve and come up with new products. It's better to have market evolution and regulators adjust to what the market is doing rather than have regulators set rules by which the markets have to operate. (R Breeden, Chairman, Securities and Exchange Commission, 1993 ISDA conference. *International Herald Tribune*, 12 March 1993.)

> Regulators should never be so risk-averse as to stop all innovation for fear that it could become a problem. We must not stifle innovation unnecessarily or impose needless regulations or burdens simply because of our nervousness about new things. (W Gramm, Chairman, Commodity Futures Trading Commission. *Risk*, October 1992.)

Although regulators and senior bank managers often fear the worst, the reality is that derivative market difficulties have been relatively few to date, lending some support to the view of participants that the regulatory fears are misplaced and out of context with the realities of the market. While a great deal of focus has been placed on the notional amount of derivatives (which, admittedly, is rather staggering), the reality is that notionals are not typically at risk; a far more relevant figure is a potential exposure measure (gross or net, depending on the laws and regulations governing a given jurisdiction), or even a mark-to-market exposure (these measures are discussed in subsequent chapters).

In July 1992, Arthur Andersen released the results of a survey on the derivatives markets commissioned by ISDA. The survey, which included 70 per cent of market participants, indicated that while the notional amount of derivatives among those surveyed reached $3.1 trillion ($4.34 trillion for the entire market) at the end of 1991, the gross mark-to-market exposure, a figure which more accurately reflects the current amount at risk (though not the amount potentially at risk for the entire span of a trade), was a much more reasonable $77 billion. Despite the availability of figures such as those provided by the Arthur Andersen survey many, rather erroneously, have chosen to focus on the $4.34 trillion in notional amount as an indication that the derivatives business is growing too rapidly. Indeed, the figure presented below, which reflects growth in the OTC derivatives business in notional terms over the past six years, is dramatic; there is little doubt that it has caught the attention of many.

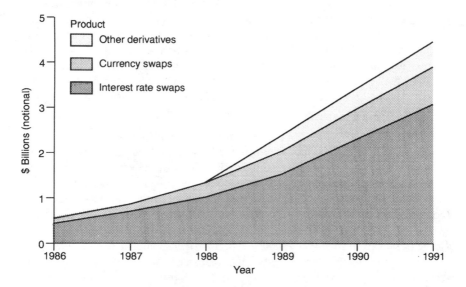

Figure 1.5   Over-the-counter derivatives growth

In addition to a relatively reasonable current exposure, as reflected in a measure such as gross mark-to-market, the losses attributable to derivatives have been relatively modest (particularly in view of the size of the markets):

- First Boston lost $50MM in OTC bond options in 1987 as a result of risk management difficulties.
- Chemical Bank reportedly lost $33MM in 1989 based on difficulties with its interest rate cap book.
- Bankers Trust set aside just under $39MM for non-performing assets in late 1991 because of problems with an interest rate swap.

- Merrill Lynch and JP Morgan each lost money on mortgage derivatives: Merrill Lynch lost $377MM in 1987 (partly due to unauthorized trading) and Morgan lost an estimated $50MM in late 1991.
- Allied Lyons, the UK conglomerate, lost £147MM on foreign exchange derivatives in 1991.
- Showa Shell, the 50 per cent owned Japanese subsidiary of Royal Dutch/Shell, lost over $1B in early 1993 as a result of massive foreign exchange losses (much due to unauthorized trading). At least two other financial institutions, Bank Negara Malaysia and the Japanese Postal Savings Bureau (Kampo), are reported to have lost several billion dollars in the foreign exchange markets during 1992 and 1993.
- Numerous banks lost heavily in the UK local authorities swap case in 1991 (with a potential £600MM at stake). Under $200MM has been lost to date, and certain cases are being settled in favour of the banks, not the local authorities (such as a recent judgement supporting Westdeutsche Landesbank in its case against Islington, and an out-of-court settlement in favor of SG Warburg by Birmingham), so the final loss figure remains to be seen.
- The 1992 ISDA sponsored survey, conducted by Arthur Andersen, indicated that total swap derivative losses to date amount to $358MM (including the UK local authorities case).

In terms of the above, derivative marketers can argue that their business has, in fact, performed much more ably than other banking businesses: high yield bonds, loans to lesser developed countries, loans to commercial real estate and energy concerns, and bridge loans, for instance, have each caused many financial institutions to post large losses (and, in some cases, have caused certain institutions to fail outright – e.g. Drexel Burnham Lambert and Bank of New England). Derivatives have not, at least not to date. Despite a relatively modest amount of losses to date, the concern is that the market is growing quickly in volume and sophistication and that additional losses could occur; some fear the interconnections might trigger a broader 'domino' or systemic effect, where failure by one counterparty to perform on a contract might cause failures by others to perform on their contracts.

Despite the differing views on the degree of risk inherent in these markets, whether or not additional regulation is required, whether standardized capital levels should be applied to all participants (only banks must currently adhere to the BIS's 8 per cent capital guidelines while others, such as investment banks and insurance companies, do not follow the same rules), and so on, it seems clear that most parties welcome additional information on these instruments. The information should cover all areas, including legal/regulatory, operations, credit, and risk management.

It is the intent of this book to focus on the credit risk aspects of these 'second generation' derivatives. This text seeks to develop a method of understanding and quantifying the credit risks which are inherent in a number of these new derivatives, including those inherent in varying options strategies, equity derivative swaps and exotic options, and complex swap derivatives. These topics will be covered in Parts

II, III and IV. By understanding the credit risk exposures which are imposed on a bank when dealing with these instruments, the reader will gain insight into the potential losses which may be incurred because of counterparty default. Such information is vital in the context of the credit decision-making process (that is, does a given derivatives trade carry too much risk to be considered appropriate for a counterparty of high, medium or low credit quality?) However, before embarking on a discussion of the specific risks of specific instruments we need to develop a framework for evaluating the credit risk which is innate in these products; this is the topic of Chapter 2.

As a final point, it should be noted that most, though not all, of the transactions considered in this book tend to be high risk in nature, by virtue of the dollar exposure they add to a bank's books, or by the long maturity horizon which they frequently cover. Credit officers and analysts seeking to consider these types of deals must always bear in mind that unaltered exposures (i.e. those which have not been modified to include risk reducing schemes) will carry either substantial quantities of so-called risk equivalent exposure (see Chapter 2) and/or a long time to final maturity. They are not, in standard form, generally acceptable for counterparties which are of weak or deteriorating credit quality. One of the reasons that the derivatives market has been so successful to date in avoiding credit losses of a substantial magnitude is the appreciation by dealers and bankers that these types of structures, in unsecured form, are generally only appropriate for institutions of higher credit quality. Although a great deal of business is transacted with counterparties of a lower credit quality, these deals are typically secured in some fashion (collateralization, periodic marks-to-market, options to terminate). Institutions which are regarded as suitable for short to long-term derivative transactions (i.e. those with a final maturity of one to ten years) are those which are rated by a credit department or an external rating agency in the middle to high investment grade category. Those institutions which have weaker investment grade ratings are generally only regarded as acceptable for short to medium term transactions (i.e. those with a final maturity between one and three to five years). In contrast, counterparties with subinvestment grade ratings are often only acceptable for very short-term derivative transactions (i.e those with a final maturity of six to twelve months) or, in many instances, no unsecured transactions at all. Although maturity restrictions as applied to varying credit qualities differ from bank to bank, most derivatives houses are cognisant of the appropriateness and suitability of different transactions and maturities for counterparties of varying credit quality.

Although there are many other ancillary issues which are necessarily a part of the topic in general, such as product suitability, risk reduction schemes, impact of netting exposures to a single counterparty, portfolio management of exposures across counterparties, these will not be covered in this text as they have already been dealt with by this author (Banks, 1993). Readers interested in exploring these important issues should consult that text.

2: Classification and Quantification of Credit Risk

BACKGROUND

In any business it is necessary accurately to classify and measure those variables which represent uncertainties to the normal functioning of operations. This is especially true in the banking industry, where the essence of the business is to reward an institution for risks taken. The accurate classification and measurement of risks is typically accomplished through a risk management framework, where an institution identifies, classifies, measures and manages the different risks inherent in its lines of business. Knowledge of risks attributable to a given business allow losses to be controlled or avoided and for profits to be maximized.

As one might expect, a bank involved in a variety of traditional banking services and products will experience a series of different risks in the normal course of business. These, at any point in time, may include credit (or counterparty) risk, sovereign risk, legal risk, operational risk, liquidity risk, hedging risk and a series of product risks which, for purposes of this text, are said to include market risk, delivery risk, inventory risk and provisional risk. In order for a bank to account fully for the exposures it assumes in the normal course of business, all risk dimensions must be considered. Different departments within a bank are generally charged with responsibility for a given set of risks. For example, the legal, regulatory and documentation departments would be responsible for aspects of legal risk; the risk management unit (generally in conjunction with individual trading desks) would be charged with oversight of liquidity risk, hedging risk and aspects of market risk (to the extent that hedged/open position and profit and loss considerations are involved); the operations and systems departments would be primarily concerned with operational and EDP risk; a central credit area would be held accountable for sovereign and credit risk as well as the evaluation of product risk (which, as indicated above, encompasses a variety of categories).

While addressing all aspects of risk is vitally important for the continuing success of a banking institution, discussion of each is beyond the purview of this text. Instead, the focus is on the topic of credit risk, knowledge of which allows an institution to quantify the amount of credit loss which may be sustained if counterparty default occurs. Within the broad topic of credit risk, which is applicable to all financial instruments, the focus is narrowed onto the area which most greatly impacts the credit risk evaluation of 'next generation' derivative products – market risk.

28

While a credit officer must always be capable of accurate assessment of counterparty risk (the risk that a counterparty in a transaction will fail to perform as expected, for reasons of financial deterioration or collapse, or fraud) and must incorporate specific details on credit quality into the decision-making process, the purpose of this book is not to review what makes a company a high or low quality credit. Instead this book seeks to provide a means of valuing the risk being assumed by a bank when it enters into a derivative transaction by facing a counterparty of a certain credit quality. In a worst-case scenario, failure by a bank's counterparty to perform on a contracted obligation will lead the bank to suffer a credit loss. The magnitude of the credit loss is a figure which is quantifiable and which will depend on the level of risk present at the time of default (less any special considerations such as collateral enhancing or securing the obligation). We shall describe below why market risk is the best measure for determining the amount a bank will lose in a derivative trade as a result of counterparty default. This text will also provide general commentary on the appropriateness and suitability of such transactions for counterparties of varying degrees of creditworthiness.

Since this text is limited in scope to derivative transactions, other forms of product risk (i.e. delivery risk, inventory risk and provisional risk) are not covered, and readers interested in delving into other products and their associated risks are urged to consult other volumes (e.g. Banks, 1993; Donaldson, 1989). Our focus for now will be on market risk, why derivative products carry market risk and how it can most effectively be measured. This chapter begins with a basic definition of market risk and then moves to a discussion of risk equivalency, which is a banker's means of placing market risk products on a loan equivalent basis. The chapter concludes by developing a method by which to measure risk equivalency.

MARKET RISK

Market risk, in simple form, may be defined as the risk of loss due to movement in market prices or rates. Note that when we discuss market risk and loss we shall confine ourselves to the topic as related to counterparty default, not to periodic profit and loss adjustments to a bank's income statement. Market risk exists because interest rates, currency rates, stock prices, index levels or commodity prices governing a given derivatives transaction fluctuate (see graphs in Figure 1.4). If there was no movement (or no movement of substance) in any of these indicators, there would be no concern over market risk (and, in reality, little use for derivative products, since these instruments seek to take advantage of, or provide protection against, market movements). When a bank enters into a transaction today, it generally expects that the market rates underlying the transaction will not be the same during the life of the trade; these instruments are said to be market risk-based and must be quantified through a process known as 'risk equivalency' or 'risk adjustment,' discussed at length below.

During the span of a given derivative trade, rates (or prices) will fluctuate. If, for example, a bank contracts to buy a call option on a stock with a strike price of 100, that option will increase and/or decrease in value as the current price of the equity moves above and/or below the strike price. As the current price level changes, the level of risk exposure, or the amount the bank stands to lose if a counterparty defaults, changes as well. If the current price of the stock moves above the strike, such that the call has value, and the counterparty fails, the bank will not receive the money it is owed (in reality it is expecting shares from the counterparty in exchange for cash at a below market price; it may then sell the shares in the market at the higher current price, or retain them in its portfolio). The bank will become an unsecured creditor of the bankrupt company and may receive some value in bankruptcy proceedings; such value, if any, will generally be far less than originally anticipated. When the current market price is above the strike price in the case of calls (vice versa in the case of puts), market risk exposure is said to be positive and implies that the bank has exposure to its counterparty. When the current market price is below the strike price in the case of calls (again, vice versa in the case of puts), market risk exposure is negative and indicates that the bank has no exposure to its counterparty. (This assumption ignores any upfront premium payment which probably accompanied the transaction, explored in greater detail in later chapters).

Market risk may therefore be positive or negative during the life of a given derivative transaction, depending on the movement of rates or prices. When positive, the bank must take account of its credit exposure, and when negative it need not be concerned. The central point to emphasize is that market movements govern market risk, which governs credit risk exposure. In a standard unsecured transaction, a counterparty default when market risk exposure is positive results in a loss to the bank in an amount equal to the market risk exposure (plus other elements where relevant, such as premium paid). A counterparty default when market risk is negative will result in no loss for the bank.

With a medium to long-term transaction (i.e. anything where the final maturity is one to two years or more in length) market risk becomes especially critical – the longer the time to final maturity, the greater the chance for market movements to occur. Since a long time horizon allows the market risk movement to become greater (which implies that a given transaction can move further in-the-money), risk exposure to the counterparty may also become greater. In addition, transactions which are governed by rates or prices which are especially volatile can also lead to an increase in market risk exposure. Many of the derivative trades common in the market today are those with a multi-year time horizon on volatile indexes, stock prices or other measures. As such, it is especially critical for all credit personnel to be cognizant of transactions with long maturities and volatile movements. Not coincidentally, these two elements play a leading role in defining our key risk equivalency measure for derivative instruments, the risk factor. The development and implementation of risk factors is discussed in greater detail below.

In order for credit officers to assess market risk accurately so that correct credit decision-making may take place, it is often helpful to segregate market risk into two separate components, potential market risk and actual market risk. Potential market risk is known variously as deemed risk, time-to-decay risk, expected exposure or fractional exposure, while actual market risk is often referred to as mark-to-market risk, replacement cost or actual exposure. Each class of market risk is defined below to enable the reader to distinguish the importance of each in the decision-making and exposure management processes.

Potential Market Risk (PMR)

Potential market risk is the risk exposure the bank must allocate against a counterparty's credit limit today, at the inception of a transaction. Why market risk exists, and why it affects the value of the derivative instruments covered in this text, has been discussed above. Potential market risk attempts to quantify future market rate movements which may impact the exposure a bank has to a counterparty. The actual calculation of PMR comes during the risk equivalency process, and is discussed at greater length in the section below. For now it is sufficient to view PMR as the most likely 'worst case' risk exposure a bank may face during the life of the transaction. PMR is vital in order for a credit officer to have ex-ante information to make a reasoned credit decision.

Actual Market Risk (AMR)

In contrast with PMR, AMR measures the true value of risk exposure once a trade is underway. Since it is well understood that the rates or prices governing an underlying transaction will move between trade date and maturity date (in a magnitude which, hopefully, will be less than that estimated by PMR through the risk equivalency process), the actual market risk figure is the amount which a bank will actually lose if a default occurs at a specific point in time. This figure, sometimes also known as a replacement cost, or mark-to market risk, can be viewed as the amount a bank will lose if counterparty default occurs or, alternatively, the amount it will cost the bank to replace the transaction in the market. Actual market risk is equal to the actual credit loss sustained by the bank in unsecured transactions once counterparty default occurs. In certain cases AMR may actually be negative, implying no risk of loss if default occurs.

Both PMR and AMR are essential to the initial decision-making process and the ongoing management of credit exposure. In longer term transactions, the total risk exposure figure will very often be reflected as a sum of the two concepts. Generally the following hold true:

At inception of a trade:

potential market risk {+} $\wedge$ *actual market risk* {0}

31

During the life of a trade:

potential market risk {↓} ∧ *actual market risk* (0,↑, ∨,↓}

At maturity of a trade:

potential market risk {0} ∧ *actual market risk* {+,-, ∨,0}

What will be clear from the above discussion is that market risk will exist in some form during the life of the trade. Market risk can either be theoretical, as measured by our PMR measure, risk equivalent exposure, or it may be real, as measured by our AMR measure, mark-to-market exposure. When a default occurs, a bank will sustain a loss only if AMR is greater than 0; to the extent AMR is negative, the bank will not sustain a loss, as it is the defaulting counterparty which is expecting performance from the bank, not vice versa. The value of PMR is not relevant at the time of default, even though it will certainly be positive (recall that PMR will only be 0 when market rates can no longer move and impact the value of the transaction; this occurs at maturity, when no more market movement, which might impact the transaction, can take place). PMR is only utilized to quantify how much a bank could lose if a bank defaults at some future point. This is vitally important for credit decision, pricing and capital allocation purposes. Without PMR a credit officer would find it difficult to make a credit decision; likewise, pricing and allocation of capital would be inaccurate. It should be noted that the following hold true for derivative transactions impacted by market risk:

$$set\ of\ \{counterparty\ risk\ CR,\ market\ risk\ MR\} \rightarrow resulting\ loss$$
$$\{min\ CR,\ min \vee 0\ MR\} \rightarrow 0\ loss$$
$$\{min\ CR,\ max\ MR\} \rightarrow 0\ loss$$
$$\{max\ CR,\ min \vee 0\ MR\} \rightarrow min \vee 0\ loss$$
$$\{max\ CR,\ max\ MR\} \rightarrow max\ loss$$

where maximum counterparty risk (defined as max *CR*) is counterparty default, and maximum market risk (defined as max *MR*) includes both AMR and PMR.

Our focus in dealing with derivative products is on market risk because, as discussed above, it is the very market movements which make derivatives function from an economic standpoint and which, in turn, add or reduce credit exposure in a transaction. The following section discusses risk equivalency, which is effectively a form by which to capture, in dollar figures, the PMR generated by a given derivative trade.

RISK EQUIVALENCY

Risk equivalency is the process by which the notional amount of a transaction is re-evaluated in light of its characteristics (e.g. maturity, initial rate, frequency of payments) to yield a figure which most accurately reflects the potential risk of the transaction. Risk equivalent exposure, the end-result of the risk equivalency process, is also referred to as risk adjusted exposure, credit equivalent risk or loan equivalent risk. Risk equivalency is necessary primarily because the derivative instruments discussed in this book are not funding transactions, such as unsecured loans or advances. In derivatives trades (with very few exceptions) the notional amounts are not involved, save as a reference point to calculate interest, currency or index amounts payable and/or receivable. Since the notional amounts are not exchanged in a one-sided fashion, as they are in a traditional bank loan, they are not at risk; therefore, risk in these transactions must be some amount which is smaller than the notional.

Risk equivalency is the process of adjusting the notional so that the actual and anticipated risks are appropriately quantified in terms which are logical to the banker or credit officer. As an example, a \$100MM five-year unsecured loan by a bank represents \$100MM of risk extended to the counterparty. A \$100MM five-year interest rate swap may only represent \$2MM of risk, since only the interest flows are being exchanged, not the notional amount. The \$2MM represents the risk equivalent exposure of the transaction; it may be quantified in different forms depending on the specific parameters involved (covered in subsequent portions of this text). It is not always accurate to say derivative instruments have far less risk than unsecured loans; most do, some do not. Cross currency swaps, zero coupon swaps, equity derivative options struck well in-the-money, and derivative options which contain 'all-or-nothing' components are all examples of derivative transactions where the risk equivalent exposure may be very high indeed. We shall not focus on the relative magnitudes of risk in these instruments at this juncture; these details will be considered in subsequent chapters. The central issue at this point is knowing and understanding that derivatives must be risk adjusted so that the correct credit and business decisions regarding the transaction may be made.

The process of quantifying the risk in a derivative transaction is twofold. First, the relevant risk factor, reflecting the underlying movement in rates or prices governing the transaction in question, must be calculated. Second, the risk factor must be used in a broader equation which is specific to the derivative in question. The risk equivalent exposure (*REE*) which results from combining these two elements is the figure which is ultimately used by the credit analyst in quantifying the risk and arriving at the credit decision. Knowing the risk equivalent exposure, the analyst may determine whether the relative risk magnitude in question is appropriate for the counterparty being considered.

The balance of this chapter is devoted to understanding the logic behind a risk factor, and how it may be developed. Parts II–IV employ the risk factor in the specific risk equations introduced for individual products and strategies. The end of this chapter returns to the concept of risk equivalency in general terms through the use of a graph, a standard equation and an example.

RISK FACTORS

Risk factors are the means by which to implement the risk equivalency process discussed above. Since we understand the necessity of risk adjusting those instruments deemed to present an institution with market risk, we need a tool to make this possible. Our discussion will focus on the development and implementation of this tool, known as the risk factor (*RF*).

In order for us to examine the potential loss which may arise from a market risk based product, it is helpful to first intuit what we are attempting to measure. When a bank enters into a derivative transaction with a counterparty, it will assume on its books an obligation which may increase or decrease in value during the course of the trade. A rise or fall in value is traced primarily to the rise or fall in rates (or prices) governing the transaction. If rates move in a certain direction, it may make the transaction more valuable to the institution and, therefore, increase the risk exposure it faces with a given counterparty. There is a positive correlation between the value of the transaction and the risk exposure generated by that transaction. As value increases risk increases, and as value decreases (or becomes negative), risk decreases (though rarely will a bank assign a negative risk figure). Thus, one of the primary parameters we need to establish in order to measure risk accurately is the value of underlying rates at certain points in time, as these will ultimately govern the value and risk of the transaction. A second item we need to consider is transaction maturity. It would seem logical that the longer the maturity of a transaction, the greater the opportunity for a given market, price or rate to move. Rates or prices can only move so far in one week, but they have the potential of moving much farther in one month or one year. Consequently, any effective measurement of risk must also include a time dimension. These two parameters, market movement and maturity, form the basis for the development of our risk exposure measure, *RF*.

In order for us to develop the risk factor measure which captures potential market movements as well as maturity, we turn to some fundamental assumptions utilized in option pricing models. Since option pricing models such as the Black–Scholes Option Pricing Model and the Binomial Option Pricing Model (and many other associated ones) are widely used in the derivatives markets, it does not seem out of line for a credit evaluation to rely on some of the same assumptions underpinning these models. Although full explanation regarding these models is not required in order for us to develop parameters to evaluate credit risk, Appendix I contains additional details on the Black–Scholes model. The original equations should be reviewed in Black and Scholes (1973) and Cox, Ross and Rubinstein (1979) for the Black–Scholes and the Binomial, respectively. In addition, there are many excellent references available which discuss different dimensions (with varying degrees of complexity) of these and other option models (Haley and Schall, 1979; Cox and Rubinstein, 1985; Hull, 1989; Merton, 1990; Gibson, 1991; Dubofsky, 1992).

We introduce concepts of option pricing models in order to achieve several goals: first to explain the background and use of a lognormal distribution; second to explain the derivation of the maturity component, represented by time *T*; third to define historical volatility in terms of option model parameters. By understanding these three items, which are fundamental to option pricing, we will be in a position to establish the risk factor (*RF*) which is central to our evaluation of risk equivalent exposure.

The Lognormal Distribution

Many option pricing models (where the underlying security might be equity, debt, foreign exchange, and so on) attempt to estimate future prices through a stochastic process; a stochastic variable is one which changes in an uncertain manner continuously or at certain points in time. A stochastic process may involve continuous time (the variable in question can change at any moment) or discrete time (the variable can only change at certain intervals) and it may involve a continuous variable (the variable can take on any value) or a discrete variable (the variable can only assume one of a set of values). A Markov process is a stochastic process which says that only the current price of a variable is relevant in determining what may happen in the future. That is, previous prices are irrelevant, as are the number of periods preceding the current observation. This 'independence' from previous price and time information is very important to certain option models.

One of the defining assumptions of the Markov process Black–Scholes Model (and others), is that the return of the variable in question follows a lognormal continuous time stochastic process (sometimes also known as a Geometric Brownian motion). Under this assumption the movement of the variable is random in continuous time; the instantaneous return (defined to be the change in the price of the variable divided by the price of the variable) has a constant mean and a constant variance (defined below). The resulting distribution of the variable is lognormal, which is equivalent to saying that the natural logarithm of the variable is normally distributed. A lognormal distribution is skewed slightly to the right; its upper bound in infinite and its lower bound is 0. This is distinguished from the normal distribution, with the traditional bell shaped curve familiar to most readers. Figures 2.1(a) and (b) show these distributions. Use of a lognormal distribution for prices and rates is generally thought to be most accurate, as one cannot have a negative price or rate and may, in fact, have a very high price or rate (the upper bound of a lognormal being infinite). A normal distribution allows for negative rates or prices, which is unreasonable for our discussion.

A continuous time stochastic process is often referred to as a diffusion process. In general terms this means that the variable exists in continuous time and that its probability density function is also continuous; the variable changes on a random and continuous basis and, as the time interval becomes larger, uncertainty in the returns increases in a predictable fashion (because we know the probability function). Returns over a long period of time are lognormally distributed while returns on an instantaneous (or continuously compounded) basis are normally distributed. Note that the diffusion process does not account for sudden 'jumps' in variables, it simply assumes they move smoothly and continuously in small increments (sudden moves

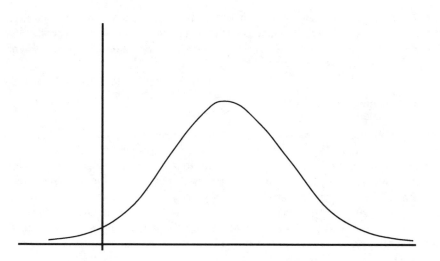

Figure 2.1(a)   Normal distribution

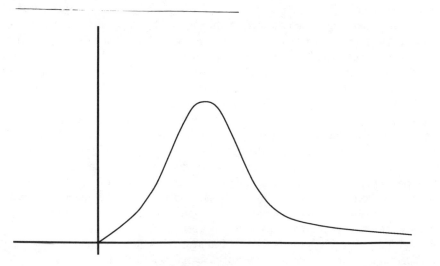

Figure 2.1(b)   Lognormal distribution

are modelled by means of a jump process, not a diffusion process). Critics argue that continuous price behaviour is not always realistic and cite sharp price movements following corporate takeovers, the October 1987 stock market crash, and so on, as examples. Other pricing models incorporate the jump process (Cox and Ross, 1975 and Merton, 1976). For purposes of our discussion, however, we shall follow the diffusion pattern. These conclusions, together with use of the lognormal distribution, mean that the variable can take any value from 0 to infinity at any point in time, T. Let us consider the movement of stock price S (though we could just as easily consider the movement of an equity index, an interest rate, a currency rate, and so on). The diffusion process may be defined as:

$$\frac{\Delta S}{S} = \mu \, \Delta t + \sigma \, \varepsilon \, \sqrt{\Delta t} \qquad (2.1)$$

where
ΔS is the change in the variable (as defined below)
S is the variable
$\Delta S/S$ is the return of the variable
μ is the expected return
Δt is a small time interval
σ is the volatility of the variable
ε is a random sample from a normal distribution with mean 0 and standard deviation 1

Since $\Delta S/S$ is equivalent to saying the return of the variable, it can be written as:

$$\frac{\Delta S}{S} = \frac{(S_{T+\Delta t} - S_T)}{S_T} \qquad (2.2)$$

with time equal to T. In qualitative terms we may say that the return of the stock price is equal to the expected return plus the standard deviation adjusted for an error term ε; ε is included as a normally distributed random sample which may impact the total return at any point in time.

We may convert the equation above into the following form:

$$\frac{dS}{S} = \mu \, dt + \sigma \, dz \qquad (2.3)$$

or

$$dS = \mu \, Sdt + \sigma \, Sdz \qquad (2.4)$$

where dz is a Weiner process and both the expected return μ and the variance of returns σ are functions of the stock price S and time t.

A Weiner process is a stochastic process which is normally distributed with expected value of 0 and variance of 1 at each time interval t. Under a Weiner process, values at time t and $t+1$ have a correlation of 0 (that is, they are independent of one another, as indicated above; thus, a Weiner process is also a Markov process). In generic form we may say that:

$$dy = adt + bdz \qquad (2.5)$$

where a is also known as an instantaneous rate of change in the random variable (and is sometimes referred to as μ or a drift coefficient), while b is the instantaneous standard deviation (or diffusion coefficient). Both a and b are constants. If a and b are not constants but are, instead, functions of certain other variables, they follow what is known as an Ito process. That is, an Ito process is defined as $a(y,t)$ and $b(y,t)$, where the values of a and b are functions of y and t. This is shown as:

$$dy = a(y,\, t)\, dt + b(y,\, t)\, dz \qquad (2.6)$$

We may add, further, that the random variable has an expected return of a and variance of b^2.

Those familiar with stochastic calculus will recognize the standard form of Ito's Lemma as:

$$dF = \left(\frac{\partial F}{\partial y}\, a + \frac{\partial F}{\partial t} + \frac{1}{2} \frac{\partial^2 F}{\partial y^2}\, b^2 \right) dt + \frac{\partial F}{\partial y}\, b\, dz \qquad (2.7)$$

For those not familiar with Ito's Lemma (or not desiring to get involved with calculus), it will be noted simply that Ito's Lemma is a form for solving stochastic differential equations; more specifically, Ito's Lemma finds the differentials of functions of stochastic variables, such as stock prices, time, interest rates, and so on.

Utilizing our equation above, where μ and σ are functions of the stock price S and time t, we substitute as follows:

$$dF = \left(\frac{\partial F}{\partial S}\, \mu\, S + \frac{\partial F}{\partial t} + \frac{1}{2} \frac{\partial^2 F}{\partial S^2}\, \sigma^2\, S^2 \right) dt + \frac{\partial F}{\partial S}\, \sigma\, S\, dz \qquad (2.8)$$

(recall that our constant, a, from the general equation is replaced not by μ, but by $\mu * S$; likewise, our constant b is replaced by $\sigma * S$).

We have said that our random variable in a Markov process is lognormally distributed. With this information, we can set our function F equal to the natural log of the stock price S, and incorporate the differentials into Equation 2.8. We solve the partial differentials when $F = \ln(S)$. These may be shown as

$$\text{if } F = \ln(S), \text{ then } \frac{\partial F}{\partial S} = \frac{1}{S}\, , \, \frac{\partial^2 F}{\partial S^2} = -\frac{1}{S^2}\, , \wedge \frac{\partial F}{\partial t} = 0$$

Substituting back into Equation 2.8, we note

$$dF = \left(\frac{1}{S}\, \mu S + 0 + \frac{1}{2} \left(-\frac{1}{S^2}\, \sigma^2\, S^2 \right) \right) dt + \frac{1}{S}\, \sigma\, S\, dz \qquad (2.9)$$

which equals

$$dF = \left(\mu - \frac{\sigma^2}{2}\right)dt + \sigma\,dz \qquad (2.10)$$

Earlier we said that our random variable has an expected return of a and variance of b^2. This means that the change in F, from one period to the next (i.e. $(T\text{-}t)$, or τ) is:

$$\phi\left[\left(\mu - \frac{\sigma^2}{2}\tau\right), \sigma^2\tau\right] \qquad (2.11)$$

or

$$\phi\left[\left(\mu - \frac{\sigma^2}{2}\tau\right), \sigma\sqrt{\tau}\right] \qquad (2.12)$$

We have set $F = \ln(S)$, so $\ln(S_T)\text{-}\ln(S)$ is precisely equal to the result above (i.e. it represents the change from one period to the next). We may conclude, therefore, that

$$\ln(S_T) - \ln(S) \approx \phi\left[\left(\mu - \frac{\sigma^2}{2}\tau\right), \sigma\sqrt{\tau}\right] \qquad (2.13)$$

which says that the difference in the natural logs of the stock prices between time T and t is normally distributed with mean of

$$\mu - \frac{\sigma^2}{2}\tau$$

and standard deviation

$$\sigma\sqrt{\tau}$$

Finally, we may calculate from above that

$$\ln\left(\frac{S_T}{S}\right) = \mu - \frac{\sigma^2}{2}\tau + \sigma\sqrt{\tau} \qquad (2.14)$$

and, through simple algebra,

$$S_T = Se^{\mu - \frac{\sigma^2}{2}\tau + \sigma\sqrt{\tau}} \qquad (2.15)$$

That is, the stock price at time T is equal to the continuously compounded stock price at $(T\text{-}t)$, normally distributed with mean and variance as defined above.

As an aside, it is important to remember that a continuously compounded return is equal to an instantaneous move up or down, with certain probabilities. We may show that a one period growth factor Z, which is simply 1 plus the interest rate i over m intervals, takes on the following form, as m moves to infinity:

$$Z = \lim_{m \to \infty} \left(1 + \frac{i}{m}\right)^m$$

$$\Leftrightarrow \quad Z = e^i$$

or

$$i = \ln Z$$

Thus, the interest rate i is exactly equal to the natural log of the growth factor Z.

Based on the rather extensive discussion above, we may say that S_T is lognormally distributed, where the standard deviation is proportional to the square root of τ (T-t). The variance about the mean is said to increase as time increases. In fact, if the variable in question follows the diffusion process, then the variance of the changes is proportional to time; thus, the standard deviation (which is the square root of the variance) of the changes is proportional to the square root of time. This is known as the 'square root rule' and the concept will be incorporated into our risk factor model. We shall also come back to this model in Appendix I, with a particular emphasis on Equation 2.15, when the Black–Scholes Model is discussed in greater depth.

Readers interested in working through calculus of the above should refer to the original work by Black and Scholes, 1973, as well as excellent discussions in Cheung and Yeung, 1992; Hull, 1989; Haley and Schall, 1979; Hull and White, 1987; Hunter and Stowe, 1992; and Merton, 1990.

The information above is provided as background to show that changes in prices and rates are lognormally distributed and vary in proportion to the square root of time. Readers who do not want to concern themselves with the mathematics or statistics presented above may wish simply to assume that future changes in prices or rates affecting the derivative transactions on our books will (a) be lognormally distributed; (b) vary with the square root of time.

These items will be very important in our development of a risk factor to quantify the potential market movements (and therefore the potential credit exposure) inherent in derivative instruments impacted by stochastic variables (such as interest rates, stock prices, currency prices, index levels, and so on).

Historical Volatility

Historical volatility measures the historical movement of price changes; this is, of course, precisely equal to the deviations about the mean, which is what standard deviation measures. When attempting to calculate the standard deviation parameters for the Black–Scholes or other models, historical volatility is often used as a proxy.

There are a number of ways by which to calculate this standard deviation measure, and one of the more common means is to focus on the mean and standard deviation of the natural log of the so-called price relatives, S_T/S_{T-1}. This may be shown as follows in Equation 2.16:

$$\tau = \text{time interval}$$
$$n = \text{number of observations}$$
$$S_T = \text{price at period } T$$
$$r = \ln (S_T/S_{T-1})$$

and utilizing s as an estimate of our standard deviation parameter

$$\sigma \sqrt{\tau}$$

above:

$$s = \sqrt{\left(\frac{1}{n-1} \sum_{T=1}^{n} (r_T - \bar{r})^2 \right)} \qquad (2.16)$$

In the equation above, $\bar{r}$ is the mean of the natural log of price relatives defined by r.

The value of s provides us with an estimate of the standard deviation of the price relatives, but only after we have adjusted the result for the time dimension denoted by τ. If the price relatives are based on daily observations, the resulting s measures the standard deviation of the daily price changes. Since most volatility figures are quoted on a per annum basis, s must be multiplied by the square root of the number of days during which the index or market is active (generally considered to be 250 active business days). Likewise, if monthly observations were taken, measuring the monthly volatility of the price changes, we would multiply by the square root of the months during which activity takes place (again, an estimate would call for 8.3 months per year). (Note that certain methodologies call for adjustment by 365 days or 12 months; it is left for the reader to employ whichever method appears most logical.) In order to obtain our per annum historical volatility estimate (HV p.a.), then, we simply need to calculate

$$HV_{p.a.} = s\sqrt{m} \qquad (2.17)$$

where m is equal to the size of the interval during which observations are taken (i.e. 250 for days, 8.3 for months, and so on). There are, of course, other ways by which to calculate historical volatility; the above method, however, provides an accurate measure of HV and is computationally simple to implement.

One of the very important topics in statistics regards the optimal number of observations taken in the development of a volatility measure. While this is a very broad and separate topic with a great many considerations, it is generally safe to say that more observations are better than less observations (with the caveat that too many historical data points may result in 'noise' or irrelevant figures being incorporated into the measure). When considering weekly or monthly data, it is not unreasonable to suppose that at least two to three years of observations points are appropriate. When dealing with daily data, it is unlikely that two to three years or more would be required to develop a meaningful sample; it is generally thought that three to six months of (rolling) data points are sufficient to provide a good estimate (Hull,1989).

At this point we have a volatility figure which is adjusted to represent a per annum movement in the price, rate or index with which we are dealing. This is obviously a crucial parameter for us in the development of our risk factor, as it provides a starting point in dictating how far, based on historical market movements and the assumptions covered above, a given variable is expected to move over a certain period of time. This, in turn, allows us to quantify how those observable market movements will increase (or decrease) the credit risk exposure we encounter in a given transaction.

Confidence Levels

Once the historical data has been identified and gathered, and the standard deviation of the price movements has been calculated, we need to adjust the volatility to the appropriate statistical confidence level. We need to elevate the findings to a degree of confidence which allows the historical volatility measure to assume a meaningful role in the decision-making process, since the volatility measure we calculate above is based on a limited sample. We want to ensure that in 90 per cent–99 per cent of cases the sample volatility is representative of the population volatility (standard deviation). If we are able to do this, we may then expect our risk factor to be representative not just of movements based on a limited sample, but of movements based on a broader population. By doing so, we would expect that a future rate or price observation (which might be relevant in a given transaction), will be less than or equal to the figure indicated by the sample standard deviation adjusted to a confidence level which is representative of a broader population standard deviation. In other words we want to be certain that the volatility measure has been adjusted such that 90 per cent–99 per cent of the time a future observation lies within the bound predicted by our adjusted volatility measure.

For those readers familiar with a normal distribution (standard 'bell shaped' curve), it will be recalled that one standard deviation on a normal distribution includes 68 per cent of all observations, while two standard deviations includes 95 per cent of all observations and three standard deviations includes 98 per cent of all observations. The parameters for two deviations are highlighted in Equation 2.18 and Figure 2.2 below.

$$P(\mu - 2\sigma \leq x \leq \mu + 2\sigma) = P(2(.3414) + 2(.1359)) = P(.9544) \qquad (2.18)$$

However, since we are utilizing a lognormal distribution in this discussion, the standard deviations which encompass 90 per cent, 95 per cent and 99 per cent confidence bands are different. From statistical theory we can derive the appropriate multiple of standard deviations which will include these confidence levels, and do so

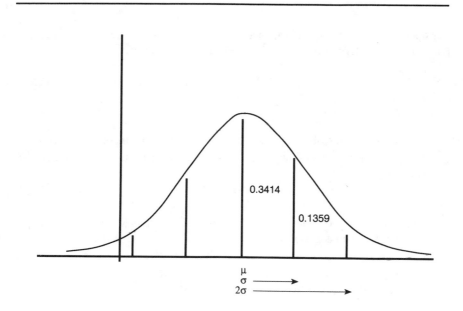

Figure 2.2   Normal distribution

via the χ^2 function. A χ^2 distribution is utilized when we want to focus our sampling distribution on the sample variance, determining the probability that the value of the sample variance will be larger or smaller than some observed value, given an assumed value for the population variance. In this process, our unbiased estimator of the population variance is shown as:

$$s^2 = \sum_{T=1}^{n} \frac{(r_T - \bar{r})^2}{n-1} \tag{2.19}$$

which is, of course, similar to the result shown in our calculation of historical volatility in Equation 2.16 above, in which we show the square root of the variance, which is the standard deviation.

The χ^2 test is shown as:

$$\chi^2_{n-1} = \frac{(n-1)\, s^2}{\sigma^2} \tag{2.20}$$

This may be interpreted as saying if the variance of the random sample (where the size of the sample is *n*) is calculated from a normal population with variance σ^2, then the χ^2 statistic above has the same distribution as a χ^2 variance with *n*-1 degrees of freedom. When constructing a two tailed χ^2 test to verify if the population variance is less than or equal to the sample variance for a given confidence level and sample size (and thus certain degrees of freedom), the equation is shown as:

$$\frac{(n-1)\,s^2}{\chi^2_{\alpha/2,\,v}} \le \sigma^2 \le \frac{(n-1)\,s^2}{\chi^2_{1-\alpha/2,\,v}} \tag{2.21}$$

In the case of a χ^2 distribution, as v, our degrees of freedom, increase over 100, the χ^2 begins to take the general appearance of a normal distribution with mean and standard deviation of:

$$\mu = v, \sigma = \sqrt{2v}$$

Since v is dependent on our sample size, and since samples we would take in the context of price movements are likely to be greater than 100, we may use a standardized z-score to evaluate our confidence level (1-α), where z(α) is the standardized normal value leaving α in the right-hand tail (and obviously (1-α) under the remainder of the curve). If sample size is less than 100, the χ^2 remains the appropriate function.

Figure 2.3 illustrates the lognormal distribution with α in the right-hand tail (where (1 - α) is our desired confidence level).

The reader familiar with statistics will recall that z-scores may be calculated via the following:

$$F(x) = P\,\{X \le x\} \tag{2.22}$$

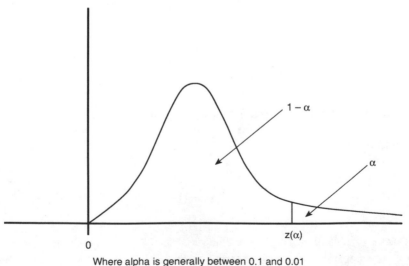

Where alpha is generally between 0.1 and 0.01
and 1 − α is our confidence level

Figure 2.3   Lognormal distribution

$$= P \left\{ \frac{X - \mu}{\sigma} \le \frac{x - \mu}{\sigma} \right\} \qquad (2.23)$$

$$= P \left\{ Z \le \frac{x - \mu}{\sigma} \right\} \qquad (2.24)$$

$$\Leftrightarrow \varphi \left(Z = \frac{x - \mu}{\sigma} \right) \qquad (2.25)$$

where μ is the mean, σ is the standard deviation and x is an observation; $\varphi(z_\alpha)$ is obtained from a table of z-scores (see Hines and Montgomery, 1990 or Mills, 1977, for example).

We also know that:

$$P\{Z > z_\alpha\} = 1 - \varphi(z_\alpha) = \alpha \qquad (2.26)$$

which simply gives us the probability our unit normal variable Z will exceed z_α with probability α.

We may also note that x may be calculated via a form of Equation 2.25 (see Mills, 1977):

$$x = \mu_x + z\, \sigma_x \qquad (2.27)$$

An examination of a table of z-scores, Table 2.1, reveals the following:

Table 2.1 Z-scores

$\varphi(z(\alpha)) =$	0.5–prob = α	$(1 - \alpha)$
$\varphi(1.28) =$	0.5–0.4000 = 0.10	1–0.100 = 0.900
$\varphi(1.64) =$	0.5–0.4495 = 0.05	1–0.050 = 0.950
$\varphi(1.96) =$	0.5–0.4750 = 0.025	1–0.025 = 0.975
$\varphi(2.33) =$	0.5–0.4900 = 0.01	1–0.010 = 0.990
$\varphi(2.58) =$	0.5–0.4950 = 0.005	1–0.005 = 0.995

Note: 1-α is our confidence level.

We may therefore say that the confidence levels (leaving α in the right-hand tail) equate to the z-scores ($\varphi(z_\alpha)$) highlighted in Table 2.2.

Table 2.2 Z-scores

z_α	$\varphi(z_\alpha)$	Confidence Level
z(0.10)	1.28	90.0%
z(0.05)	1.64	95.0%
z(0.025)	1.96	97.5%
z(0.01)	2.33	99.0%
z(0.005)	2.58	99.5%

Note: We shall refer to $\varphi(z_\alpha)$ as z below, and throughout the text.

Utilizing the information above, we may elevate the sample volatility measure so that it is representative of the population volatility, by utilizing the appropriate z score against the sample volatility. For example, if the sample standard deviation is 10 per cent, and we employ a 90 per cent z statistic of 1.28, we may say that the 90 per cent estimate of the population standard deviation is 12.80 per cent.

In summary form, in order to elevate the volatility measure to a certain confidence level, we need only multiply the standard deviation (which we have termed *HV*) by the relevant standard deviate factor above. This is done via:

$$HV = HV_{p.a.} \times z \qquad (2.28)$$

(where we assume s has been adjusted to the appropriate time interval m, as shown in Equation 2.17, to yield *HV* $_{p.a.}$).

If we want to adjust a volatility measure of 15 per cent to a 95 per cent confidence level, we would simply multiply 15 per cent by 1.64 to obtain 24.6 per cent. Within our total risk factor framework, this may then be interpreted as saying we are confident, with 95 per cent certainty, that a future price or rate observation governing a transaction will be within 24.6 per cent of the level on trade date. This implies that our risk factor will be meaningful in at least 95 per cent of all cases, which adds a high degree of comfort to the credit decision-making process. Institutions opting for a more conservative or rigorous standard may elect to increase the confidence level to 97.5 per cent or even 99 per cent; the associated confidence level factors, as we have shown above, are 2.33 and 2.58 respectively. Once again, for those not wishing to delve into the statistics presented above, it will be sufficient to remember that a volatility measure can be adjusted to a confidence level by utilizing one of the z-score 'multipliers' highlighted above, depending on specific confidence level requirements.

Transaction Maturity

We know from our discussion above that the standard deviation of the changes in our variable is proportional to the square root of time; this is our 'square root rule'. In order for us to take account of the maturity of a given transaction, we must incorporate the 'square root rule' into our volatility estimate. That is, if we obtain an *HV* of 15 per cent (recalling that *HV* has already been annualized by Equation 2.17 above, and has been adjusted to the relevant confidence level), we know the expected movement of the index based on past historical movements during the next 12 months will be within 15 per cent of the starting point. If a particular transaction is executed for final maturity in two years, or in six months, we know that we must adjust the *HV* (or standard deviation) measure to account for this change in time. The change we need to make is done by:

$$HV_{adj} = HV\sqrt{T} \qquad (2.29)$$

where T is the maturity of the transaction, in fractions or multiples of 1 year (i.e. a 2-year trade would set T at 2, while a 6-month trade would set T at 0.5). In our example above, *HV* of 15 per cent for a 2-year trade would translate into an HV_{adj} of 21.2 per cent; a 6-month trade would imply an HV_{adj} of 10.6 per cent.

The Complete Risk Factor

Having discussed the development of volatility based on a lognormal distribution, confidence levels associated with bringing the volatility measure to a 90 per cent–99 per cent level and transaction maturity to capture the essential time dimension, we have effectively created all the components of the risk factor RF. We summarize these elements as:

$$RF = HV\sqrt{T} \times z \qquad (2.30)$$

(Note that we shall continue to separate *HV* and $\sqrt{T}$, instead of using HV_{adj}, for purposes of clarity).

With this information we are in a position to measure the potential future market movements for a given rate or index, with a 90 per cent (or higher) confidence level, for any maturity which may be proposed.

In the framework of an example, we can imagine developing a risk factor to quantify the potential future market movements of the Nikkei index. If we observe a series of 180 days of closing price information where the standard deviation of the natural log price relatives, as measured by s in Equation 2.16, results in 1.25 per cent, we may proceed as follows. Since daily price information was used, and recalling that the resulting 1.25 per cent represents the standard deviation of the daily price moves, we adjust this measure by the square root of the number of trading days, per Equation 2.17. This will yield an annualized $HV_{p.a.}$ of

$$1.25\% * \sqrt{250} = 19.76\%$$

Thus, the annualized standard deviation of price moves is 19.76 per cent.

We next adjust *HV* to a 90 per cent confidence level by multiplying by the 1.28 *z*-score, as outlined in Equation 2.28. This yields a 90 per cent confidence level volatility measure of 25.3 per cent. We are thus certain that in 90 per cent of future cases, the 1-year market movement will be no more than 25.3 per cent from our starting level.

Finally, we take account of the time dimension by multiplying by the square root of transaction maturity *T*, per Equation 2.29. If we are attempting to create a one-year risk factor, we know there will be no change to our confidence-level-adjusted risk figure of 25.3 per cent. A six-month figure, however, would be calculated as:

$$25.3\% * \sqrt{0.5} = 17.9\%$$

while a two-year factor would be:

$$25.3\% * \sqrt{2} = 35.8\%$$

At this point we have developed a series of risk factors for the Nikkei, within the confines of our defining Equation 2.30. We interpret the above as saying that we would expect, with 90 per cent certainty, the 6-month, 12-month and 24-month movement of the Nikkei to be within 17.9 per cent, 25.3 per cent and 35.8 per cent of our starting

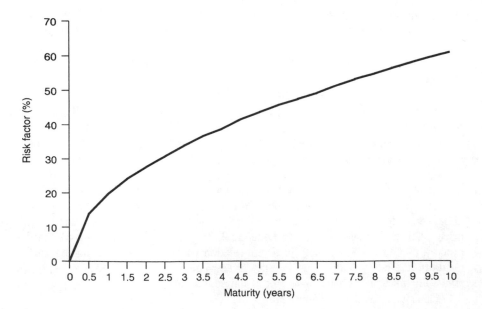

Figure 2.4   Risk factor, HV$_{adj}$ 15 per cent, 90 per cent confidence level

point, respectively. This is our measure, then, of how estimated future index levels may impact the value of a market risk derivative transaction involving the Nikkei. If our bank enters into a 6-month Nikkei trade with a counterparty today we would expect, with 90 per cent confidence, market movements during the transaction to be within 17.9 per cent of today's starting point. This, then, allows us to quantify the maximum expected market movement in the index and, as we know from above, the maximum potential market risk exposure on the transaction. The same logic may, of course, be applied to any stochastic variable which is evaluated through the *RF* framework (e.g. interest rates, stock prices, currency rates).

As additional information, we present graphs which capture the path of the risk factor at varying confidence levels so the reader may observe the interaction between the two and see the position of the risk factor.

The reader will recognize the shape of the curve to be equivalent to the exponential curve (with the function $y = \ln(x)$). This is to be expected, given the use of the natural log throughout our discussion in this chapter.

As one might expect, the movement to a higher confidence level results in an upward shift in the entire risk factor curve.

At this point we have developed a complete risk factor as defined by Equation 2.30. At the ends of both Chapter 5 and Appendix II, the reader will find sample risk factors for major equity indexes and interest rate swaps, respectively. Using the methodology above it is relatively simple to develop risk factors for other instruments and markets as well.

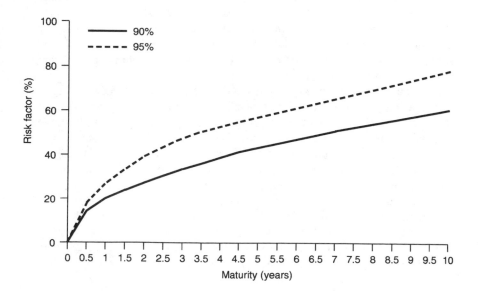

Figure 2.5 Risk factor, HV 15 per cent, varying confidence levels

The risk factor we have developed may now be used in the appropriate risk equivalency calculation, which is dependent on the specific derivative product or strategy with which we are dealing. The general form of the equation is

$$REE = RF \times N$$

where   *REE* is the risk equivalent exposure,
                  RF is the risk factor,
                  N is the notional amount of the transaction.

Thus, if we were presented with a derivative transaction where the notional was $100MM and we determined the risk factor to be equal to 5 per cent, our *REE* would be $5MM. This would be the maximum we would expect to lose at any point during the life of the trade, based on our complete *RF* framework. If our counterparty defaults during the life of the swap, we would expect our maximum credit loss to be less than, or equal to, $5MM. This figure is also, of course, precisely equal to the potential market risk (PMR) discussed earlier in the chapter. This *REE* measure is the ex ante figure we require in order to make a credit decision regarding the acceptability of a transaction for a given counterparty, and it represents the maximum credit exposure we would expect to face during the life of the deal. Knowing the *REE* is equal to $5MM, for example, an analyst considering a transaction (and bearing in mind other items such as transaction maturity, product suitability, and so on) would arrive at a rational credit decision. Without an *REE* measure, it would be impossible for the analyst to know how to evaluate the risk on a $100MM swap. Actual market risk (AMR), though vital once a trade is underway, is equal to 0 at inception and is, therefore, unsuitable for decision-making purposes. It should be noted that the standard *REE* equation above is very often modified for individual products, as we shall note in the following chapters. The form given above is generic.

Figure 2.6 summarizes, in graph form, our discussion on *RF* and *REE*.

A note at this point: the above discussion relies on a number of assumptions in order to create a workable framework. Many of the assumptions can be altered to suit the individual requirements of a given institution. What we have discussed above is by no means the only effective representation of a risk equivalency framework. Having said this, we now have one straightforward method by which to begin quantifying potential market movements and, by definition, the potential credit risk exposure which might be encountered in a given derivative transaction under normal conditions.

Obviously, the financial markets exhibit a fair degree of volatility. While the framework we have created above relies on a volatility measure to yield its final result, it is true that on occasion volatility exceeds the boundaries of what is considered 'normal'. Instances of turmoil or chaos in certain markets lend some weight to this: the global equity crashes in October 1987 and October 1989, the junk bond market crash in October 1989 and, most recently, the currency turmoil in Europe in September 1992 (when overnight interest rates in certain currencies reached dramatic levels, e.g. Sterling at 160 per cent, Euro escudos at 1500 per cent, Swedish krona at 600 per cent).

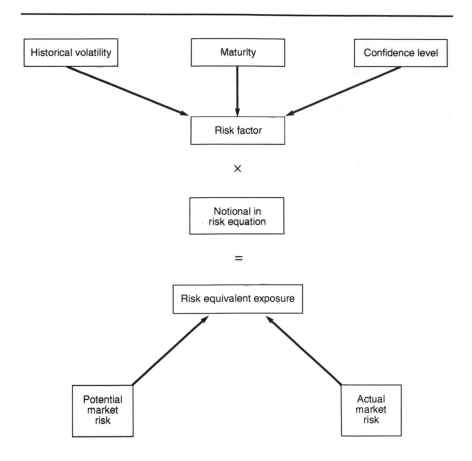

Figure 2.6   The risk equivalency process

No model is perfect, as derivative practitioners have found, particularly in times of extreme volatility. However, we can be comfortable that the above provides us with an accurate measure when conditions are normal; since most credit and exposure management decisions take place during times of relative tranquility (if 15 to 20 per cent volatility is considered tranquil), the approach highlighted above serves our purposes. If decision-making and transaction execution must occur in periods of extreme volatility, then the credit professional involved in a transaction must take account of this fact and modify the approach or decision accordingly.

PART II

THE CREDIT RISK OF OPTIONS

3: A Review of Credit Exposure Evaluation for Options

We will discuss, at several points in this text, the use of options in derivative structures. Puts (giving the holder the right, but not the obligation, to sell a given underlying instrument at a certain strike price) and calls (giving the holder the right, but not the obligation, to buy a given instrument at a certain strike price) are fundamental to many transactions and structures in the capital markets, and are used by a broad range of participants. Since over-the-counter options can be bought and sold on virtually any instrument (the same not being true, obviously, for exchange listed options), they are logical components of a tailor-made package designed to yield very specific results for either investor or issuer. Given the importance of options, it is worth reviewing some basic approaches to valuing credit risk in standard contracts. This chapter serves as a brief review of the evaluation of credit risk exposure in general options transactions, for use in subsequent chapters (including Chapter 4 on the credit risk of varying options strategies and Chapter 6 on equity derivative options).

As the reader might suspect, options are impacted by movements in rates (whether interest or currency rates, stock prices, index prices, and so on). As a result, they are defined as market risk products and have to be risk adjusted through the risk equivalency method in order to obtain an accurate measurement of the credit risk assumed by a bank. As discussed in Chapter 2, the risk equivalency calculation will focus on the risk factor RF in the relevant risk equation. Below we present models for the valuation of risk exposure in options, one which is generic and is a standard for options struck at-the-money, and a second which is somewhat more detailed and applicable to options struck in- or out-of-the-money. Either method may be employed in estimating the level of credit risk an institution faces when dealing with these instruments. We also adapt these equations to account for situations when a transaction is based on a notional amount, rather than a specified number of contracts (as is very common in the options market).

In virtually all OTC options, risk exposure is one-sided (the only exception being currency options, where exercise may result in the option seller being exposed to delivery risk; such a discussion, however, is not relevant to our work in this text and we shall not consider this special situation). In all cases it is the buyer of an option, be it a put or a call, which suffers the credit risk exposure. The role of the option seller is to provide the buyer with a certain economic payoff should a certain strike level be attained; in exchange for providing this payoff, the seller will earn premium income. Once the seller receives its premium, it is no longer dependent on the buyer for any future performance and, as such, has no credit exposure to the buyer. Most options which are not part of an interest/currency swap or equity derivative swap structure are 'independent' contracts, so it is most common for premium to be paid in an upfront sum, within a five-business-day settlement period. (If an option is packaged within a swap structure, premium may be deferred or amortized over a longer period of time, implying different risk parameters; we shall explore such special cases in subsequent chapters). Thus, there is no credit risk exposure from non-receipt of the premium since, if the seller fails to receive what it is owed within five days, it will cancel the option contract and no longer be obligated to provide the buyer with any possible economic payoff in the future.

The buyer, in contrast, is paying the seller for a potential financial benefit should a market move in a particular direction; it is the buyer which is expecting to receive a certain payment once the target level is reached. If the option moves in-the-money during the life of the transaction and the buyer exercises its rights under that option, it will expect performance by the seller in order to derive its economic gain. Since it is looking to the seller to 'make good' on its contract, it has exposure to the seller as its counterparty. If the seller defaults when the option is in-the-money, the buyer will not receive what it is rightly owed and, as a result, will suffer an economic loss. In addition, the payment it made to secure the option, its premium, will have been sacrificed as well. Thus, any option buyer has credit risk exposure on two fronts: exposure to loss of premium and exposure to loss of the economic gain resulting from the option moving into-the-money. Only if the option premium is deferred until the end of the transaction (in some sort of a net payment fashion) will it be able to avoid its premium exposure. Unless an option is embedded in another structure, it is uncommon for premium payments to be deferred or amortized.

Focusing on these two points, then, we know that a bank's credit exposure in dealing with OTC options occurs when it is long, (i.e. the purchaser of the call or put). Short options carry no risk to the bank, to the extent premium is received in a normal cash settlement time frame. For purposes of this chapter we shall assume that derivative options purchased by a bank will be made with an upfront premium payment; likewise, options sales will be done with an upfront premium receipt. The reader should always bear in mind the differences which occur when premium payments are either deferred or amortized during the life of the transaction (such as a Libor flow embedded in a swap, as discussed in later chapters). Adjustments should be made as required in order to compensate for these non-standard differences.

With these comments as a general background we shall focus on the credit risk exposure of long options. If we turn to our general risk equivalency Equation 2.31, which says that $REE = RF * N$, we can adapt it slightly to create the basic form for long options, which is also equivalent to the more complex equation for long at-the-money transactions. The form of our equation focuses on defining our notional, N, in two components, NC and SP, where NC is equal to the number of contracts and SP equals the strike price of the contracts. The multiplication of NC and SP will yield a figure which is equivalent to the generic notional term N. Since option buyers and sellers often speak in terms of contracts bought and sold, it is helpful and accurate to separate the terms. We shall present an adjustment for equations executed on a notional basis later in the chapter.

If we apply the correct *RF* to our option's notional value, we will obtain the first part of our risk equivalent exposure calculation; that is, we will have a figure which provides an estimate of the maximum dollar market exposure we encounter when dealing with a transaction characterized by *NC* contracts at a given strike price *SP*. We know from above that we must also add in the premium which is paid out in upfront form to the option seller, as this represents additional risk the buyer has to the seller. The form of our general long options equation is, therefore:

$$REE = Premium + (RF \times (NC \text{ x } SP)) \tag{3.1}$$

where   *RF* is the relevant risk factor,
         NC is the number of contracts,
         SP is the strike price of the contracts.

To put the above in the context of an example, we can consider the following: Bank EFG, wishing to receive the appreciation in the S & P 500 over a price level of 400, decides to buy 1000 call contracts at a current level of 390. In order to enter into this obligation it will pay its counterparty, Bank Q, a premium of $50,000 (note that we shall not concern ourselves with the specific calculation of the premium value. For our purposes this is a figure provided by the derivatives trader from an option pricing model). We may assume for this example that a 12-month option on the S & P yields a risk factor of 20 per cent. The risk equivalent exposure on this simple equation is, therefore:

$$REE = \$50,000 + (0.20 * (1000 * 400))$$
$$REE = \$50,000 + \$80,000$$
$$REE = \$130,000$$

In other words, an option exposure on the S & P for 12 months equal to $400,000 notional will create a credit risk equivalent exposure of $130,000 for Bank EFG. If Bank Q fails to perform at some point during the life of the transaction, EFG will lose, with certainty, its $50,000 premium payment. In addition, it stands to lose the intrinsic value of its option when, and if, it goes in-the-money. According to our risk factor the S & P can move by 20 per cent in a 12-month time frame, to a level no higher than 468 (i.e. 20 per cent above 390, our starting point). Should the option move to its maximum point during the life of the trade, and should Q default at that point, EFG will sustain its maximum loss. It should be noted that this is a relatively simple, and static, risk equation, which is generally only useful in evaluating the risk of an option at inception. It does not take into account future changes in either the current market price or the risk factor, nor the fact that the call being purchased is 2.5 per cent out-of-the-money (nor would it make an adjustment for an option which was purchased in-the-money). Nonetheless, it is a suitable equation for those wanting to obtain a quick estimate of the maximum risk scenario at the inception of the transaction. This is often sufficient for decision-making purposes though it will result in some understatement or overstatement of risk; in addition, it is unlikely to be sufficient for ongoing credit exposure management purposes. Note that we assume that counterparty default occurs when the index has moved to its maximum level. Although the probability of both events occurring simultaneously is small this is, nonetheless, a very common approach when utilizing a conservative credit risk posture.

In order to evaluate the credit risk exposure of an option position in a more precise fashion, both at inception and on an ongoing basis, we can make certain refinements to Equation 3.1. The refinements we make include adjusting the risk factor on a continuous basis in order to account for the decreasing maturity of the trade. This is done by substituting RF with RFc, a constantly adjusted risk factor which declines with the passage of time. This should make intuitive sense to the reader, because as time passes and there is a shorter span until maturity, the chance for future market movements begins to decline as well; such will be represented by a lower RFc.

The second refinement we need to make is related to the intrinsic value of the option at inception, and at subsequent points during the life of the trade. This may be thought of as measuring actual market risk (AMR) outlined in Chapter 2. When an option is entered into initially, it may be out-of-the-money, at-the-money or in-the-money; options struck out-of-the-money (i.e. those with no intrinsic value) have less economic value than those struck at-the-money or in-the-money. An option with less value is also one which carries less credit risk exposure; an option with more value is one with more credit risk exposure. Again, this should make sense to the reader: if a bank purchases an option which is deeply out-of-the-money, it has less value and it stands less chance of finishing in-the-money. If an option does not move in-the-money, the option buyer will never need to look to the option seller for performance; when the buyer is not looking to the seller for performance (or is not expecting to look to the seller for performance), its associated risk exposure will be lower. Conversely, options which are struck in-the-money have a greater chance of ending with value; since it is highly probable such instruments will be exercised, the buyer places increased reliance on the performance of the seller in such instances. In addition, since the option is already in-the-money, counterparty default immediately after the commencement of the trade will result in a certain credit loss (over and above the loss of premium). Our new equation takes account of these facts.

For those options which are deeply out-of-the-money, particularly with a short time to maturity (i.e. little time value), it is entirely reasonable to suppose that market risk exposure will never be positive; that is, the option will not move in-the-money and the buyer will not look to the seller for performance. In such instances it seems appropriate to value only the risk of the premium as credit exposure. Our new equation takes account of this fact by assigning credit risk exposure equal to the greater of 0 or the potential market risk movement (calculated by applying our risk factor to the current market price CMP, which is our starting point), adjusted for the in- or out-of-the-money portion of the option (which is calculated by comparing CMP and SP). Our new equation, then, takes the form of Equation 3.2 for calls, and Equation 3.3 for puts:

$$REE = Premium + 0 \vee (NC \times [(RFc \times CMP) + (CMP\text{--}SP)]) \tag{3.2}$$

and

$$REE = Premium + 0 \vee (NC \times [(RFc \times CMP) + (SP - CMP)]) \tag{3.3}$$

where RFc is a constantly adjusted risk factor,
             NC is the number of contracts,
             CMP is the current market price,
             SP is the strike price.

Note that we designate CMP as the starting point in tracking market movement, and apply RFc to that starting point. Intuitively this should make sense, since our percentage RFc, applied to the current market level, provides us with the maximum upward or downward movement we can expect during the life of the transaction. Use of $(RFc * CMP)$ provides a slight upward bias when CMP is higher than SP, a slight downward bias when CMP is lower than SP (this logic is borne out by examining extreme cases: for instance, the equations above, for a call and put struck equally deep in-the-money on the same strike, will assign the incrementally higher risk to the call, on the assumption that the put faces a lower bound of zero but the call has an upper bound of infinity). Those not wanting to bias the risk factors may use $(RFc * SP)$; there is no single correct answer, and it is dependent on one's view of the matter. Note that regardless of the method used, the intrinsic value component $(CMP\text{-}SP)$ or $(SP\text{-}CMP)$ remains unchanged. Although it is left for the reader to decide which method is most relevant, in this text we shall continue to value options via the equations detailed above. (Note further that we shall utilize a similar approach in developing swap risk factors in Appendix II, where 'up' movements shift at a greater rate than 'down' movements.)

Returning to our discussion, let us put the above in the context of actual practice, through the following example:

Bank J buys 10,000 out-of-the-money put contracts on the Nikkei, struck at 15,000 in a 16,500 market (10 per cent out-of-the-money). The maturity is 12 months and the premium paid to the seller, Bank Y, is $200,000 (note that the notional principal involved in this transaction is approximately $1.2MM, which is derived from 10,000 contracts * 15,000 current price, divided by 125 yen/$). The risk factor used at inception is 25 per cent. The initial risk faced on this transaction, per Equation 3.3, is captured by the following (note that the index values of 16,500 and 15,000 are divided by an exchange rate of 125 yen/$ in the second step in order to yield a dollar equivalent REE):

$$REE = \$200,000 + 0 \text{ or } (10,000 * [(0.25 * 16,500) + (15,000 - 16,500)])$$

$$REE = \$200,000 + 0 \text{ or } (10,000 * [(4125) + (-1500)]$$

$$REE = \$200,000 + \$210,000$$

$$REE = \$410,000$$

Although the option is struck 10 per cent out-of-the-money (which subtracts from the total market risk exposure faced by Bank J), the long time to expiry translates into a 25 per cent risk factor on market movements. This, in turn, more than offsets the out-of-the-money portion of the trade and adds potential risk exposure to the transaction (over and above the premium). It is relatively simple to imagine that a short term trade, which is struck 10 per cent out-of-the-money, would have less time for market movement to force the option in-the-money; this, in turn, would translate into less credit risk to the institution buying the option (which, again, would be captured by a lower risk factor). If, in the example above, the maturity of the trade was lowered from 12 months to 1 month (with the associated risk factor falling from 25 per cent to 7 per cent), the second portion of the equation would be negative. In such an instance the only credit risk exposure likely to be encountered would be loss of premium.

Returning to our original example, we can track the credit risk exposure of the option trade every quarter, remembering to substitute a new risk factor at each valuation point. The results are shown in Table 3.1 (yen/$ is assumed to remain constant in order to isolate the effects of the option risk):

Table 3.1   Ongoing credit risk of Nikkei put ($ in Ms), 10,000 contracts

Day	REE	Premium	RFc	CMP	SP
t=0	$410	$200	0.25	16,500	15,000
90	$402	$200	0.22	16,000	15,000
180	$404	$200	0.17	15,000	15,000
270	$391	$200	0.13	14,500	15,000
360	$280	$200	0.00	14,000	15,000

Through this example we can see how the option's risk changes over time. The premium remains static throughout the life of the transaction, as this is a sum which Bank J will have at risk until the conclusion of the trade. The *RFc* declines each quarter (or each month, week or day) in line with the declining maturity of the option. As the *CMP* of the Nikkei decreases, we note that the actual credit exposure of the option begins to increase, until the strike level is breached on day 180; from that point on the option is in-the-money, and the second portion of Equation 3.3, (*SP-CMP*), will be positive. Note the movement of the total *REE* over time: there is a gradual decline, a slight increase as actual market movements offset the time-to-decay element (*RFc*) and then a continued decline until maturity, when the total risk ($280,000) is represented by the premium paid, and the actual intrinsic value of the option. If Bank J exercises the option at maturity it will receive an equivalent payout of $80,000, the difference between the strike (15,000) and the market price (14,000) times the number of contracts (divided by 125 yen/$ for our purposes). If the put were denominated in dollars at a predetermined fixed rate, this would be an opportunity to see a 'quanto' convert the yen proceeds back into dollars at a fixed rate of 125 yen. We shall discuss this further in Chapter 6.

Had Bank Y, the put seller, defaulted at maturity, Bank J would have sustained a certain loss of $280,000, or its premium plus the intrinsic value of the option. Had Y defaulted on day 180, J would have faced a certain loss of its premium and nothing more, since the option had not yet moved into the money. However, not knowing when the option will move into the money, and when the counterparty will default, results in a credit officer having to assign a potential worst case risk exposure scenario to the transaction through the risk equivalency framework. In some instances an institution will assign a probability of counterparty default to the risk exposure figure it calculates. The stronger the counterparty, the lower the probability of default, the lower the resulting risk exposure. The probability of counterparty default may be estimated through default probability factors. These factors may be based on an historical review of counterparty default as related to credit ratings from external rating agencies or internal credit departments, credit spreads in the fixed income markets, and so on. While defaults in the derivatives market have been relatively few to date and do not provide suitable information for this purpose, proxies in the form of bond defaults (which are more widespread) can be of use. While this is certainly a valid approach, we shall not adjust our *REE* figures in this text for probability of default and will continue to focus on an unadjusted, worst case, *REE* scenario.

It should be noted that this model we have just described is generally more useful in providing an accurate reading of the actual, and remaining, credit exposure in a given option transaction and, as such, is more useful than Equation 3.1 above. Further note that Equations 3.2 and 3.3 actually condense to Equation 3.1 when the strike and the current market prices are equal; thus, as we have already mentioned, Equation 3.1 is a standard form of valuing credit risk in at-the-money options.

A note is relevant at this point regarding exchange traded option contracts where contract multipliers are automatically set. For example, if a bank purchases an exchange traded S & P 500 option, the price is multiplied by a contract multiplier of 500 to yield the dollar value of the contract. Thus, to achieve a notional of $400,000 based on a strike price of 400 (as in our first example), a bank would only have to purchase two exchange contracts (i.e. 2*500*400 = $400,000), not the 1000 OTC contracts previously mentioned. Care must be taken to utilize correct multipliers when dealing with exchange contracts, as failure may result in severe overstatement of the notional required. Since our discussion is based on OTC contracts and products we shall create a discussion on the basis of *NC* unrelated to a contract multiplier, only *SP* and *CMP*.

There are times when an option is not expressed in terms of the number of contracts, but in terms of some set notional amount. In such cases, we need to make an adjustment to the equations covered above. We have indicated in the paragraphs above that a notional equivalent of contract size may be derived by multiplying the number of contracts (*NC*) by the strike price (*SP*). This should make sense to the reader, since the purchase of 100 OTC contracts of the S & P 500, with a strike of 400, does not imply a notional of 100, but of 100 * 400, or $40,000. With this in mind, and using some simple algebra, we note that the number of contracts *NC* is actually equal to the notional divided by the strike price (i.e. \$40,000/400 = 100). In order to adjust Equations 3.2 and 3.3 to a notional base, we need simply divide by the strike price:

$$REE = Premium + 0 \vee \left(N \times \left[\frac{(RFc \times CMP)}{SP} + \frac{(CMP - SP)}{SP} \right] \right) \qquad (3.4)$$

and

$$REE = Premium + 0 \vee \left(N \times \left[\frac{(RFc \times CMP)}{SP} + \frac{(SP - CMP)}{SP} \right] \right) \qquad (3.5)$$

If we return to our original Nikkei example and say that Bank J is buying a 12-month 10 per cent out-of-the-money put option (*SP* of 15,000 in a 16,500 market) on \$1.2MM notional ((10,000 * 15,000)/125) for \$200,000, our risk exposure (assuming an *RF* of 25 per cent and 125 yen/\$) would be:

REE = \$200,000 + 0 or (\$1.2MM * [(0.25 * 16,500)/15,000 +
      (15,000 − 16,500)/15,000])

REE = \$200,000 + 0 or (\$1.2MM * [(0.275) + (−0.10)]

REE = \$200,000 + \$210,000

REE = \$410,000

The result is, not coincidentally, identical to the one from our example above. Thus, Equations 3.2 and 3.3 are useful when dealing with numbers of contracts, while Equations 3.4 and 3.5 are useful when dealing with notional amounts. We shall use both approaches throughout the text.

As a final note, it should be highlighted that the approach taken above is algebraically identical to the current market price approach assumed by certain other works (e.g. Arak, Goodman and Rones, 1986; Banks, 1993), which value credit lines for options in terms of a current market price, as opposed to a strike price. For instance, Arak, Goodman and Rones (p.450) define their adjustment to the out-of-the-money portion of a call option as (*SP-CMP*)/*CMP* (subtracted from the original risk factor value), while this author defines the adjustment as (*CMP-SP*)/*CMP* (added to the original risk factor value). These are consistent with the discussion above when expressed as a percentage of the market value of the underlying. This may be accomplished, for example, by Equation 3.6 for calls, and Equation 3.7 for puts.

$$REE = Premium + 0 \vee ((RFc \times NC \times CMP) + (\frac{(CMP - SP)}{CMP} \times (NC \times CMP))) \qquad (3.6)$$

$$REE = Premium + 0 \vee ((RFc \times NC \times CMP) + (\frac{(SP - CMP)}{CMP} \times (NC \times CMP))) \qquad (3.7)$$

Note that our notional N is now the product of NC multiplied by CMP, not SP.

In our Nikkei example we may show that the result is identical (recalling our 125 yen/$ exchange):

REE = \$200,000 + 0 or ((0.25 * 10,000 * 16,500) + ((15,000 − 16,500)/16,500)
  *(10,000 * 16,500)))

REE = \$200,000 + 0 or ((\$330,000) + (-\$120,000))

REE = \$200,000 + \$210,000

REE = \$410,000

We can see that the above formula yields the same identical risk exposure as our original equations; if we examine two other data points from our Nikkei put chart above, say t=90 and t=270, we obtain total REEs of \$402,000 ((\$200,000 + (\$282,000) + (-\$80,000))) and \$391,000 ((\$200,000 + (\$151,000) + (\$40,000))), respectively; these are precisely equal to the results obtained above.

Although algebraically identical and consistent, it is perhaps intuitively simpler to discuss the above in terms of strike prices, not current market prices. As such, this text will focus on the formulae presented in Equations 3.2 to 3.5 when valuing the credit risk of option positions.

At this point the reader has at his or her disposal some basic equations which may be employed in the valuation of credit risk for options of any type. There are, of course, many other fashions by which to value such risks, but the equations above are intuitively easy to understand and mathematically simple to employ. We shall return to these equations in Chapters 4 and 6.

4: The Credit Risk Inherent in Varying Options Strategies

PRODUCT DESCRIPTION

An institution active in the use of over-the-counter or listed options for investment or risk management purposes will very often find itself utilizing more than simple put or call positions. Depending on the precise results it is attempting to achieve, a bank may be involved in using options in packaged combinations which, when taken, together, yield very specific results not possible through simple positions. In Chapter 3 we have discussed the credit risk aspects inherent in standard put and call transactions. In this chapter we seek to explore the credit risks which are imposed on an institution which actively combines puts and calls in various combinations. As we shall highlight, the credit risks inherent in these varying strategies can, in certain instances, be far greater than those found in simple option positions; in certain other instances credit risks will, in fact, be lower than the straightforward put and call positions.

Our discussion of the credit risk aspects of varying option strategies begins with an overview of the most commonly used combinations of options. For purposes of this discussion we begin with simple relationships and then move to the more complex, or multiple, option strategies. The reader should note that the strategies covered in this chapter are applicable to any underlying security or market, and relate equally to listed as well as over-the-counter options (although OTC options clearly provide a great deal more flexibility and access than listed options).

Simple Positions

It is well known that taking positions (short or long) in puts (an option to sell a certain instrument at a certain strike price) or calls (an option to buy a certain instrument at a certain strike price) implies taking a certain view of a market. We review these in brief, for the time being ignoring the consequences of credit risk exposure. Note that when we indicate limited risk or unlimited risk, we are referring to price risk which would cause a capital gain or loss to the investor, not credit risk. While price risk has a bearing on credit risk, it is not the sole determinant. Full credit risk considerations will be addressed later in the chapter.

Long call: a position taken when a market is expected to rise. Premium is exchanged for upside potential, so economic loss is limited to premium paid; upside returns are theoretically unbounded.

Short call: a position taken when a market is expected to fall, and is a means by which to earn premium income. Return, in the form of premium income, is modest, but risk of having to perform is theoretically unlimited.

Long put: a position taken when a market is expected to fall. Premium is exchanged for downside potential, again with economic loss limited to premium paid. Total returns are limited only to the point when market prices reach 0.

Short put: a position taken when a market is expected to rise. Premium income is earned, but risk is the downside in the market to the point when prices reach 0.

These four variations are often grouped as 'price driven' positions, as they seek to take advantage only of absolute price levels. Long calls and short puts are established by a bank when it is bullish; short calls and long puts are taken when a bank is bearish. Short positions in general may also perform well when there is a steady market; markets with little or no movement for a period of time will not push puts or calls in-the-money, meaning that premium income earned on the options will not have to be given up. The profit/loss paths of the basic positions described above are highlighted in Figure 4.1.

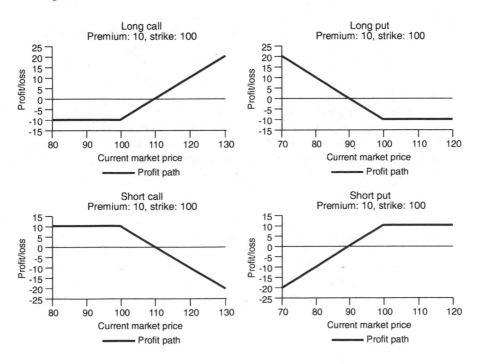

Figure 4.1   Profit/loss paths

Compound Positions

Combining puts and/or calls into groups of two or more results in different outcomes being achieved; specific outcomes are dependent on whether puts and/or calls are used, whether long or short positions are established, whether strike prices are equal or different, and whether or not exercise dates are equivalent. Various combinations are explored below.

Price Driven Strategies

Among the most common of the price driven strategies (i.e. those which seek to take advantage of absolute price movements in certain directions) are vertical spreads.

Vertical Spreads

Vertical spreads (also known as price or money spreads) always consist of a long and short position utilizing the same type of option with the same expiry date. Spreads may be bullish or bearish, to reflect a certain view of the market's anticipated direction.

Bullish Vertical Call Spread

A combination of a long call with a low strike and a short call with a higher strike (implying that the long position is closer to-the-money and, therefore, more expensive; in fact, there will be a net outflow of premium for the bank; this is often called a debit). As an example, a bank might purchase a call struck at 101 (when the current market price *CMP* is 100) and sell a call struck at 105. Once *CMP* exceeds 101, the bank will have an in-the-money position, which will only be offset once *CMP* exceeds 105; the long position will always be worth 4 points more than the short position once the short call strike has been reached. This type of strategy is suitable when a bank is bullish, wants to earn potential income within a limited range, and wants a prespecified level of price risk.

Bullish Vertical Put Spread

A combination of a long put with a low strike and a short put at a higher strike. Since the short position is struck closer to-the-money, there will be a net inflow of premium from the bank's perspective (this is known as a credit). Again, this is a bullish strategy where the bank is expecting the market to rise: if the long put is struck at 95 and the short put at 100 (when the *CMP* is 101, as an example) and the market rises to 105, both puts remain out-of-the-money (but the bank will have been a net earner of premium income).

Bearish Vertical Call Spread

Simply the reverse of the *bullish vertical call spread* above, where a bank is short a call with a low strike (say 101) and long a call with a higher strike (say 105). This is a bearish position, because the bank expects the market to fall: if *CMP* falls to 99, both positions will remain out-of-the-money but, again, the bank will be a net earner of premium (since it sold the more expensive closer-to-the-money call).

Bearish Vertical Put Spread

Again, the reverse of the *bullish vertical put spread above*, where the bank establishes a short put with a low strike (e.g. 95) and a long put with a higher strike (e.g. 100, when the *CMP* is 101). Since the bank's long put is struck closer-to-the-money, it will be a net payer of premium, but will achieve profitability on its position first; with such a spread, the bank is obviously expecting the market to fall.

Volatility Driven Strategies

Volatility driven strategies are those which seek to take advantage of movements in volatility, as opposed to absolute prices or price directions. Many institutions actively measure and react to an option's delta, gamma, theta and lambda. Although a detailed discussion of these measures is not required for our outline of risk exposure aspects and is beyond the scope of this text, we introduce below some simple definitions of each (and explore some of the mathematical relationships, as related to the Black–Scholes option pricing model, in Appendix I):

Delta: the rate of change (or percentage change) in the price of the option for a unit change in the price of the underlying instrument. Options struck at-the-money typically have a delta of 0.5; that is, for a price change of 1 in the underlying instrument, the option price moves by 0.5. Options struck further in-the-money have deltas which are greater than 0.5; they converge on 1.0 as time to expiry approaches. Options struck out-of-the-money generally have deltas of less than 0.5, and converge on 0 as expiry draws closer. Long calls have deltas which are positive, as do short puts; long puts and short calls have negative deltas. Delta is often employed in the calculation of appropriate hedging levels. As an example if an option has a delta of 0.5, it means that 0.5 short units of the underlying hedge 1 long option. Delta is also often interpreted as the probability a given option will end in-the-money; this, in turn, implies that delta is related to the level of volatility, the time to expiry and the intrinsic value of the option.

Gamma: the rate of change (or percentage change) in the delta of the option for a unit change in the price of the underlying instrument. Gamma effectively measures the risk of an option, while delta measures the risk of the underlying. Options struck at-the-money carry the highest gammas, while options in- or out-of-the-money have lower gammas which decrease to 0 as time to expiry draws near. Gamma is always a positive figure and is often used to gauge how frequently a delta-hedged position will have to be rebalanced.

Theta: the rate at which an option loses value with the passage of time (also known as time to decay). Options which are struck at-the-money have the highest thetas; in- or out-of-the-money options have lower thetas. With each passing day, as time to maturity draws closer, the value of the long option decreases, at a rate measured by theta. The higher the theta, the greater the decay in the option's value over time. Theta decreases at a rate equal to the inverse of the square root of time, T, which, the reader will recall from Chapter 2, is a form of the 'square root rule'. Long options have negative thetas, short options positive thetas.

Lambda (sometimes called zeta, vega or kappa): the rate at which the value of the option changes for a unit percentage change in volatility. Options struck at-the-money have much more sensitivity to changes in volatility and, as such, have higher lambdas. Options which are struck in- or out-of-the-money have lower lambdas. As maturity grows nearer, lambda begins to decline; option values are less sensitive as expiry draws near since volatility declines. Lambda is always positive and increases as volatility increases.

Returning to our discussion on option strategies, the most commonly used compound option positions for taking advantage of a view on market volatility are straddles, strangles, butterflies, condors, ratio horizontal and vertical spreads and backspreads.

Straddles

Straddles are formed by a combination of puts and calls, with equal strike levels and identical maturity dates. Long straddles are established by buying puts and calls and are taken in anticipation of a market movement of substance (i.e. significant volatility), when the actual direction of the movements in uncertain; long straddles are positive gamma strategies. To the extent the market moves by an amount greater than that dictated by the volatility reflected in the price of the options, the position will result in a gain. As an example of a long straddle, a bank might purchase a put at 100 and a call at 100, in market of 100 (implying that the call and the put and the straddle are all at-the-money). If the market remains relatively stagnant (i.e. it displays little volatility), the position will not be profitable for the bank. However, to the extent there is a price move of some magnitude, either up or down, the position will be profitable. From a pure profit perspective, a long straddle has limited downside risk and unlimited profit potential.

A short straddle is, as one might expect, the reverse of a long straddle, and is taken by a bank which believes that the market will remain relatively quiet for a period of time (that is, it will show little or no volatility). As long as there is little volatility, the

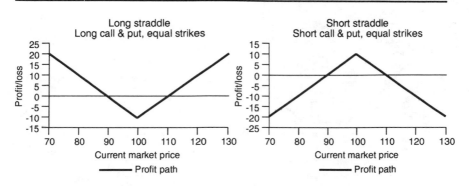

Figure 4.2   Long and short straddle positions

short put or call positions will not move significantly and will therefore result in little or no payout to the buyer. Naturally, the bank selling a straddle earns premium income; however, profits are limited to premium income earned, while downside risk is theoretically unlimited.

Strangles

Strangles are very similar to straddles except they are generally more aggressive for the long side, as greater volatility is required to put a position in-the-money (or deeper in-the-money). Long strangles are established by buying puts and calls with the same expiration dates but different strike levels. As an example, a bank may buy a put struck at 90 and a call struck at 110; it will not gain on either position when the *CMP* trades in a range of 90 to 110 and, as such, must wait until there is a very large market movement which pushes *CMP* below 90 or above 110 (in contrast to a straddle, which may have both strikes at 100 in a market of 100, indicating that a small move to 101 or 99 will easily push one side of the straddle in-the-money). Long strangles have positive gamma.

Short strangles are the reverse of long strangles and are, like short straddles, taken when market volatility is expected to be minimal. The seller of a strangle typically has more market volatility with which 'to play', before one side or the other moves in-the-money (assuming the original strangle was struck out-of-the-money; strangles where there is an in-the-money portion at the outset are sometimes referred to as 'guts' and result in greater premium income to the seller (as well as greater risk of payoff)). The profit path of long and short strangles is show in Figure 4.3.

Butterflies

A butterfly, long or short, is a combination of 4 separate puts and calls, designed to provide results which are similar to straddles or ratio verticals (covered below). In fact, a long butterfly is very similar to a short straddle, with the exception that risk is more limited. A bank believing market volatility will remain low can be short a straddle or

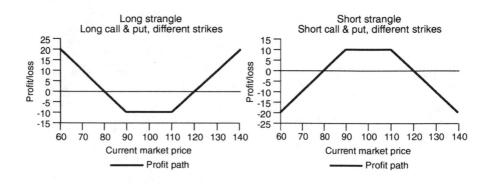

Figure 4.3   Long and short strangles

long a butterfly, but a short straddle exposes it to much greater downside risk should volatility actually occur. This behaviour suggests a long butterfly has negative gamma. A long butterfly can be created by one of several means, and is done by buying the low and high strikes and selling the middle strikes (all with the same exercise date). The creation of a butterfly is always done in the same ratio (i.e. 1 low strike, 2 middle strike, 1 high strike):

- Long call with low strike (say 100);
- Short 2 calls with middle strike (say 105);
- Long call with high strike (say 110).

This has the effect of providing the buyer of the butterfly with gains between 100 and 105. If the *CMP* of the security or index in question falls below 100, the spread will be worthless; if *CMP* rises above 110, the two long calls of 100 and 110 will be offset by the two short calls at 105, for a net of 0. The only profit position in a butterfly is the range between the two long strikes, with the maximum profit coming right at the middle strike of 105 (the long call with the 100 strike will be worth 5 points, the two short calls expire worthless, as will the long high strike). The profit profile is highlighted in Figure 4.4. Readers should contrast this profile with the straddles highlighted in Figure 4.2 to get a clear view of the different risk profiles of the two strategies. Note that a long butterfly spread can also be constructed with:

- Long put with low strike (say 100);
- Short 2 puts with middle strike (say 105);
- Long put with high strike (say 110).

A short butterfly is the reverse of a long butterfly, and requires selling the low and high strikes and buying the middle strikes (with puts or calls); this strategy is akin to a long straddle with limited risk. As before, all options mature at the same time. A short call butterfly is shown in Figure 4.4.

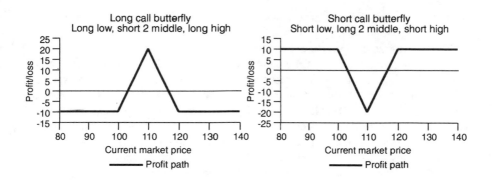

Figure 4.4   Long and short call butterflies

Condors

Condor spreads are similar to butterfly spreads, except strikes of the various options are further apart. This results in a greater potential gain within the defined parameters of the option combinations; it also implies, of course, greater loss should the market move the opposite direction. A long condor can be established via the following:

- Long call with low strike (say 100);
- Short call with middle low strike (say 103);
- Short call with middle high strike (say 107);
- Long call with high strike (say 110).

Long condors can also be established with puts instead of calls. Note that the profit profile of a long condor is similar to a short strangle (in the same way a long butterfly is similar to a short straddle), except that downside risk is limited.

Short condors are created with the sale of the high and low puts or calls and the purchase of the two middle puts or calls. The profit profile is similar to a long strangle with limited risk.

Ratio Horizontal Spreads

Ratio horizontal spreads are created when a bank buys or sells the option closer to expiry while doing the opposite with the option further to expiry; these spreads are also known as 'time' or 'calendar' spreads. The strategy behind this combination is to take advantage of expected changes in volatility which might occur over a period of time; the spreads are often done in various multiples, not simply 1 buy and 1 sell; the greater the multiple, for example 1 buy and 2 sells, the greater the potential risk and the potential return. Spreads are established by utilizing the same type of option (i.e. puts or calls, but not both), together with the same strike price.

The long horizontal spread is one resulting in a net outflow of premium (i.e. a debit), a short spread in an inflow of premium (i.e. a credit); a long spread is typically characterized by negative gamma and positive theta. As an example, a long spread might be one where a bank is long the far call (say September 105s) and short the nearer call (say March 105s); its hope is that volatility will remain low. One of the key considerations motivating horizontal spreads is the notion of theta, discussed above. Theta, which is an option's time decay, is central to time spreads, as a short term option generally loses value more quickly than a longer term option (i.e. a short term option has a higher theta). A long horizontal spread is established by institutions believing that volatility will remain very modest; if this happens, as in our March and September 105s above, the short term option, with a higher theta, will lose more value and the spread will widen.

The opposite occurs with short horizontal spreads, which seek greater volatility in order for a gain to be made. If volatility is high, time value begins to shrink as positions move sharply in- or out-of-the-money. As an example, if the short spread is call based and the market moves up sharply, the two options will lose their time value and the spread will be worth 0. Ratio horizontals attempt to take advantage of volatility as related to time.

Backspreads

Backspreads are created when an institution buys more contracts than it sells, whether puts or calls; all contracts have the same expiry date but, in order to remain delta neutral, a call backspread would require buying calls with higher strikes (and selling the lower strike ones) or buying puts with lower strikes (and selling the higher strike ones). A call backspread, for instance, would be created if a bank bought 10 March 100 calls and sold 5 March 95 calls. As the market makes a large upward move, the call backspread increases in value; if it makes a sharp downward move, the long and short calls expire worthless, but the bank is left with premium income from selling the closer-to-the-money options; most backspreads are credit (as opposed to debit) transactions with positive gamma. In a backspread, an institution will generally gain as long as there is volatility. If the market is reasonably static, there is a chance that the spread will expire with no gain. The gains on a call backspread increase as *CMP* rises and, in a put backspread, increase as the *CMP* declines. The opposite of a long backspread is generally referred to as a ratio vertical spread; ratio verticals are created as more contracts are sold than purchased. The comparison between a call backspread and a call ratio vertical spread is highlighted in Figure 4.5.

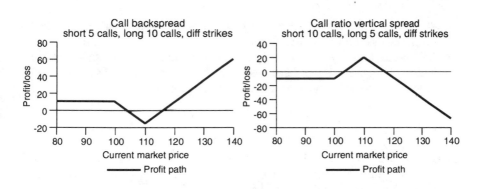

Figure 4.5   Comparison between call backspread and call ratio vertical spread

Ratio Vertical Spreads

Ratio vertical spreads occur when a bank establishes a greater sold than bought position in puts or calls with the same expiry date, precisely the opposite of a backspread; such spreads have negative gamma. The intent of this strategy is to take advantage of a market with low volatility. In a call ratio vertical spread, as an example, a bank may buy 10 March 100 calls and sell 20 March 105 calls. Since it is buying closer-to-the-money calls (albeit a smaller quantity), it will be a payer of premium. If there is little market volatility the bank will not be forced to pay the upside on the short calls; it earns its maximum profit when the *CMP* expires at the strike of the sold calls. If, in contrast, there is a great deal of upside movement in *CMP*, the bank faces risk. A put ratio vertical spread is the opposite, where a bank sells more puts at a lower strike than it buys at the higher strike price. The downside profit risk in this position is unlimited should *CMP* decline sharply.

Other Variations on the Theme

As one might imagine, there are many other combinations of options which can be assembled to create very specific results corresponding with a given view of market direction or volatility. The ones discussed above are among the most common in the OTC and listed options market, but there are others we can mention briefly:

(a) long strap: long one put and long two calls with the same strike; unlimited profit potential, limited downside risk;

(b) short strap: short one put and short two calls with the same strike; unlimited downside risk, limited profit potential;

(c) long strip: long one call and long two puts with the same strike; unlimited profit potential, limited downside risk;

(d) short strip: short one call and short two puts with the same strike; unlimited downside risk, limited profit potential;

(e) box spread: long one call and short one put with same low strike and short one call and long one put with same high strike; or long one put and short one call with same low strike and long one call and short one put with same high strike.

Synthetics

As institutions active in the market know, being long or short the underlying instrument and combining such positions with long/short puts or calls on the same underlying can result in synthetic options being created.

Consider the following: if a bank is long a put and long the underlying instrument, it is effectively long a call. Assuming the put is stuck at 100 and the current market price is 100, the following may happen: if the *CMP* rises to 105, the put moves further out-of-the-money (and expires worthless), but the underlying rises in value to 105. If *CMP* falls to 95, the bank will not gain on the underlying, but will gain on the long put as it moves in-the-money; hence the two scenarios result in profit positions characteristic of long calls.

If a bank is long a call and short the underlying, it has created a synthetic long put. Again, if the strike is 100 and the current price is 100, the following may occur: if *CMP* falls to 95 the call moves out-of-the-money and expires worthless but the position gains on the short underlying, which is worth more when prices fall; this is the behaviour of a long put.

If a bank is long the underlying and short a call, it has created a synthetic short put. If the *CMP* and strike are initially 100, and the *CMP* falls to 95, the underlying will have declined while the call will be out-of-the-money: this is the equivalent of being short a put, where the bank loses as *CMP* falls.

In a fourth scenario, if a bank is short the underlying and short a put, it is short a call. Again, with *CMP* and strike set at 100, if the *CMP* rises to 105, the short underlying will be worth less; at the same time, the short put will have moved out-of-the-money and will expire worthless. Thus, the above is the equivalent of being short a call, where the bank loses as the price of the instrument rises.

The synthetic relationships, which are an important part of creating option strategies, are highlighted in Table 4.1.

Table 4.1   Synthetic options

Synthetic	=	Underlying	+	Option
Long call	=	Long underlying	+	Long put
Long put	=	Short underlying	+	Long call
Short put	=	Long underlying	+	Short call
Short call	=	Short underlying	+	Short put

As one might expect, synthetic instruments can also be created by establishing long/short put and call positions. For instance, if a bank is long a call and short a put, both struck at 100 with the same expiration, it has created a synthetic long instrument: if the *CMP* increases to 105, the call gains in value, which is the behaviour of a long underlying position. The put will remain out-of-the-money, of course, and will therefore have no impact on the position.

Conversely, if a bank is short a call and long a put, it is equivalent to being short the underlying: if the strikes are set at 100 and expirations are equal, and the *CMP* falls, the put gains in value, which is precisely equal to the behaviour of a short position in the underlying. Once again, the option portion of the trade (short call) moves out-of-the-money. These synthetic relationships are captured in Table 4.2.

Table 4.2 Synthetic underlying

Synthetic	=	Option	+	Option
Long underlying	=	Long call	+	Short put
Short underlying	=	Short call	+	Long put

CREDIT RISK EVALUATION

Our discussion of the credit risk inherent in varying options strategies will, for the most part, take two forms: compound positions which are created by an institution with a single counterparty, and those which are created 'synthetically' by splitting the position between two separate counterparties. There will, in certain instances, be different credit risk assessments for each scenario. Although it is far more common for specific strategies to be executed with a single counterparty, on some occasions the same effects are replicated synthetically using two or more different counterparties. In many of the risk discussions below we shall refer back to the original risk equations for calls and puts developed in Chapter 3. These, for contract-based calculations, are:

$$REE = Premium + 0 \vee (NC \times [(RFc \times CMP) + (CMP - SP)]) \qquad (3.2)$$

for calls, and

$$REE = Premium + 0 \vee (NC \times [(RFc \times CMP) + (SP - CMP)]) \qquad (3.3)$$

for puts,

where
RFc is a constantly adjusted risk factor,
NC is the number of contracts,
CMP is the current market price,
SP is the strike price.

Vertical Spreads

A vertical spread is a combination of a long and short put (put spread) or a long and short call (call spread), where the puts or calls have the same expiry dates. In the case of a bullish call spread, the long position is struck closer to-the-money than the short position, indicating a net outflow of premium (debit). A bullish put spread has the short position struck closer to-the-money, implying a net inflow of premium (credit). Bearish spreads are the reverse.

Single Counterparty Transaction
If a bank transacts a put or call spread with a single counterparty, and the transaction is documented as a single deal, the credit risk evaluation is as follows:

BULLISH VERTICAL CALL SPREAD Our bank stands to lose the net outflow of premium (not a gross figure, since the deal is being executed with one counterparty) plus market risk exposure on the long call position. However, we must recall that the upside gain will be limited once the short call position is in-the-money. Therefore, the maximum market risk which can occur is equal to the difference between the long call strike and the short call strike. We may show this as:

$$REE = Net\ Premium + (NC \times (SP_{call2} - SP_{call1})) \qquad (4.1)$$

where $SP_{call\ 1}$ is the strike price on the closer to-the-money long call,
$SP_{call\ 2}$ is the strike price on the short farther-from-the-money call,
NC is the number of option contracts,
and where $SP_{call\ 2} > SP_{call\ 1}$.

Let us consider an example, where Bank EFG buys a call on the S&P 500 struck at 400 (in a 400 market), and sells a call struck at 405. The notional is based on 100,000 contracts, and net premium paid is $200,000. The maximum *REE* Bank EFG will encounter over the life of the transaction is limited to the differential between the two strikes:

$$REE = \$200,000 + (100,000 * (405 - 400))$$
$$REE = \$200,000 + \$500,000$$
$$REE = \$700,000$$

Since the maximum payoff of this contract, on a net basis, will be the differential between the strikes, times the notional (once both legs are in-the-money), we do not apply the same formula detailed in Equation 3.1. Note that the above is a generic formula with no adjustments for in- or out-of-the-money elements. It is unlikely that we would want to incorporate such adjustments (as we might with standard options) because our maximum risk is bounded by the differential between the two options, not by the market movements as measured by RFc (which is more sensitive to the starting point and final maturity of the transaction). If a particular spread was struck well out-of-the-money, it is conceivable that an institution would only count the premium as risk. However, we shall assume that the spreads are struck at-, in- or slightly out-of-the-money, so our focus is only on the differential. Note that the only exception to this approach would occur in instances when the spread between the long and short positions is excessively large (that is, when the spread is wider than the amount dictated by *RFc*). In such instances, the risk valuation would follow the standard formula for calls indicated by Equation 3.2.

BULLISH VERTICAL PUT SPREAD   In this instance our bank has no risk. Net premium inflow is received (not paid) since the bank is selling the nearer to-the-money put; although it has a long put position which would normally add risk, it is farther out-of-the-money than the short and, as such, will only have value once the short position is further in-the-money. If counterparty default occurs once a bank's long position is in-the-money, the bank will not receive what it is owed on the long position but it will not make the larger payment on the short position. There is therefore no credit risk.

BEARISH VERTICAL CALL SPREAD   This transaction is the reverse of the bullish vertical call spread, where the bank is short the closer to-the-money call and long the farther out-of-the-money call. As such, it would be a net earner of premium and, following the logic developed for the bullish put spread, would have no risk.

BEARISH VERTICAL PUT SPREAD   In this type of structure, the bank has risk which closely resembles that of a bullish call spread. Since the bank is long the closer to-the-money put and short the farther out-of-the-money put, it is a net payer of premium. It will also suffer market risk exposure to a maximum level equal to the difference between the long and short strikes. We may show the equation as:

$$REE = Net\ Premium + (NC \times (SP_{put1} - SP_{put2})) \qquad (4.2)$$

where $\qquad$ $SP_{put\ 1}$ is the strike price on the closer to-the-money long put,
$\qquad\qquad$ $SP_{put\ 2}$ is the strike price on the farther-from-the-money short put,
$\qquad\qquad$ NC is the number of options contracts,
$\qquad\qquad$ and where $SP_{put\ 1} > SP_{put\ 2}$.

If the spread between the long and short puts is particularly large (e.g. in excess of that dictated by *RFc*), valuation could occur via Equation 3.3.

Multiple Counterparty Transaction
It is, of course, possible for a bank to create a synthetic put or call spread by booking a long position with one counterparty and a short position (with matching notional and maturity date) with a second counterparty. If such occurs the profit payout (or loss) will be the same to the bank as in the traditional single counterparty vertical spread discussed above, assuming both counterparties continue to perform. However, the credit risk parameters will be different.

BULLISH VERTICAL CALL SPREAD In this instance our bank will be a receiver of premium equal to x, and payer of premium equal to $x + y$. In a single counterparty transaction the net payment premium by the bank to the client was simply $(x + y) - x$, or y. In a multiple counterparty transaction, the bank would ignore receipt of premium x from the first counterparty and focus simply on what it is paying the second counterparty, $x + y$. In addition, the bank will no longer have the benefit of a nettable transaction, so the potential market risk on the deal is no longer the difference between the two strike prices times the number of contracts. An accurate assessment would indicate that the full amount of the long position must be counted, since failure by the counterparty to perform once the long position is in-the-money will mean the full amount of intrinsic value is lost. The bank will be required to perform on its short once that leg moves in-the-money and, as such, can no longer look simply at the strike differences. The risk of this transaction will equal that of a standard long call, as shown by Equation 3.2.

BULLISH VERTICAL PUT SPREAD The analysis in this case is, once again, identical to that discussed immediately above. Risk on this transaction would focus on the long put established with one of the two counterparties, together with premium paid for that put, while ignoring the short put and the premium received from the second counterparty. The equation for puts is shown as Equation 3.3 above.

BEARISH VERTICAL CALL AND PUT SPREADS In both instances the risk on these transactions will again focus on the full credit risk inherent in the long call and put portions of the transaction, as in the discussion on bullish spreads.

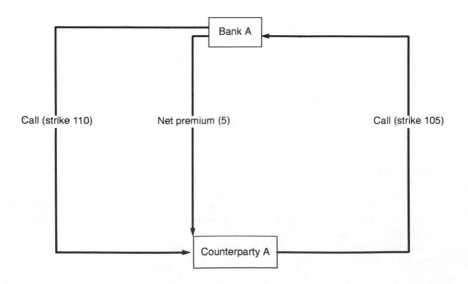

Figure 4.6(a)   Call spread, single counterparty risk

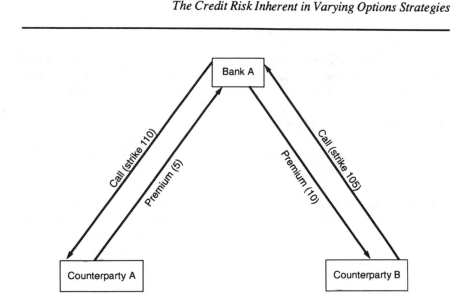

Figure 4.6(b)   Call spread, multiple counterparty risk

Figures 4.7 (a) and (b) clarify the risk differences between a bullish vertical call spread transacted with one and two counterparties.

Straddles

The credit risk of straddles focuses exclusively on long positions. Short straddles result in the sale of a put and a call with matching strikes and expiry dates. To the extent premium is received in a normal cash-settlement time frame, the straddle seller will not encounter any credit risk as it is the seller which must perform should one side of the straddle move in-the-money. It will also be irrelevant for the straddle seller whether the position is synthetic (i.e. one side sold to one counterparty, the second to a different counterparty). Thus, our discussion focuses exclusively on long single and multiple counterparty straddles.

Single Counterparty Transaction
In a long straddle involving a single counterparty our institution will be long both a put and a call, and will have paid premium for the two positions. From our discussion above we know that the premium will immediately be at risk. However, the market risk portion of our transaction will focus on only one leg of the straddle. We know this is true because only one side can finish in-the-money. Since both the put and the call are struck at the same level, it will only be possible, in a worst case scenario, for one side to be in-the-money at any point in time. Therefore, our risk equation will include a component which values the risk of either the put or the call, whichever is closer to-the-money, or in-the-money, on an ongoing basis. Utilizing Equations 3.2 and 3.3,

we can effectively combine them to reflect both the call and the put positions which define a straddle; however, we shall only take the greater of the two as our risk, since we know that we shall not exercise both at the same time. By the parameters of our equation, it is also possible that a deeply out-of-the-money straddle will cause us to only value the premium paid out as our credit risk:

$$REE = Premium + 0 \vee greater\ of\ (NC \times [(RFc \times CMP) + (CMP - SP)]\ ) \qquad (4.3)$$
$$\wedge\ (NC \times [(RFc \times CMP) + (SP - CMP)])$$

Let us consider the following example in order to demonstrate use of Equation 4.3. Bank Q purchases an at-the-money straddle on the German DAX stock market index, with both the put and call legs struck at 1600 in a 1600 market. The premium paid for the 10,000 contracts is $1MM, the maturity is 12 months and the initial RFc is 22 per cent (note that we shall convert the proceeds to $ in this equation at DM1.5/$). Our initial REE is:

REE = $1MM + 0 or greater of (10,000 * [(0.22 * 1600) + (1600 – 1600)])
    and (10,000 * [(0.22 * 1600) + (1600 – 1600)])

REE = $1MM + greater of [$2.35MM and $2.35MM]

REE = $3.35MM

If we assume that 6 months from now the *CMP* of the DAX has risen to 1700 (and our *RFc* has declined to 15.5 per cent), we know that our call will be in-the-money while our put will be out-of-the-money. Returning to our equation we note:

REE = $1MM + 0 or greater of (10,000 * [(0.155 * 1700) + (1700 – 1600)])
    and (10,000 * [(0.155 * 1700) + (1600 – 1700)])

REE = $1MM + greater of [$2.42MM and $1.09MM]

REE = $3.42MM

If, at maturity, the DAX finishes at 1750, we know that the only portion of our straddle which has value is the call; the put expires worthless. One day prior to maturity we might show our risk as:

REE = $1MM + 0 or greater of (10,000 * [(0.0 * 1750) + (1750 – 1600)])
    and (10,000 * [0.0 * 1750) + (1600 – 1750)])

REE = $1MM + greater of [$1MM and –$1MM]

REE = $2MM

If Bank Q's counterparty defaults at this point, Bank Q will lose its $1MM in premium, plus the intrinsic value of the call, $1MM. The put is out-of-the-money and therefore represents no credit risk at the point of default. It is easy to imagine the opposite scenario, where the put finishes in-the-money, but the call expires worthless; Equation 4.3 takes account of this as well.

Multiple Counterparty Transaction
A bank can create a synthetic straddle by entering into a long call with one institution, and a long put (with identical strike and maturity details) with a second institution. From a credit standpoint the risk assigned to the transaction is dependent on whether the institution in question chooses to view the trades as a single strategy, knowing that only one side can be in-the-money at any point. If such is the case, it would likely continue to utilize Equation 4.3, substituting the sum of the premiums paid (which should theoretically be close to the original premium paid for the single counterparty transaction above). Direct assignment of Equation 3.2 for the call portion and 3.3 for the put portion would be unnecessarily conservative if a bank is truly viewing the positions as a straddle, albeit with different counterparties. Default at a point in time by one of the two counterparties will never result in a situation which is worse than that captured via Equation 4.3 for a single institution. For instance, if the call went in-the-money but the put counterparty defaulted, our institution would only lose premium (which we have already accounted for via Equation 4.3); if the call counterparty defaulted while the call was in-the-money, we would lose premium plus the intrinsic value of the call which, as we know, is already reflected via Equation 4.3. If we return to our original example above and separate the call and put and evaluate via Equations 3.2 and 3.3 (and keeping our FX conversion in mind and splitting our premium in half between two institutions), we would note:

Call risk

$$REE = \$500M + 0 \text{ or } [10{,}000 * ((0.22 * 1600) + (1600 - 1600))]$$
$$REE = \$500M + [\$2.35MM]$$
$$REE = \$2.85MM$$

Put risk

$$REE = \$500M + 0 \text{ or } [10{,}000 * ((0.22 * 1600) + (1600 - 1600))]$$
$$REE = \$500M + [\$2.35MM]$$
$$REE = \$2.85MM$$

Total REE = $2.85MM + $2.85MM
Total REE = $5.7MM

Thus, *REE* of $5.7MM (versus $3.35MM at inception via Equation 4.3) represents a significant overstatement of potential credit risk.

Strangles

A strangle, like a straddle, will only carry credit risk on the long, not the short, position. A strangle, as we have discussed, is simply a put and call combination with different strikes but the same maturity. The rationale for calculating credit risk is similar to that discussed in the section immediately above.

Single Counterparty Transaction
If a bank establishes a strangle with a single counterparty, it will be long both a put and a call at different strikes. It will naturally pay premium for the transaction, so this becomes a portion of the *REE* calculation. Thereafter, our logic is identical to that developed for straddles: since only the put or the call stands a chance of being in-the-money at exercise, only one side of the transaction need be counted for credit risk purposes. We may, in fact, utilize Equation 4.3 to calculate the *REE* for a strangle.

Utilizing Equation 4.3 in an example helps illustrate the calculation. Assume Bank B purchases a strangle on the S&P 500 from Bank Z, with the following parameters: *CMP* is 400, the call is struck at 405 and the put is struck at 390 (i.e. the call is struck closer to-the-money than the put). The straddle is comprised of 10,000 contacts with a final maturity of 12 months; the S&P 12 month risk factor at inception is 20 per cent. Premium paid for this strangle is $150,000.

$$REE = \$150,000 + 0 \text{ or greater of } (10,000 * [(0.20 * 400) + (400 - 405)])$$
$$\text{or } (10,000 * [(0.20 * 400) + (390 - 400)])$$
$$REE = \$150,000 + [\$750,000 \text{ or } \$700,000]$$
$$REE = \$900,000$$

Since the put is further out-of-the-money, the risk equation only values the call market risk (less the out-of-the-money portion) plus the premium. If we assume that 9 months into the trade the S&P has fallen to 375 (and our *RFc* is 10 per cent), the *REE* would be:

$$REE = \$150,000 + 0 \text{ or greater of } (10,000 * [(0.10 * 375) + (375 - 405)])$$
$$\text{or } (10,000 * [(0.10 * 375) + (390 - 375)])$$
$$REE = \$150,000 + [\$75,000 \text{ or } \$525,000]$$
$$REE = \$675,000$$

The reader will note how drastically the call has fallen out-of-the-money; this, of course, implies that the put is moving further in-the-money, increasing credit risk exposure on the put leg. It also illustrates why we cannot, and should not, attribute risk to both portions of the structure.

Multiple Counterparty Transaction
As above, a bank may create a synthetic strangle by establishing long put and call positions with different institutions. Since the theoretical premia paid for the two legs should approximate the premium paid for the single counterparty strangle, and since at most only one side of the transaction can end in-the-money (or be in-the-money during the life of the trade, when default may occur) we need only attribute risk to either the put or call, whichever is closer to-the-money. Given these parameters, the risk of a multiple counterparty strangle would be calculated via Equation 4.3. The logic followed is identical to that for a multiple counterparty straddle, where separate risk calculations for both the put and the call (via Equations 3.2 and 3.3) might be considered overly conservative.

Butterflies

Butterflies, as all other option strategies, must be broken into long and short positions. A long butterfly (put or call), consists of buying the low and high strike options and selling two middle strike options. Depending on the individual strike prices, there may be a net payment of premium for the long butterfly position.

Single Counterparty Transaction
A long call or put butterfly with a single counterparty will result in a defined amount of *REE* being assumed during the life of the transaction. Since a long butterfly means buying the low and high strikes, and selling two middle strike options, we know the following may occur in the case of a call (the opposite in the case of a put): if *CMP* is below the lowest strike, all options will be worthless. If it is above the highest strike, the gains from the long low strike and high strike calls will be exactly offset by the losses from the two short middle strike calls. Thus, the only opportunity for profit (and, therefore, credit risk) occurs when the *CMP* is between the two long strikes. In fact, the greatest profit and credit risk will occur when *CMP* is precisely equal to the two middle strikes, as the difference between the long low strike and the short middle strike will be maximized. Thus, our *REE* calculation is relatively easy to develop for long positions, and is shown simply as:

$$REE = Premium + (NC \times (SP_{call\ mid} - SP_{call\ low})) \qquad (4.4)$$

for calls, and

$$REE = Premium + (NC \times (SP_{put\ high} - SP_{put\ mid})) \qquad (4.5)$$

for puts, where NC is the number of contracts,
$SP_{call\ mid}$ is the strike price of the short middle call,
$SP_{call\ low}$ is the strike price of the long low call,
$SP_{put\ high}$ is the strike price of the long high put,
$SP_{put\ mid}$ is the strike price of the short middle put.

Consider the following: Bank F buys a call butterfly on a stock with a *CMP* of 99 for $100,000; the transaction size is 100,000 contracts (one each end, 2 * 100,000 contract short in the middle, utilizing only closer-to-the-money NC in our equation). F is long a call at 100, short two calls at 105, and long a call at 110. The initial, and maximum, *REE* on this deal is:

$$REE = \$100,000 + (100,000 * (105 - 100))$$
$$REE = \$100,000 + \$500,000$$
$$REE = \$600,000$$

If *CMP* reaches 105, and F's counterparty defaults, the bank will have lost its premium of $100,000 plus the anticipated payout of the butterfly, $500,000. If *CMP* rises to 110, and the counterparty defaults, F will simply lose its premium of $100,000; although it was expecting to receive the differential between *CMP* and SP (110 – 100), times 100,000, for a total of $1MM, it will not pay its obligation on the short calls ((105 – 100) * 2 * 100,000, or $1MM), and will therefore face no loss other than premium. If *CMP* only reached 109 before default, F would be owed ((109 – 100) * 100,000, or $900,000), but would have expected to pay ((109 – 105) * 2 * 100,000, or $800,000); F would then lose $100,000 of premium plus $100,000 of market value on the butterfly. It should be clear, then, that Equation 4.4 above represents the maximum risk a bank can face on a long call butterfly. The logic is identical in the case of long puts, utilizing Equation 4.5. Note that if a bank wanted to take account of the short position once it moves in-the-money (which will subtract from total *REE*), it would simply subtract the intrinsic value of the short positions from Equations 4.4 or 4.5, being careful to adjust for the greater number of options. As in the case of call or put spreads, if the differential between the strikes is larger than that dictated by our *RFc*, we might elect to value the structure as an independent long position. However, most butterflies are written with narrower, as opposed to wider, spread differentials.

The credit risk analysis of a short butterfly is considerably different from that of a long transaction. Assuming premium is received in a cash settlement period, there is no risk to a butterfly seller. Although the seller is long two middle strike options, it is short the low and high strike options. In the case of a put, for example, if the short low strike is 90, the short high strike is 100 and the long middle strikes are 95, the following may occur: if *CMP* moves to between 100 and 95, the butterfly seller will be obliged to pay out. If *CMP* moves below 95 (but not to 90), when the seller's long puts move in-the-money, it will still be a net payer to the buyer (assume *CMP* travels to 93; the seller's payoff is ((95 – 93) * 2, or 4), while the buyer's payoff from the seller is ((100 – 93), or 7). Thus, the buyer has risk to the seller, not vice versa. Lastly, if *CMP* moves below the low strike of 90, the butterfly's payoffs will net to 0, implying no risk to the seller (or buyer). Thus, short butterflies carry no risk, to the extent they are transacted with a single counterparty and premium is received in a cash settlement time frame.

Multiple Counterparty Transactions

If a synthetic long butterfly is established with separate counterparties, the transactions must be looked at in isolation. Since the position involves the establishment of long and short positions of either puts or calls, and since they cannot legally be netted out as they can in the case of a single counterparty transaction, each leg must be analyzed on its own. In the case of a long butterfly, a bank will have at risk the premium and market risk components associated with the long low and high strike positions; these may be evaluated by Equations 3.2 and 3.3. The two short middle options are, of course, of no credit concern to the institution and can effectively be ignored.

In the case of a short synthetic butterfly, a bank can ignore the short low and high strike options, but must account for the two middle strike long options; this would again imply premium and market risk movement as calculated by Equations 3.2 and 3.3.

Given the differences in calculating risk on multiple counterparty butterflies, particularly for short positions, care must be taken when considering the credit risk implications.

Condors

Our analysis of the credit risk of condors approximates what we have covered above for butterflies, given our understanding that a condor is similar to a butterfly with the exception that the middle strike puts or calls are spread further apart.

Single Counterparty Transaction

Under a single counterparty condor, our focus once again is on long positions. Under a long call condor, for instance, our bank will pay premium for the right to enter into the transaction. It will buy the low strike and high strike calls (the same as in a long call butterfly), but it will sell the middle strike low and middle strike high calls (instead of selling two calls at the same middle strike as in the case of the butterfly). The maximum credit risk will, once again, be based on the difference between the long low strike on the call and the short middle strike; in the case of a call condor, the maximum profit (and credit risk) will be reached with the middle strike low call.

Consider the following: Bank Z buys a long call condor of 100,000 base contracts (each leg is comprised of 100,000 contracts, as in our previous example) from Bank J for $500,000. The long call strikes are set at 100 and 110, while the short middle strikes are set at 103 and 107. If we assume the *CMP* is 99, the position is out-of-the-money for Z. Once *CMP* moves to 103, J will owe Z (103 − 100) ∗ 100,000, or $300,000. As CMP moves to 105, J will owe Z (105 − 100) ∗ 100,000, or $500,000, but Z will owe J (105 − 103) ∗ 100,000, or $200,000, which results in a net gain of $300,000 for Z. As *CMP* moves to 108, J will owe Z (108 − 100) ∗ 100,000, or $800,000, but Z will owe J on two different options: (108 − 103) ∗ $100,000, or $500,000, and (108 − 107) ∗ 100,000, or $100,000, for a total of $600,000. This implies a net gain of $200,000 for Z. Once *CMP* moves past 110, the positions will equal 0, with no gain to either party. Thus, the maximum risk Z will encounter in being long the condor is the difference between the long low strike call and the short middle strike low call (this presumes that the strikes are set at 'even' intervals between long and short positions; this is the normal way of constructing a condor). As always, added to this is the risk of premium which may be lost in the case of default. We may show the long call condor risk as Equation 4.6:

$$REE = Premium + (NC \times SP_{call\ mid\ low} - SP_{call\ low}))$$ (4.6)

For puts, the equation focuses on the difference between the long high strike put and the short middle strike high put, as in Equation 4.7:

$$REE = Premium + (NC \times (SP_{put\ high} - SP_{put\ mid\ high}))$$ (4.7)

where NC is the number of contracts,
          $SP_{call\ mid\ low}$ is the strike price of the short middle low call,
          $SP_{call\ low}$ is the strike price of the long low call,
          $SP_{put\ high}$ is the strike price of the long high put,
          $SP_{put\ mid\ high}$ is the strike price of the short middle high put.

Short condors with a single counterparty, although they include two long positions in the form of the middle strike high/low puts or calls, do not result in credit risk being assumed by the condor seller, as long as premium is received in a timely fashion. The reason for the absence of credit risk follows along the lines discussed immediately above for short single counterparty butterflies.

Multiple Counterparty Transactions
As in the case of a synthetic butterfly established by booking discrete transactions with more than one counterparty, the establishment of a synthetic condor with several institutions requires an examination of the individual long positions in a normal framework such as presented in Equations 3.2 and 3.3. The logic for evaluating the individual components fully is discussed in the section above.

A short condor with multiple counterparties requires the risk evaluation to focus on the long middle strike high/low calls or puts, again per Equation 3.2 or 3.3. Once again, care must be taken when evaluating the risk of single and multiple counterparty short condors, as the risk levels are substantially different.

Ratio Horizontal Spreads

A ratio horizontal, or calendar, spread, results in an institution buying and selling the same type of option with the same strike, for different delivery months. We know that a calendar spread can be developed by buying the near month and selling the far month, or vice versa, and that it can be done in multiples, not simply 1:1. As one might expect, the credit risk difference in dealing with one counterparty and multiple counterparties is significant.

Single Counterparty Transaction

In a single counterparty calendar spread, we presume that the long and short components are documented as a single transaction, where an event of default by one counterparty on its obligation leads to the cancellation of required performance from the second counterparty. If this is, in fact, the case, the analysis of credit risk takes the following form:

For a long calendar spread (which results in a premium debit), an institution will initially be exposed to loss of premium. Thereafter, much depends on the direction of the spread: if a bank is short the near month and long the far month, it will focus its credit risk evaluation on the long portion of the transaction, in a traditional valuation such as Equation 3.2 or 3.3. For instance, if Bank X pays $1MM to enter into a calendar spread where it sells an at-the-money call for 2 month delivery and buys an at-the-money call for 4 month delivery on 100,000 contracts we can imagine that a default might occur on the third month, after X performed on the short call, but before it received performance from its counterparty on the long call. In such an instance, X will have experienced normal credit risk attributable to a long call position. In the example above, if we assume the relevant risk factor for a 4-month trade is 14.5 per cent (and a 2-month trade is 8 per cent), the at-the-money short and long calls are struck at 100 and the net premium paid is $1MM, the risk via Equation 3.2 would be:

$$REE = \$1\text{MM} + 0 \text{ or } [100{,}000 * ((0.145 * 100) + (100 - 100))]$$
$$REE = \$1\text{MM} + \$1.45\text{MM}$$
$$REE = \$2.45\text{MM}$$

Although X has sold 2-month calls to its counterparty in this instance, it will have no bearing on what X expects to receive (if anything) from its counterparty at or near maturity. Thus, Equations 3.2 and 3.3 are appropriate for long calendar spreads for calls and puts, respectively. Note that the premium paid above is net, not gross.

Short calendar spreads are those which result in a premium inflow to the institution. Depending on the individual ratios of buys versus sells, we can imagine a short calendar spread where our institution is long the near month and short the far month. In such an instance, the quantification of risk exposure is largely dependent on the conservatism of an institution: if it wants to assign credit risk for the long near month call or put, it may do so via Equation 3.2 or 3.3, with the following adjustment:

For calls:
$$REE = (NC \times [(RFc \times CMP) + (CMP - SP)]) - Premium \vee 0 \qquad (4.8)$$

For puts:
$$REE = (NC \times [(RFc \times CMP) + (SP - CMP)]) - Premium \vee 0 \qquad (4.9)$$

The adjustment, of course, subtracts premium received from the short leg (or subtracts 0, if the institution wants to be more conservative).

Some analysts might view the above as overly conservative, and suggest that a short ratio horizontal has no risk once premium is received. The underlying rationale for this would be if the ratio horizontal is documented as a single nettable trade, any default by the counterparty on the bank's near month long position once it moves in-the-money will be offset by the bank's far month short position, which by definition will also be in-the-money (since ratio horizontals are constructed with the same strike on the long and short positions). Thus, the two positions will net to a figure of zero, where the gain on the long position lost through counterparty default will be offset by the payment owing the counterparty by the bank on the short position. This presumes the transaction is appropriately documented as a single transaction giving right of offset against future amounts which might be due the defaulting counterparty on an in-the-money short leg, where a bankruptcy receiver is unable to 'cherry pick' the short position. It is for the reader to determine which approach is most logical for a given situation.

Multiple Counterparty Transactions
As with most other multiple counterparty transactions we have discussed, the long or short calendar spread will focus on the long position established at either the near or far month, per our normal risk Equations 3.2 and 3.3. Since these are discrete transactions with individual counterparties, there is clearly no netting involved which may be used to offset (or eliminate) credit risk exposure. Full valuation of long positions (whether for the near or far months) should be employed.

Backspreads

A backspread occurs when an institution buys more options than it sells; the options that it buys are always farther out-of-the-money than those which it sells and as such, generally results in a net inflow of premium. Strikes will be different in a backspread, but maturity will be identical. Our credit risk discussion below is only on long backspreads; a short backspread is, in fact, a ratio vertical spread, and is covered in the section immediately following.

Single Counterparty Transaction
When an institution establishes a backspread with a single counterparty, the premium it receives from selling the nearer-to-the-money options is generally greater than the premium paid for the larger quantity of farther out-of-the-money options. As such, premium may be set at 0 in our *REE* equation, or it may, in fact, be subtracted from our *REE*.

An example of a call backspread might be one where our bank is long 100,000 call contracts struck at 105 and short 50,000 call contracts struck at 100. If *CMP* moves from 99 to 101, the short position moves in-the-money. When *CMP* reaches 105, our bank will be a payer of (105 − 100) * 50,000, or $250,000. However, once *CMP* exceeds 105 and reaches 110 the profit profile begins to shift: though our bank will have to pay ((110 − 100) * 50,000) or $500,000, it now expects to receive (110 − 105) * 100,000, or $500,000, for a net of $0. When *CMP* moves up to 115, the pace of receipt increases further: payout will be $750,000, but receipt will be $1MM, for a net receipt of $250,000. Thus, our bank is exposed once the long positions move heavily in-the-money. Until they pass the point of outpacing the value of the short positions, however, there is no credit risk. Thus, any credit risk evaluation must focus on the maximum movement of the long position (times the number of contracts, which is central to backspreading), less the amount payable on the short positions, less premium received (or 0, in the case of a more conservative stance). We may document the risk via Equation 4.10 for calls:

$$REE = [NC_{long} \times ((RFc \times CMP) + (CMP - SP_{long}))] - \qquad (4.10)$$
$$[NC_{short} \times ((RFc \times CMP) + (CMP - SP_{short}))] - Premium \vee 0$$

And via Equation 4.11 for puts:

$$REE = [NC_{long} \times ((RFc \times CMP) + (SP_{long} - CMP))] - \qquad (4.11)$$
$$[NC_{short} \times ((RFc \times CMP) + (SP_{short} - CMP))] - Premium \vee 0$$

where NC_{long} is the number of contracts associated with the long position,
SP_{long} is the strike associated with the long position,
NC_{short} is the number of contracts associated with the short position,
SP_{short} is the strike associated with the short position.

Returning to our example above, if we assume that on trade date the *RFc* is 20 per cent, the *CMP* is 99 and that our bank received $100,000 in premium for selling the nearer to-the-money calls, our *REE* would be:

$$REE = [100,000 * ((0.20 * 99) + (99 - 105))] -$$
$$[50,000 * ((0.20 * 99) + (99 - 100))] - \$100,000$$
$$REE = [\$1.38MM] - [\$940,000] - \$100,000$$
$$REE = \$340,000$$

If, during the life of the trade, *CMP* moves to 115 (with the *RFc* declining to 10 per cent), our new *REE* would be:

$$REE = [100,000 * ((0.10 * 115) + (115 - 105))] -$$
$$[50,000 * ((0.10 * 115) + (115 - 100))] - \$100,000$$
$$REE = [\$2.15MM] - [\$1.325MM] - \$100,000$$
$$REE = \$725,000$$

REE is beginning to rise because the intrinsic value of the long calls, multiplied by the far greater quantity of contracts, is outweighing the value of the higher strike, lower volume short calls. If our counterparty defaulted today, we would lose with certainty the difference between $((115 - 105) * 100,000)$, or \$1MM, less $(115 - 100) * 50,000$, or \$750,000, less the premium, or \$150,000. In addition, our *REE* equation still includes a potential factor which allows for the *CMP* to move even further during the remaining life of the trade (before default occurs). For instance, if *CMP* rose to 120 just prior to maturity (when our *RFc* is set at 0), the *REE* would be:

$$REE = [100,000 * ((0.0 * 120) + (120 - 105))] -$$
$$[50,000 * ((0.0 * 120) + (120 - 100))] - \$100,000$$
$$REE = [\$1.5MM] - [\$1MM] - \$100,000$$
$$REE = \$400,000$$

If default occurs at this point, our bank will lose with certainty \$500,000 on the net difference between the long and short positions, less the \$100,000 taken in premium.

Multiple Counterparty Transactions
In order to evaluate the risk of multiple counterparty transactions, we simply need to isolate the long and short positions. On the short positions we will have no credit risk exposure and will be a receiver of premium. On the long positions, however, we will value the risk in the same fashion as any long put or call position, via Equation 3.3 or 3.2 respectively. In addition, though our single counterparty backspread results in a net inflow of premium (as a result of selling more expensive options, albeit in lower quantity), the long position established with an institution as a way to create a synthetic backspread will result in an outflow of premium (and cannot be legally offset by inflow from the sale of the more expensive options to the second counterparty).

Ratio Vertical Spreads

A ratio vertical spread is the opposite of the backspread discussed above, and occurs when an institution sells more options than it buys. The options it buys are closer to-the-money than those it sells and, as such, a ratio vertical normally results in a net outflow of premium.

Single Counterparty Transaction
Under a single counterparty transaction a bank may, as an example, buy 100,000 call contracts struck at 100 while selling 200,000 call contracts struck at 105; though it is selling more calls, it is likely that the lower volume of closer to-the-money calls it is buying will result in the bank paying a premium. Note that in a ratio vertical, the expiry of all options is the same. The credit risk exposure of a ratio vertical spread is easily quantified, and is best illustrated by following the path of *CMP* on the positions: if *CMP* rises to 105, our bank will be expecting a payout of $(105 - 100) * 100,000$, or \$500,000. However, as *CMP* rises above 105, the ratio of sold versus bought calls will begin to shift the profit profile from a gain to a loss for our bank. For example, if

CMP reaches 115, our bank will expect a payoff of (115 – 100) * 100,000, or $1.5MM. However, because it has a short position as well, it will owe (115 – 105) * 200,000, or $2MM. Thus, there is a net outflow of $500,000 to the counterparty (and no longer any credit risk except premium paid). This logic is, of course, precisely the reverse of that discussed immediately above in the section on backspreads. The maximum risk for our bank, therefore, will be the point at which market price and volume are maximized; in fact, this occurs when the short position is precisely at-the-money. Thereafter, it will reduce until it is negative, implying that our counterparty has credit risk exposure to the bank, and not vice versa. When this occurs, the only item at risk to the bank is the premium. Note that the ratio of bought versus sold contracts is important in determining how much price movement it will take before exposure is negative. We discuss this at greater length in our example below. Our ratio vertical risk equations, for calls and puts, are shown as:

$$REE = Premium + [NC_{long} \times (SP_{short\ call} - SP_{long\ call})] \qquad (4.12)$$

for calls, and

$$REE = Premium + [NC_{long} \times (SP_{long\ put} - SP_{short\ put})] \qquad (4.13)$$

for puts,

where NC_{long} is the number of long contracts,
$SP_{short\ call}$ is the strike price of the short call,
$SP_{long\ call}$ is the strike price of the long call,
$SP_{long\ put}$ is the strike price of long put,
$SP_{short\ put}$ is the strike price of short put.

In our example above, if we assumed premium paid to be $500,000, maximum *REE* would be:

$$REE = \$500,000 + [100,000 * (105 - 100))]$$
$$REE = \$500,000 + [\$500,000]$$
$$REE = \$1MM$$

If the bank's counterparty defaults when *CMP* is equal to the strike of the short call, the bank will lose $1MM. While the above represents the maximum level of risk attributable to the transaction we may choose to value the risk on an ongoing basis as the difference between the long and short positions. To do so, we may simply utilize Equation 4.14:

$$REE = Premium + 0 \vee [(NC_{long} \times (CMP - SP_{long})) - \qquad (4.14)$$
$$(NC_{short} \times (CMP - SP_{short}))]$$

for calls, and Equation 4.15:

$$REE = Premium + 0 \vee [(NC_{long} \times (SP_{long} - CMP)) - \qquad (4.15)$$
$$(NC_{short} \times (SP_{short} - CMP))]$$

for puts,

where $\qquad$ NC_{long} is the number of long contracts,
NC_{short} is the number of short contracts,
SP_{long} is the strike price of the long put or call,
SP_{short} is the strike price of the short put or call.

For instance, if in our example above the CMP moves to 107, the actual *REE* would be:

$REE = \$500,000 + 0$ or $[(100,000 * (107 - 100)) - (200,000 * (107 - 105))]$

$REE = \$500,000 + 0$ or $[\$700,000 - \$400,000]$

$REE = \$500,000 + \$300,000$

$REE = \$800,000$

This is, of course, less than the $1MM calculated above, which is a maximum *REE* figure. Note that we do not employ any *RFc* figures in this calculation, since the maximum risk is bounded on the upside, not by market movements (as dictated by *RFc*), but by the short position established in the ratio vertical. Note further that we take the greater of 0 or the market risk portion of the equation because, as the *CMP* moves further in-the-money, the buy:sell ratio will cause the risk to become negative (i.e. the bank is not expecting any performance from its counterparty; it is, in fact, expecting to perform for its counterparty). In such a situation, the only item at risk is the premium.

Multiple Counterparty Transactions
As in the case of backspreads, a synthetic ratio vertical created by dealing with more than one institution will involve a focus on the long and short positions. On the higher volume short positions the bank will have no credit risk exposure and will be a receiver of premium. However, on the lower volume, more expensive, long positions, the bank will value the risk in the same fashion as any long call or put position, via Equation 3.2 or 3.3.

A Note on Synthetics
From a credit risk perspective, synthetics created by a combination of long or short options and long or short underlying do not require any special analysis. For instance, if our institution is long the underlying and long a put, we know that it is actually long a synthetic call. Since our credit risk evaluation will not focus on the long underlying (as there is no credit risk inherent in the position as long as the issuer of the underlying does not default), the focus will be exclusively on evaluating the long put, via Equation 3.3, for example. Although the relationship of the underlying and the put translates into a synthetic instrument which acts like a long call, this is irrelevant to the credit

officer. From a risk management standpoint it may well be a consideration, as it might affect the direction and posture of hedging. However, from a strict credit perspective we need focus only on the original long option, not on the resulting synthetic option.

To summarize the discussion we have presented above, it should be clear to the reader that the most vital component in the credit risk analysis of varying option strategies is to understand the potential payoffs which may be made or received during the course of the transaction. This will assist in determining whether maximum risk should be calculated via a risk factor, whether it will be capped by the sale of another option, whether premium is ever at risk, and so on. When dealing with multiple counterparties, which is more unusual when creating a given option strategy, it is vital to decompose the package of options to the individual level, so that long and short positions can be viewed separately, and risk attributed accordingly.

Note that no presentation of risk factors is included for this chapter, as the topic we have addressed is generic in nature. Risk factors should be obtained from individual product chapters, such as those dealing with equity indexes or swaps.

PART III

THE CREDIT RISK OF EQUITY DERIVATIVES

5: The Credit Risk of Standard Equity Derivative Swaps

PRODUCT DESCRIPTION

Equity derivatives, which were developed and refined in the late 1980s by several prominent commercial and investment banks, are today a fast-growing segment of the financial derivatives market. While many of the swap structures common in today's markets are by now very standard in nature (such as 'plain vanilla' currency and interest rate swaps), equity derivatives tend to have far more 'tailor-made' details about them, which makes them fundamentally more difficult to generalize and categorize from a credit risk standpoint. Nonetheless, for purposes of this text, we shall divide our discussion into two broad areas, so-called standard equity derivative swaps, and the more complex derivatives with exotic or embedded options ('embeddos' as they are known among market participants). In this chapter we begin with a background discussion of convertibles, warrants and equity-linked debt which were the precursors of equity derivatives, and then move to a descriptive and risk discussion of standard equity derivative swaps. In Chapter 6 we turn to a discussion of the more complex structures with embeddos.

Convertible Bonds

Convertible bonds were among the earliest of the debt-equity instruments and have been utilized by issuers for several decades. In standard form, a convertible is a bond which enables the holder (investor) the right to convert the debt instrument into a prespecified number of shares should a certain conversion price be reached. When this occurs, the equity generated by the issuer extinguishes the debt held by the investor. Convertibles are often considered debt-equity hybrids, since they may, at given points in the life of the instrument, be either a debt or equity instrument. A convertible which has not been converted into equity is effectively a bond with an option or warrant attached; the market conversion price (i.e. the level at which the bond may be exchanged for equity) is akin to the strike price of an option. While the convertible contains an embedded instrument which acts like a call option, it should be noted that the conversion of the debt instrument into equity results in the issuer actually generating new equity; it is not simply a reallocation of equity shares from a third party to the investor, as in the case of a pure call option. We shall discuss this at greater length below. Convertibles, which are often issued as debentures, may also be issued in zero-coupon form (i.e. deeply discounted instruments which pay no interest but are redeemed at par at maturity if conversion never occurs).

Equity Warrants

Equity warrants have been in use for several decades and give the holder the right to purchase a company's stock at a set strike price within a fixed time frame (typically one to several years). Warrants, which are often exchange listed and traded, are sold by the company itself, and require the issuance of new equity (in exchange for cash) if an investor's warrant is in-the-money and exercise takes place. They are distinguished from call options by the fact that a call option does not result in the issuance of new equity at exercise; it simply reallocates an equity holding from one party (the seller) to another party (the buyer) if exercise occurs. The company is not involved in the issuance of new equity in such circumstances. During the 1960s and 1970s, when warrant issues were especially popular, a company would often issue a 'package' of securities when raising new capital; such packages typically consisted of a bond yielding a certain coupon and detachable warrants allowing for the issuance of new equity when and if exercise occurred. Such warrants have often acted as 'sweeteners' to entice investors to acquire a company's underlying debt. In many instances warrants can be stripped, valued and traded independently. Valuation models for warrants typically examine such variables as the underlying stock price and its volatility, the life of the warrant and the growth and earnings potential of the stock. Models must also take account of the fact that warrant holders are not entitled to receive dividends if the underlying stock pays dividends and that earnings dilution will occur should exercise take place. Such models also determine whether the warrant in question has an anti-dilution clause, which will protect the warrant holder from further dilution resulting from stock splits or stock dividends.

Bonds with Warrants

Although equity warrants have been issued by companies for several decades, the product saw renewed interest during the 1980s when many firms issued bonds with warrants attached. Japanese companies were especially heavy users of the Eurobond-with-warrant concept, raising massive amounts of capital through the structure. The issuance of Eurobonds with such warrants allowed many Japanese firms to raise debt with very low interest coupons. Estimates of the amount Japanese companies raised during the mid- to late 1980s are staggering: 1986 saw approximately $10B in warrants issued, 1987 just under $25B, 1988 just under $30B, 1989 over $65B and 1990 approximately $20B (Connolly and Philips, 1992). Another estimate indicates that between 1987 and 1989 Japanese companies issued $115B in warrants, to add to $25B already outstanding (*The Economist*, 1990). The Securities Public Information Center of Japan estimates that 90 per cent of all private placement bonds issued by Japanese companies between 1984 and 1989 included some type of equity related component, such as a warrant or convertible feature (Rowley, 1991). Despite such spectacular issuance figures, many warrants have expired worthless as the Nikkei has fallen from nearly 40,000 to its current level of 17,000, with the stock prices of many individual warrant issuers following suit. The actual issuance of Eurobonds with warrants has seen a sharp decline in the past two years. In the first nine months of 1992, equity-linked issuance by Japanese companies was down to just over $6B (Treanor *et al*, 1992). Given that many of these warrants have expired worthless, issuers who were expecting to float new equity as warrants were exercised (with proceeds available to repay the maturing bonds) are finding themselves having to redeem the bonds by obtaining alternate, higher cost funds such as bank borrowings. This phenomenon will continue during much of 1993, 1994 and 1995 when many warrants come due.

Covered Warrants

Another segment of the derivatives market, so-called covered warrants, has been gaining in popularity in recent years. Covered warrants are, in reality, not warrants in the traditional sense described above. That is, they are not instruments issued by companies which may eventually be converted into new equity. Covered warrants are third party transactions, where a bank may write (sell) a warrant backed by the underlying stock (or perhaps warrants or options) of a given company, hence use of the word 'covered'; these warrants are exercisable into either the underlying shares or cash. Such instruments are, in fact, options, not warrants, as they will result in the reallocation of stock by the writer (typically a bank), not in new issuance of stock by the company. Although many covered warrant transactions are straightforward, there have been increasingly sophisticated covered warrant structures brought to market in the past few years, with varying redemption features. A glance at the weekly listing of new covered warrant deals in financial trade publications reveals a substantial and ongoing number of warrant deals on specific equities, American Depository Receipts (ADRs), debt instruments, emerging markets securities and reverse floating securities (which we shall discuss in the context of swaps in Chapter 8). Such issues cater to the very specific needs of investors and are a significant source of revenue for many of the commercial and investment banking institutions arranging such transactions.

Highlighted in Table 5.1 is a summary of the major instruments which result in the issuance of new equity, or in the reallocation of existing equity (in all cases, this presumes the exercise or conversion level has been reached).

Table 5.1

Instrument	If Exercise Level Reached
Convertible	New equity issued
Call option	Existing equity reallocated
Equity warrant	New equity issued
Bond with warrant	New equity issued
Covered warrant	Existing equity reallocated

Covered Index Warrants

In addition to the issuance of 'true' warrants by individual issuers and covered warrants by third party institutions on individual stocks and other instruments, the 1980s also witnessed the writing of covered index warrants on indexes such as the Japanese Nikkei 225, the German DAX, the French CAC–40, the US S&P 500 and the UK FTSE 100. In such transactions, major financial institutions such as Bankers Trust, Salomon Brothers and Merrill Lynch packaged and sold put or call warrants, enabling investors to benefit from the appreciation or depreciation in a given index. In virtually all cases exercise of the warrant has been into cash, not delivery of the underlying index. Some indexes, such as the German DAX, previously had no futures contracts, making investor participation in the movement of the actual index difficult. The purchase of a warrant on the DAX allowed investors actually to participate in the movements of the German stock market in absence of a futures contract.

With indexes as the starting point, banks have started becoming more creative, assembling baskets of stocks in particular industrial or geographical sectors and selling warrants on those baskets. Again, this has served a specific need by enabling portfolio and pension fund managers to invest in markets, or segments of markets, which have previously been 'off limits'. As an example, foreign investors have been prohibited from buying registered shares on the Finnish stock market, having instead to buy bearer shares at a premium. One early warrant issue allowed foreign investors to buy into the Finnish market at a premium to registered shares but a discount to bearer shares, thereby allowing somewhat more equitable participation in that market.

Nikkei-linked Bonds

The Japanese Nikkei was an early and frequent target market for index warrants. In addition to covered warrants on the Nikkei (both puts and calls), it was only a short time before index-linked bonds on the Nikkei were issued for a variety of companies (such instruments being different from the Eurobonds with warrants described above, which were related to a company's own shares). Under a typical equity-linked bond structure, an issuer would sell bonds with a call warrant (for example) which would allow cheaper funding for the company and an opportunity for the investor to receive capital gains in the Nikkei (and, in certain cases, dividends as well). In some structures, if the Nikkei fell, investors would still receive a nominal interest payment and would have their principal investment returned, but would obviously receive no capital gains. If, in contrast, the Nikkei rose, the company would be forced to pay the investor the additional capital gains. In reality, the company could hedge the transaction by entering into an equity derivative swap (as discussed below) with a financial institution, where it would receive Nikkei appreciation and pay either the depreciation, or nothing at all. Alternatively, particularly for shorter term bonds, it could establish a position in Nikkei futures, where it would benefit if the market rose (and pass such benefits to its investors). As another option, it could remain unhedged, and take a chance that the Nikkei would fall instead of rise. Those who issued Nikkei-linked bonds with call warrants in late 1989 and early 1990, when the Nikkei was near its peak of almost 40,000, would have found themselves paying only nominal coupons and no capital gains to investors holding now worthless call warrants.

A second type of Nikkei-linked bond, with a put instead of a call, also proved popular with issuers and investors; the structure is depicted in Figure 5.1. Under this type of transaction, a bank would approach an institutional investor interested in writing a put on the Nikkei and would then find an issuer needing to raise funds (and in some cases also willing to 'take a view' on the Japanese market). The issuer would then sell a bond with repayment tied to the level of the Nikkei. If the Nikkei fell below a certain level, the issuer would exercise the put and only have to repay the investor a reduced principal amount instead of par at maturity; in certain instances, it would simply pay the investor a lower coupon instead of reduced principal. In exchange for the put on the market, the issuer compensated the investor via a higher coupon

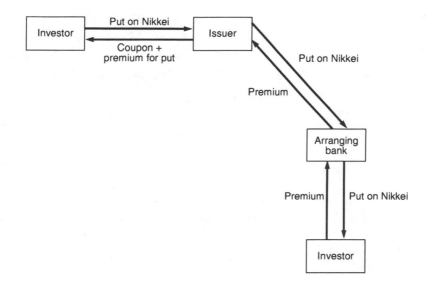

Figure 5.1   Nikkei-linked bond with puts

payment, which was effectively the option premium. On the other side of the transaction, the issuer would very often sell its own put warrant to the bank arranging the financing, again in exchange for premium income which it could pass to the original investor. The bank itself, in a third leg of the deal, could write its own Nikkei puts and sell them to a different set of investors with a different view of the market. (Note that in certain instances the original investors wrote puts which were purchased directly by the arranging bank, and did not flow through the original issuer.) The effect of the above at its conclusion was, of course, to provide the issuer with a more favourable cost of funds than would otherwise have been possible, and to allow investors another financial vehicle through which to take a view on the market. In the late 1980s, when these structures were popular, many investors were convinced that the markets would continue to rise and were therefore eager to write puts as a way to earn extra income. Other investors were eager to buy puts, as they were quite convinced that the levels of the market were out of touch with fundamental economic considerations. In short, there were benefits (or expected benefits) to be gained by all participants, hence the economic rationale and success of such products. Only in hindsight would certain investors or issuers question the advisability of buying or selling certain warrants at certain points in time.

In Table 5.2 we summarize some of the major equity-linked instruments which have been utilized by financial institutions in recent years.

Table 5.2 Major equity-linked instruments

Instrument	Benefit to Investor
Convertible	Coupon and/or value of equity
Call option	Existing equity at lower than market price
Equity warrant	New equity at lower than market price
Bond with warrant	Coupon and/or equity at lower than market price
Covered warrant	Upside/downside of equity/index/basket
Covered index warrant	Upside/downside of index
Index-linked bond	Coupon and up-/downside in index

Equity Derivative Swaps

From the issuance of convertibles, equity warrants, index-linked bonds, covered index warrants, and covered basket warrants, the financial sector turned to equity derivative swaps as the next 'logical' step in the evolution of equity derivatives. The fundamental structure in the equity derivative swap market is one which allows one or both swap parties to achieve financial gains based on the financial appreciation or depreciation of an equity, a basket of equities, or an equity index; maturities typically range from one to five years, though transactions can be structured with longer or shorter terms.

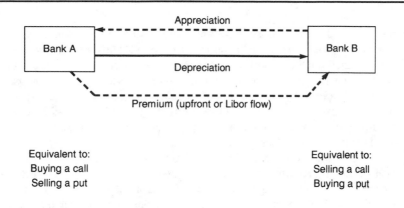

Equivalent to:
Buying a call
Selling a put

Equivalent to:
Selling a call
Buying a put

Figure 5.2   Equity derivative swap, two-sided swap

In the same way covered warrants have allowed investor participation in equities, equity derivative swaps allow the same type of exposure to baskets and indexes. In addition, swaps are also utilized by certain investors (e.g. pension fund managers) holding equities or indexes as a logical way to hedge downside exposure.

In a typical equity derivative swap, highlighted in Figure 5.2, Bank A (as buyer of the swap) will pay Bank B premium in exchange for receiving appreciation in the underlying equity or index. The payment of premium may be in the form of an upfront cash payment, or it may be spread over the life of the swap in the form of a Libor flow. If a transaction is two-sided, Bank A would have to pay Bank B any resulting depreciation in the equity or index. This may be thought of as Bank A buying a call (i.e. receiving value as the market price of the equity rises above a certain strike price) and selling a put (i.e. paying value as the market price of the equity falls below a certain strike price). The receiver of the appreciation is generally the payer of the premium, though this may depend on the intrinsic value of each component.

In a standard two-sided swap, Bank A and Bank B may exchange payments periodically. For example, every quarter the two institutions might compare the strike level of the index established at trade date with the index level prevailing at the

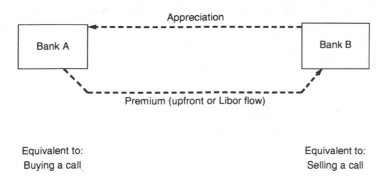

Equivalent to:
Buying a call

Equivalent to:
Selling a call

Figure 5.3 Equity derivative swap, call swap

quarterly interval, and make a payment in one direction or the other. This may be thought of as a series of periodic forwards, since the index differential is settled each quarter and then continues until the next period, when another measurement and settlement occurs. Alternatively, the two institutions may elect not to compare the index values at any time during the life of the transaction, except at maturity. At that point an examination would take place and one party or the other would make the required payment. The risk implications of the two structures are different and are explored in the credit risk section below.

As indicated above another version of the equity derivative swap where Bank A is receiver of the appreciation and payer of the depreciation is one where Bank A is receiver of the appreciation (again, in exchange for premium payment), but is not payer of depreciation. This, in essence, is Bank A buying a call and not selling the associated put, as discussed above; this is often referred to as an equity call swap. The diagrammatic illustration is depicted in Figure 5.3. As one might expect, it is also possible to structure a put swap where Bank A is receiver of depreciation in exchange for premium; in such instances, index appreciation would be irrelevant.

As already mentioned, the equity derivative swap market is enormously custom-driven. Figure 5.4 demonstrates a variety of ways in which an investor, currently holding a portfolio of US Treasury notes yielding 5.5 per cent, could elect to participate in the appreciation of a given stock market, say the Nikkei 225, by entering into a 2-year swap with Bank Z. Depending on the investor's view of the Nikkei, it could choose to pass on the interest received from the bonds in exchange for appreciation in the Nikkei (e.g. buying a call swap struck at 19,000 in a market of 19,000). Alternatively, if it believes that the Nikkei's upside potential is somewhat limited, it may choose to cap its upside gain by writing a call at a higher strike (e.g. 23,000), in exchange for premium income (which will enhance total return). If, however, the investor is quite certain the market will continue to rise, and does not want to cap the upside (but still desiring some premium income), it may choose to write a put (that is, pay Bank Z any depreciation in the index, say below 17,000) and earn premium. If two years from now the Nikkei is at 22,000 and our investor had elected the first scenario, it would have realized a gain of approximately 15.5 per cent for two years, which is superior to the gain from the Treasury notes (11 per cent assuming no compounding). However, if our investor had selected the third scenario and the market had fallen to 16,000, the investor would not have realized any gain on the transaction, except for the premium received from selling the put at 16,000. In addition, it would have foregone 11 per cent in interest on the Treasury notes and would have made a 5.2 per cent payment to Bank Z for depreciation in the Nikkei. Thus, depending on the type of results a given investor is interested in achieving (which ultimately depends on the investor's view of a particular index or equity), a derivative swap can be structured to meet most any desire.

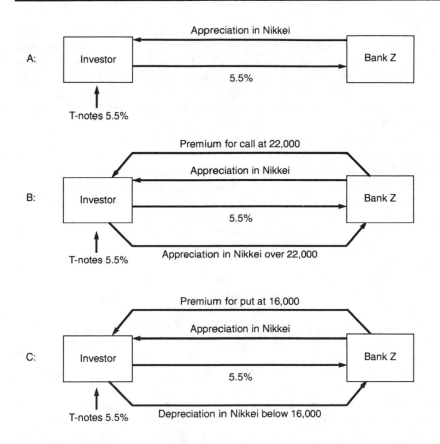

Figure 5.4   Customized derivative swap

CREDIT RISK QUANTIFICATION

The Credit Risk of Equity Derivative Swaps

We know from our discussion in Chapter 2 that equity derivatives are susceptible to market risk movements. This is, in fact, what makes an equity derivative function from an economic standpoint. If there were no market movements, there would be no reason to have an equity derivative to provide up- or downside market exposure, investment enhancement or lower funding. Since equity derivatives of all types are subject to market movements, and since the notional amounts of the contracts are not exchanged, they need to be risk adjusted in order to allow a credit analyst to judge the appropriate level of risk attributable to a given transaction and make an informed credit decision.

Many equity derivative transactions are longer term in nature; that is, their maturities go beyond twelve months, into an area of the maturity spectrum where great care must be taken when considering counterparties of lesser credit quality. Equity derivatives also carry, in general, reasonably large amounts of risk adjusted credit exposure, as we shall explore below. This combination of characteristics generally implies that unsecured structures are only suitable for counterparties of middle or higher credit quality.

Referring once again to our initial discussion in Chapter 2, we know that the credit risk equivalent of a given transaction will be a function of several items, including the volatility of the underlying rate or market index related to the derivative structure, the appropriate confidence level which an institution decides is required in order to render a statistically significant adjustment to the volatility measure, and the square root of the maturity of the trade. These three components help create our risk factor RF, which is then applied to the notional amount of the transaction to yield a credit risk equivalent. In certain instances we must also consider other flows in our risk equation, such as upfront premium payments.

In our discussion of credit risk of equity derivative swaps, we begin first with the simpler call swap (note that the same concepts may also be applied to a put swap; we shall not include a special discussion on such swaps, since the logic and formulae follow from the call swaps). Recall from above that a call swap involves our bank receiving appreciation in an index above a certain level, with no corresponding payment to the counterparty should the index depreciate. In other words, the bank has purchased a call but has not sold a put. In exchange for the right to receive any appreciation in the index, the bank will pay its counterparty a premium, which is very often transferred in the form of a Libor flow against the notional amount of the trade.

Consider the following example: Bank Z enters into a transaction where it is expecting to receive appreciation in the Hong Kong Hang Seng Index over 5000 in one year; in other words, it has purchased a 12-month European call swap on the Hang Seng struck at 5000, in a current market of 4500. The call swap is 10 per cent out-of-the-money and, as such, Bank Z will be paying its counterparty a premium of 12-month US $ Libor minus 50 basis points, on a notional of $50MM (with 12-month Libor currently 3.50 per cent). The premium will not be paid in an upfront lump sum, it will be paid at the conclusion of the transaction, on a net basis if necessary (that is, if the Hang Seng moves in-the-money, the counterparty will subtract its expected premium from the amount it owes Bank Z; depending on how far the index moves, there will be a net payment in one direction or the other). One year from now we can assume one of the following results:

(a) The Hang Seng moves to 5200, or 200 points above the strike level. This equates to a 4 per cent increase over the strike, against a notional of $50MM; Bank Z will receive 4 per cent of $50MM, or $2MM, from the counterparty. However, Bank Z owes the counterparty its Libor-based premium payment, which amounts to 3 per cent of $50MM, or $1.5MM. Thus, Bank Z expects to receive a net payment of $500M from its counterparty, the net profit on the transaction.

(b) The Hang Seng ends the 12-month period at 5000, the precise strike level of the call swap. Although the chances of the current market price equalling the strike price at maturity are rather unlikely, for purposes of this example it would mean that Bank Z would gain nothing from the swap, and would simply make a $1.5MM premium payment to its counterparty.

(c) The Hang Seng falls to 4200, implying a call which is now 16 per cent out-of-the-money. Once again, the call swap expires worthless to Bank Z, which will still have to forward a $1.5MM payment to its counterparty.

The above example should illustrate that any equity derivative call swap can end in one of three positions, two of which will imply no gain, and therefore no market risk exposure (save premium), for the call swap purchaser.

At this point it is worth highlighting several items which will assist in developing a risk equation for the equity derivative call swap structure: firstly, the timing of the Libor-based premium payment to the counterparty is of consequence in determining the credit risk of the transaction. In the example above, Bank Z structured a transaction where it would not have to pay its premium payment upfront; such a scheme reduces risk by not having to deliver a payment before anticipated performance by the option writer. It is fairly simple to envision a scenario where Bank Z delivers its premium payment upfront and, prior to conclusion of the transaction, experiences counterparty default. Such a structure would imply the loss of premium at the very least (together with possible loss of market gains if the index moved in-the-money). It is essential for the credit officer always to be certain when premium is to be paid, even on a Libor-based structure. To the extent the Libor flow can be incorporated as a net payment whenever the value of the index is measured, such is preferable in controlling risk levels. Secondly, the fluctuation of the index is what ultimately determines whether the transaction has value to the appreciation receiver (call swap purchaser). This is clearly a market risk comparison since, as indicated above, the transaction can terminate with value to the call purchaser or with no value to the call purchaser. For transactions which finish with value (i.e. the index is in-the-money), credit risk exposure for the bank is higher since this is value which the bank expects to receive from its counterparty.

Our measurement of market risk movements is captured by *RF*, which is our statistically adjusted volatility measure, calibrated to the maturity of the transaction in question. If, in the above example, we calculate the annual historical volatility of the Hang Seng to be 30 per cent and, taking a 90 per cent confidence level on a lognormal distribution (which, the reader will recall, yields a *z* value of 1.28), the risk factor of our 12-month derivative swap will be equal to 38.4 per cent. This indicates that, based on historical movements of the Hang Seng, we are certain that a future observation taken 12 months from now, when Bank Z's call swap expires, will be within 38.4 per cent of our current starting point (4500), at least 90 per cent of the time. Through this procedure we are able to quantify the likely worst case market movement on our swap and, therefore, our maximum market risk exposure and maximum expected credit loss. If we apply the 38.4 per cent to our starting point of 4500 on the Hang Seng we obtain a maximum likely upper bound of 6228. If this were to occur, Bank Z would expect a net payment of approximately \$10.8MM from its counterparty; that is, it would expect to receive the appreciation in the index over and above the strike price of 5000 (nearly 25 per cent on a notional of \$50MM, for a total of almost \$12.3MM less the premium payment of \$1.5MM). The above measure, through its adjustment to a 90 per cent confidence level, ensures that risk in these volatile transactions is not understated (but remains sufficiently accurate so as not to cause business to be sacrificed through erroneous credit decision making).

To generalize our risk equation from the discussion above, we know that a bank's risk in entering into equity derivative call swaps is, therefore, twofold: premium payment and market risk movement, where potential market risk movement is captured by our risk factor *RF*. The premium payment may be in the form of a known lump sum payment (indicated as 'premium' in the equation below), or it may be derived from Libor flows during the life of the transaction; in the case of the latter, our bank would be required to estimate the maximum expected Libor movement during the life of the transaction. Such an estimate should generally be conservative and focus on current Libor, plus the anticipated upward movement which might occur during subsequent payment periods. An analyst may choose to apply the adjusted historical volatility framework from Chapter 2 to Libor movements in order to determine the maximum likely movement of the benchmark rate over the life of the swap. Alternatively, the analyst may want to utilize a forward-forward method for estimating the floating rates. Though we shall not cover this method in our text, it is a common approach among swap traders for pricing deals based on a net present value basis, and could be used in this context as well. We shall return to Libor estimates in our discussion of differential swaps in Chapter 8. Our complete risk equation is shown as:

$$REE = (RF \times N) + Premium \vee \sum (Libor_{max} \times N) \qquad (5.1)$$

where
RF is the relevant risk factor,
N is the notional amount of the transaction,
$Libor_{max}$ is the maximum anticipated Libor rate during the transaction (or the relevant period).

Note that the latter term is a summation of periodic interest payments if they occur more than once during the life of the transaction. Further note that in Equation 5.1 (and all others in this chapter) we may elect to substitute RF for RFc, a constantly adjusted risk factor which declines continuously as the transaction reaches maturity. This should appear logical to the reader, as a lesser time to maturity implies a lesser chance for market movements which, in turn, translates into a lower RFc. Note that whenever RFc is utilized, we must also include some measure to account for the actual mark-to-market exposure which may be increasing, or we will be understating the risk of the transaction. This may be accomplished through an adjustment to the REE to reflect the ongoing value of the transaction (as shown in Equation 5.3 and 5.4 below), or through the use of a fractional and actual exposure framework (this concept is discussed at the end of the chapter). For ease we shall continue to present *RF*, with the knowledge that *RFc* may be substituted as necessary. As a final note, it should be clear that a multi-year risk factor is generally discounted back to the present utilizing a discount rate which an institution deems most appropriate. While this is vital, we do not include any discounting of our *RF*, for ease of presentation.

If the premium is payable as a net flow at the appropriate evaluation interval(s), credit risk will simply focus on market risk movements, under the assumption that failure by the counterparty to perform on its payment of index appreciation will result in the bank withholding payment of its Libor flow. The second version is captured as:

$$REE = RF \times N \qquad (5.2)$$

where $\qquad$ *RF* is the relevant risk factor,
$\qquad$ *N* is the notional amount of the transaction.

If we return to our previous example and assume that Bank Z was required to pay the Libor-based flow upfront (and no longer had the benefit of a nettable final payment), the *ex-ante* risk attributable to the transaction for credit risk evaluation purposes would be calculated as \$20.7MM (\$1.5MM in premium plus 38.4 per cent of \$50MM for the market risk component) per Equation 5.1. When compared with standard interest rate swaps, which typically carry risk of 1–5 per cent for a short to intermediate term swap, it should be clear that even standard equity derivative swap structures may carry substantial amounts of risk.

Certain institutions may elect to assign a risk value which is somewhat lower or higher than standard factors would dictate if a particular swap entered into is far out- or in-the-money. This logic parallels the approach taken in our discussion of in- and out-of-the-money options in Chapter 3. In the example above we showed a bank entering into a Hang Seng index swap which was 10 per cent out-of-the-money on the start date. Our normal risk factor for such a transaction was calculated as 38.4 per cent (plus the relevant premium amount). This is a decidedly conservative stance when the transaction is starting 10 per cent out-of-the-money. If our risk factor indicates that the maximum likely movement of the index is 38.4 per cent, then a transaction which is structured 10 per cent out-of-the-money is unlikely to end 38.4 per cent in-the-money. To take account of the intrinsic value, an institution may wish to utilize Equation 5.3 for call swaps:

$$REE = N \times \left(\frac{RFc \times CMP}{SP} + \frac{CMP - SP}{SP} \right) + Premium \vee \Sigma \left(Libor_{max} \times N \right)$$

$$(5.3)$$

or 5.4 for put swaps:

$$REE = N \times \left(\frac{RFc \times CMP}{SP} + \frac{SP - CMP}{SP} \right) + Premium \vee \Sigma \left(Libor_{max} \times N \right)$$

$$(5.4)$$

where   *CMP* is the market level of the index at trade date,
             SP is the strike level of the index,
             N is the notional of the transaction,
             $Libor_{max}$ is the maximum anticipated Libor rate during the
             transaction (or the relevant period).

These equations, which should look familiar to the reader from our discussion of options in Chapter 3, allow an institution to track the ongoing exposure resulting from an increase or decrease in intrinsic value. Use of an adjustment to *RFc* means that a fractional/actual exposure framework, such as the one described at the end of this chapter, need not be utilized.

Returning to our original example, and utilizing Equation 5.3, we note the following *REE* calculation:

$$REE = \$50MM * (((0.384 * 4500)/5000) + ((4500 - 5000)/5000)) + \$1.5MM$$
$$REE = \$50MM * (0.3456 + (-0.10)) + \$1.5MM$$
$$REE = \$12.28MM + \$1.5MM$$
$$REE = \$13.78MM$$

This compares with the risk of \$20.7MM from our original example. As the reader might suspect, the above has a relevant effect when indexes are very deeply out-of-the-money, and will ensure that risk is not overstated by an unnecessary amount. In addition, the above equations allow institutions to increase the risk exposure by the same means for those indexes which are struck far in-the-money. (The reader should recall from our discussion in Chapter 3 that the *RFc*s in Equations 5.3 and 5.4 are calibrated by an amount which reflects the additional in- or out-of-the-money portion of the transaction. If desired, *CMP* in the numerator may be replaced by *SP* to preserve the original *RFc*). While we have presented these additional equations, the reader should note that other examples in this chapter will be based on the generic Equation 5.1.

Returning to our previous discussion on call swaps, the risk discussion presented in Equations 5.1 and 5.2 does not hold true, obviously, if our bank is payer (instead of receiver) of index appreciation (i.e. seller of the call). In such instances it will be the bank's counterparty which will be looking to the bank for performance should the index move in-the-money. In such instances the bank will need to focus only on receipt of premium; if it occurs in an upfront lump-sum fashion the trade should be viewed as normal cash settlement risk, which is minimal (e.g. if the counterparty fails to deliver the cash within a five-day time frame, which is normal, the bank would simply unwind the transaction and is unlikely to have suffered any ill effects from market movements in a five-day time span). If, however, payment of premium follows the more traditional convention and is paid out in a Libor stream over the life of the transaction (or simply at the end of the transaction), the bank may elect to estimate the anticipated value of that Libor stream as indicated above and count that figure as its risk. Some banks may choose to ignore the risk of the Libor stream on the assumption that if Libor is not received, appreciation in the index will not be made. However, if no appreciation occurs and the Libor flow is not received, the bank will have effectively lost money.

For purposes of the second standard equity derivative swap structure discussed above, where our bank is receiver of appreciation on an index and payer of depreciation on the same index (that is, it has purchased a call and sold a put), we can consider the following scenario: Bank A is expecting to receive appreciation in the S&P 500 over 340 in one year from Bank X; that is, it has purchased a 12-month call on the S&P, struck at 340 (in a current market of 335). The call is 1.5 per cent out-of-the-money and the notional amount of the transaction is $100MM.

At the same time, Bank A is willing to pay depreciation in the index below 325 in one year; in option terminology, it has sold Bank X a 12-month put on the S&P, struck at 325 (again, in a current market of 335). The put is 3 per cent out-of-the-money.

In order to compensate for the more expensive call option (which is struck closer-to-the-money), Bank A agrees to pay Bank X 6-month Libor less 75 basis points, semi-annually (assume for this part of the example that 6-month Libor at trade date is 2.75 per cent and it remains constant during the life of the transaction; we shall loosen this assumption when we return to the example in the section below); it will pay the Libor flows at t=0 and t=180. Twelve months from now we can envision one of the following scenarios:

(a) The S&P reaches a high of 362 at maturity of the transaction. Bank A, receiver of the appreciation, is entitled to the 6.5 per cent appreciation over the strike and will receive a gross payment of $6.5MM from Bank X. Net of the Libor flows, Bank A receives $4.5MM at maturity ($1MM in Libor was paid at t=0 and a further $1MM at t=180).

(b) The S&P falls to 320 at maturity. Bank A, which is receiver of appreciation and payer of depreciation, finds that the index is 1.6 per cent below the put strike price of 325 and, as such, will be forced to pay Bank X $1.6MM for the depreciation and $2MM for the premium on the now-worthless call portion of the transaction.

From a credit risk standpoint we again divide the issue into two perspectives: Bank A, as receiver of appreciation and payer of depreciation and Libor, and vice versa. When Bank A is receiver of index appreciation in exchange for Libor, the analysis is identical to the one presented in Equations 5.1 to 5.4 above (depending on the particular circumstances of the transaction and the method used to value the risk). The fact that the Bank is also a payer of depreciation does not enter into the credit risk consideration, as we must always expect that the transaction will move in the favour of the Bank, which implies increasing exposure.

If, in contrast, Bank A is receiver of depreciation and Libor, and payer of appreciation, the analysis shifts somewhat. Once again, we assume a worst case scenario which, in this instance, would be that the index falls and our bank expects to receive the depreciation below the strike. This element can be captured by the same risk factor framework discussed above, because volatility implies both upward and downward movements. In addition, the bank must also consider the nature and timing of the premium payment. If it is an upfront payment, this amount can effectively be subtracted from the risk equivalent exposure yielded by the $(RF * N)$ component of our equation if desired (as it is money in hand which can be used to defray any amounts due in the future from the counterparty which are not paid because of default). The resulting formula is shown as Equation 5.5:

$$REE = (RF \times N) - 0 \vee premium \tag{5.5}$$

where RF is the relevant risk factor,
                     N is the notional amount of the transaction.

If the swap contains a normal Libor premium flow which occurs during the life of the transaction, or even at the conclusion of the transaction, it is important that the additional exposure be reflected in the risk calculation, since non-receipt of premium in a normal cash time frame implies an amount at risk for the seller. Once again, this is a variable which can be estimated using an adjusted historical volatility measure on Libor movements, or it can be approximated by the amount of lump sum premium which would normally be owing on a long-date option with similar time and intrinsic values. We may use Equation 5.1 or 5.4 to value the risk of equity derivative swaps when our bank is receiver of depreciation and premium over time.

If, in the example above, Bank A is expecting to receive appreciation from Bank X against payment of Libor premium (in two semi-annual instalments) and depreciation we would obtain the following:

S&P 500 risk factor = 25.6%
6-month Libor volatility = 10%
Adjusted to 90% confidence level for second payment = 12.80%

Libor amounts estimated during transaction (we assume it is no longer constant):

First 6 months (no adjustment required): 2.75%–.75% = 2.00%/2 = 1.00%
Second 6 months (estimated): (2.75% * 1.128) – .75% = 2.35%/2 = 1.18%
Total estimated Libor payments: (1.00% + 1.18%) * $100MM = $2.18MM

$REE = (0.256 * \$100MM) + (0.0218 * \$100MM)$
$REE = \$25.6MM + \$2.18MM$
$REE = \$27.8MM$

Thus, the total risk on a $100MM transaction where Bank A expects to receive appreciation in the S&P 500 in one year against payment of 6-month Libor less 75 basis points every semi-annual period (together with index depreciation) is equal to just under $28MM. Note once again that there is no credit risk implication for Bank A on the index depreciation of the transaction. From the standpoint of Bank X, risk exposure focuses on the second Libor payment (recall the first one is received at $t=0$), as well as index depreciation which Bank A might have to pay. This *REE* can be shown as $1.18MM (for the second premium payment) and $25.6MM (for index depreciation), for a total of $26.78MM; X might choose to subtract the original premium of $1MM from its *REE* if it so desires.

The Credit Risk of Equity Derivative Swaps Structured as Forwards

In our discussion above we have focused on transactions where an index is evaluated at one point in time, the maturity date of the swap. This means that the strike level of the index and the market level of the index are measured at the conclusion of the transaction, with appropriate flows being made in one direction or the other (depending on whether appreciation and/or depreciation are involved). When an equity derivative swap is structured in this fashion, the potential for single, continuous market movement without interruption is far greater than if the index is measured at periodic points in time, with settlement of the index appreciation or depreciation taking place during these intervals.

An equity derivative can be structured as a series of linked forward transactions, where the strike and market prices are compared at periodic intervals. At such pre-agreed periods, the two parties would evaluate the relevant prices and a payment would be made in one direction or the other (or, quite possibly, no payment in either direction at all if the swap called for only one-sided movement of the index). Following the period comparison, a typical agreement might call for the strike of the structure to effectively be set at the new market level. That is, the next forward would only have value equal to the difference between the current market price at the end of the second settlement period and the strike price set at the beginning of the second period, not the original strike price set at the beginning of the transaction. Any transaction structured as a forward with periodic settlement has the effect of not allowing the mark-to-market or intrinsic value of the swap (the excess of market over strike in the case of a call, market below strike in the case of a put) to build up in an overly significant fashion. This, in turn, has the effect of allowing a lower amount of risk equivalent exposure to be allocated to a transaction.

We can consider the following example: Bank J enters into a call swap structured as a series of forwards where it will receive appreciation in the Nikkei over 20,000, and will pay Bank Y 6-month Libor flat each semi-annual period for 2 years. Under the agreement, Bank J and Bank Y will compare the market value of the Nikkei every semi-annual period when the Libor payments are due. If the value of the Nikkei is in excess of the strike level, Bank Y will make a payment of the appreciation to Bank J (less any Libor amounts Bank J owes Y), the new strike level of the index will be set at the current market level and the evaluation process will continue for the next period. This is a common structure when dealing with equity derivatives as a series of forwards. Note that the two banks could agree to set the new strike level in advance at any particular position, for example the original level, the new market level plus 200 points, 102 per cent of the new market level, and so on. This will clearly change the risk parameters of the transaction by forcing it in- or out-of-the-money, so care must be taken when considering these 'less common' arrangements, with adjustments to the risk factor as necessary (via Equation 5.3 or 5.4). If, for example, the strike remains at the original level, the succeeding period will have an *RFc* which reflects the in-the-money portion of the transaction since the swap will already have intrinsic value; this type of structure, however, is not especially common.

Under our example above the risk equivalency calculation would focus on the possible market movements in the Nikkei from period to period, instead of the full two-year time horizon. Since settlement will occur on each comparison date, and the transaction will effectively be 're-written' at new market levels, exposure on the swap is not permitted to accumulate.

If the 2-year *RF* for the Nikkei is 54.3 per cent (30% $* 1.28 * \sqrt{2}$) and Bank J's estimated Libor payments for those two years are 5 per cent p.a. (payable each semi-annual period), the risk on an unaltered standard 2-year $100MM Nikkei call swap (via Equation 5.1) would be:

$$REE = (0.543 * \$100MM) + ((0.05 * \$100MM) + (0.05 * \$100MM))$$
$$REE = \$54.3MM + \$10MM$$
$$REE = \$64.3MM$$

If, however, the swap is reviewed and settled every 6 months (and the new strike equals the current price), our risk falls to $27MM. This is calculated by reducing the maturity factor applied to our risk factor. The change focuses on reducing $\sqrt{T}$ from 2 years to 0.5 years, or 6 months; this is the maximum amount the index can move during the semi-annual period, according to our *RF* model. Since the maximum movement in the underlying index is what ultimately determines our market risk exposure, this adjustment is critical to ensure accuracy in measuring a call swap structured as a series of forwards. In the example above, the $27MM is derived from (30% $* 1.28 * \sqrt{0.5}$).

A simple way to illustrate the difference between the series of forwards and the unaltered two-year swap comes from an examination of the level of the index at a select point in the transaction. Let us assume that after the first six months the index has moved to 23,000 (from its starting point of 20,000). Bank J receives 15 per cent, or $15MM, in the form of index appreciation, less $2.5MM in premium (Libor of 5 per cent p.a./2 $* $100MM). The new strike is set at 23,000, instead of the 20,000 still in existence under the unaltered transaction. Assume, further, that just before the second evaluation date, the Nikkei falls to 22,000, at which time J's counterparty defaults. Since the forward is out-of-the-money, J has no credit exposure which may cause a loss. In addition, since J has not yet paid its periodic premium, it has not sustained a loss on that front, either; its first premium payment is effectively ignored, since J already obtained performance during the first evaluation period. The unaltered swap, in contrast, has value of $10MM (the difference between the *CMP* and the original *SP*), plus $2.5MM in premium from the first semi-annual period, for a total loss of $12.5MM. It should be clear, then, that the risk of an equity derivative established as a series of forwards carries less risk than a swap which is unaltered.

Returning to our example, we note that the $10MM in expected Libor payments are not included in the risk calculation since two years of interest payments in the equation would represent an overly conservative, and unreasonable, stance. This is especially true when the swap agreement calls for net payments of Libor and the index on each settlement period (which, in practice, is how many structures function). In such instances, one of three positions may occur at the time of counterparty default:

(a) the index appreciation is greater than the Libor payment to be made – in such cases the credit loss experienced by Bank J from non-receipt of the index will be partially offset by the Libor payment it was meant to have made to Bank Y. The risk factors used to calculate market movement will more than account for any potential loss in such a scenario;

(b) the index appreciation is equal to the Libor payment to be made – in this case there will be no movement of funds from Bank J's perspective and it will, in fact, be 'ahead of the game' as it was expecting no index receipt and is making no premium payment (although a bankruptcy receiver is likely to demand such a payment be made in any event);

(c) the index depreciates – in such instances Bank J was expecting no payment from Bank Y and was, in fact, prepared to make a net payment of Libor; once again, it is likely that any bankruptcy receiver would insist on the proper payment being made. The central point is that valuation of the premium interest payments to be made to Bank Y need not be included in a credit risk calculation unless they occur in upfront fashion.

Based on the above, we can establish the appropriate risk equivalency equation for equity derivative forwards (simply equity derivative swaps with periodic settlements) as:

$$REE = RF_{adj} \times N \tag{5.6}$$

where RF_{adj} is a risk factor adjusted to reflect the relevant settlement period (i.e. the maximum period during which the index can fluctuate),
N is the notional.

Note: for a series of transactions where premium is not paid as a Libor stream but, rather, as an upfront payment, we add the value of the premium to *REE*. As a reminder, if the second in a series of forwards retains the original strike as the new starting point, (instead of the new current market level), the RF_{adj} must be calibrated for the in-the-money portion by Equation 5.3 or 5.4.

As a final note it is important to emphasize two points: first, the appropriate fractional portion of a year should be used to correspond with the settlement period when deriving the adjusted *RF*; second, the above framework is useful for either pure call or put swaps or call/put swaps, as long as the bank is long (i.e. it is expecting appreciation and paying Libor and/or depreciation). In situations where the bank is short a put/call structure (i.e it is expecting depreciation and Libor and paying appreciation), the analysis must focus on an adjusted *RF* framework plus receipt of periodic Libor, since a default by the counterparty when the index has depreciated will result in the loss of both the mark-to-market portion of the swap (captured by RF_{adj} times the notional) plus nonreceipt of the contracted Libor flow for the period. The appropriate equation for a short put/call forward is, therefore, equal to:

$$REE = (RF_{adj} \times N) + (Libor_{per} \times N) \tag{5.7}$$

where RF_{adj} is the risk factor adjusted to reflect the relevant settlement period,
N is the notional,
$Libor_{per}$ is the periodic Libor flow expected by the bank.

When a short call (or put) structure is involved, the risk exposure will focus exclusively on the expected Libor receipt each period. If there is a counterparty default when the index is out-of-the-money, that is, it does not owe the counterparty any sum because the index has not appreciated (or depreciated), the bank will lose its Libor premium payment for the period; the benefit of a netting arrangement will be of no use in such situations. Only if the index is in-the-money and sums due the counterparty are sufficient to cover the Libor payment (which the bank never receives) will it not sustain a loss.

A Potential Exposure Framework for Separating Risk

One method which is widely used in tracking credit risk exposure on standard interest and currency swaps (and which we shall discuss in Chapter 7 of this text), is a potential exposure framework, which separates risk into two distinct components, potential market exposure and actual exposure (these same terms can be substituted by others commonly used in the market, such as time-to-decay exposure and mark-to-market exposure, respectively).

Potential market exposure (PME) seeks to measure the risk exposure which may occur throughout the life of the transaction due to market movements; this is equal to the potential market risk measure discussed in Chapter 2. At the beginning of a transaction, such exposure is calculated by the risk factors and the *REE* equations we detail above. That is, it is exposure which is unknown to an analyst at the beginning of the transaction, but which must be attributed to the deal in order for the correct credit decision to be made (i.e. our ex ante information). As we have discussed, potential market exposure is always positive, but declines over time as the chance for market movements to occur begins to reduce. If in a three-year derivative swap transaction the potential for market movements to occur during the life of the deal (as measured on day one) are 35 per cent, we expect this potential for movement to fall to 0 per cent at maturity.

Actual exposure (AE), in contrast, measures the true exposure which is present at any point during the life of the transaction. This sum represents the economic cost of replacing the transaction in today's markets should the counterparty default. Depending on market rates at the time of default versus those at inception, this figure may either be positive or negative; if positive, the bank will sustain a loss and if negative it will have no exposure and therefore no loss. Actual exposure, which is also known as mark-to-market risk, is generally calculated as Equation 5.8 for interest/currency swaps:

$$MTM = \sum_{x=1}^{p} \left(\frac{N \times \dfrac{(r_n - r_0)}{t}}{\left(1 + \dfrac{r_n}{t}\right)^x} \right) \tag{5.8}$$

where

N is the notional,

r_n is the new rate in period x,

r_0 is the original rate,

p is the number of periods until maturity,

t is the frequency of payments under the transaction.

This equation represents a discounted annuity of what a bank may be owed by a counterparty if default occurs (see Chapter 7 for another form of calculating this same value). Actual exposure components, particularly in the context of interest and currency swaps, may also include an accrued interest receivable component, if there is a mismatch between the payment and receipt of a flow between a bank and its counterparty. To the extent a bank makes payments more frequently than it receives them, this represents additional exposure which has been assumed by the bank, and is added to actual exposure. These concepts are discussed in more detail in Chapter 7.

A potential market exposure framework is perfectly applicable to our discussion of risk on equity derivative swaps, as it allows a bank to continue valuing its credit exposure to a given counterparty on an ongoing basis, with considerably more accuracy than a simple ($RF * N$) calculation at the beginning of the transaction. For equity derivatives structured as forwards with periodic settlement this type of framework is not generally required, since the actual exposure is not allowed to build up beyond a given settlement period, and since potential market exposure is always limited to the risk attributable to one settlement period's movements (although in theory the potential market exposure component could be reduced on a monthly basis and the actual exposure could be valued on a monthly basis. However, it is unlikely that a bank would do this when dealing with a transaction which will be limited to market movements of three or six months). Standard equity derivative swaps, in contrast, are excellent candidates for this analysis and will yield ongoing accuracy in measurement of credit risk exposure. This type of framework is used in conjunction with a constantly adjusted risk factor *RFc*, as indicated earlier (though one which is not adjusted via Equations 5.3/5.4 as this would result in 'double counting'). Naturally, in place of r_n and r_O in the equation above, we focus on the index levels denoted by current market price *CMP* and strike price *SP*.

Consider the following transaction: Bank EFG enters into a $100MM 2-year call swap on the Australian All Ordinaries Index with a strike of 1500, with evaluation taking place at maturity. In exchange for this call, EFG will pay its counterparty Libor flat every 12 months, with the first payment based on Libor at commencement and payable on trade date, and the second based on Libor levels existing 12 months hence and payable on that date. The All Ords is currently at 1350 and 12-month Libor is 4 per cent. Under our normal fractional exposure the credit officer at Bank EFG would estimate the initial *REE* (which is our potential market exposure on day 1) to be the following:

All Ords adjusted historical volatility is 32% (25% * 1.28)
The *RF* for a 2 year transaction is 45% (32% * $\sqrt{2}$)
12-month Libor adjusted historical volatility is 12.8% (10% * 1.28)

Based on Equation 5.1 (but not adjusting the 10 per cent out-of-the-money portion via Equation 5.3, since our actual exposure framework will eventually yield similar results – this is discussed below), our initial *REE* (or PME) is:

$REE = (0.45 * \$100MM) + ((0.04 * \$100MM) + (0.045 * \$100MM))$
$REE = \$45MM + \$8.5MM$
$REE = \$53.5MM$

The sum of $53.5MM is how much the analyst must assign as potential risk exposure at the inception of the transaction, before any market movements have taken place. We can now create Table 5.3, which indicates the quarterly path of the All Ords (and Libor) in order to demonstrate how the potential exposure framework aids in tracking credit exposures. In practice, most institutions would value these positions at least monthly, and perhaps more frequently if required. Note that for clarification purposes PME and AE each include separate valuation columns for the index and the interest payment. Since the transaction starts with a 4 per cent payment to the counterparty, that is immediately shown as an AE; since EFG will also be required to make a second payment in one year, the estimated payment is shown as a PME component and will shift to an AE component at the end of quarter 4.

Table 5.3 Tracking potential exposure of a derivative ($ in MMs)

Date	All Ord	Libor	REE =	PME Index	+ Int	AE Index	Int
Trade	1350	4.00%	$53.50	$45.0	$4.5	$ 0.0	$4.00
Qtr 1	1370	4.00%	$50.80	$42.3	$4.5	$ 0.0	$4.00
Qtr 2	1425	4.25%	$47.50	$39.0	$4.5	$ 0.0	$4.00
Qtr 3	1550	4.75%	$47.60	$35.8	$4.5	$ 3.3	$4.00
Qtr 4	1600	4.75%	$47.45	$32.0	$0.0	$ 6.7	$8.75
Qtr 5	1600	4.75%	$43.15	$27.7	$0.0	$ 6.7	$8.75
Qtr 6	1550	4.75%	$34.65	$22.6	$0.0	$ 3.3	$8.75
Qtr 7	1625	4.75%	$33.00	$16.0	$0.0	$ 8.3	$8.75
Qtr 8	1650	4.50%	$18.75	$ 0.0	$0.0	$10.0	$8.75

It should be noted that in this example, if the index is out-of-the-money (such as during the first 2 quarters), the AE component for the index is not negative, it is set at 0. In addition, recall that for clarity no discounting is shown.

Table 5.3 highlights the actual losses which might be sustained at various points in time. For example, if EFG's counterparty defaults during quarter 3, EFG will lose, with certainty, $3.3MM from index appreciation, and $4MM from Libor premium payments. If the counterparty does not default in quarter 3, EFG still has positive actual exposure equal to $7.3MM; it also has potential exposure of $35.8MM for possible future market movements in the index, and $4.5MM for the second premium payment which will be payable at the end of the quarter.

Note that instead of utilizing the fractional/actual exposure framework, we may employ Equation 5.3 or 5.4 during the life of the trade. The figure yielded by Equation 5.3 will equal $35.3MM, or $700,000, more than in Table 5.3, for the reasons discussed in Chapter 3 (recall that use of *SP* in the numerator of Equation 5.3 will yield the same result as in the Table).

Naturally, it is unnecessary to utilize both procedures at the same time, as such would 'double count' exposure. Note that an unadjusted RF_c, together with a fractional/actual exposure framework, will result in some overstatement of credit risk at the beginning of a transaction if it is struck out-of-the-money.

RISK FACTORS

Highlighted In Table 5.4, for informational purposes, are sample risk factors used in the calculation of *REE* in standard equity derivative swaps based on major indexes. The risk factors were developed using historical volatilities adjusted to a 90 per cent confidence level on a lognormal distribution. Note that to the extent a transaction is structured as a series of forwards with either quarterly or semi-annual settlement (which are most common in the marketplace), the risk factors for the 3- month and 6-month columns are appropriate as RF_{adj} in the equations above. Note also that these risk factors may be employed with the equity derivative option structures discussed in Chapter 6.

Table 5.4   Risk factors for equity derivatives on major indexes (per cent)

	Three months	Six months	One year	Two years	Three years	Four years	Five years
S&P500 HV=17	10.9	15.4	21.8	30.8	37.8	43.6	48.7
Nasdaq HV=13	8.3	11.7	16.6	23.5	28.8	33.2	37.1
Hang Seng HV=30	19.2	27.1	38.4	54.3	66.5	76.8	85.8
Nikkei HV=22	14.1	19.9	28.2	38.0	48.8	56.4	63.0
All Ords HV=14	8.9	12.7	17.9	25.3	31.0	35.8	40.0
Milan MIB HV=22	14.1	19.9	28.2	40.0	48.8	56.4	63.0
DAX HV=21	13.5	14.8	26.9	38.0	46.6	53.8	60.2
CAC 40 HV=18	11.5	16.3	23.0	32.5	39.8	46.0	51.4
FTSE HV=20	12.8	18.1	25.6	36.2	44.3	51.2	57.2
Swiss SMI HV=14	8.9	12.7	17.9	25.3	31.0	35.8	40.0

6: The Credit Risk of Equity Derivative Options and Complex Structures

PRODUCT DESCRIPTION

Having reviewed standard equity derivative swaps in Chapter 5, the reader should be acquainted with the basic structures of the equity derivative swap market. In this chapter we seek to explore some of the more complex and interesting features which have been incorporated into standard equity derivative transactions to yield very specific results for issuers and investors. Many of the risk features of these instruments are rather different from those we have discussed so far and warrant a close examination. Indeed, some of the structures we shall mention below, such as 'all-or-nothing' options, carry substantial amounts of risk. Credit officers evaluating the appropriateness of such deals must be fully aware of the credit exposures which are assumed when booking such transactions.

This chapter will cover in greater detail the use of exotic or embedded options ('embeddos') which are characteristic of tailor-made derivatives packages. (Many of the structures described in this chapter are not only specific to equity-related transactions; some may also be found in the interest and currency markets. However, we will present them in the context of equity structures in this text.) Before describing such embeddos, we shall begin with a discussion of conventional OTC options on equities and equity indexes, which are often used by banks to obtain hedging 'cover' on other transactions they may position on their books. We shall then turn to a discussion of the more popular embedded options common in today's market, including path dependent barrier options (e.g. 'knock-outs,' 'knock-ins,' 'lookbacks'), binary options (e.g. 'all-or-nothings'), time dependent or 'preference' options, deferred payment American options, outperformance and basket options, quantos, and equity call and put spreads. Following a brief description of each, we shall turn to the credit risk quantification of these options.

Conventional Options

The category of conventional options is by now well known to the reader following our discussion in Chapters 3 and 4. Puts and calls on individual equities, and on equity indexes, are widely used by participants in the equity derivatives market acting as either investor, issuer or hedger. While many equity options (on both individual stocks and on broader indexes like the S & P 500) are listed, much of the activity in these instruments takes place in the over-the-counter market, which allows for greater flexibility in setting strike prices and maturity dates. Puts and calls on equities may be struck in-, at-, or out-of-the-money, and they may be for European or American exercise. Maturities in the OTC market may range from several weeks to several years. These options are central to the marketplace and are particularly useful as hedging tools (in either OTC or listed form) for banks creating derivative structures.

Path Dependent Barrier Options

Path dependent options are options with a payout directly related to the movement of the underlying security. This category of embeddos is generally said to include four separate 'knock-in/out' options, as well as lookback options.

A barrier option is an option which either comes into existence, or is eliminated, when a market price reaches a pre-determined strike price. The four primary barriers include the '*up and out*,' where an option is cancelled (out) if an index rises above a certain level (up); the '*down and out*,' where an option is cancelled (out) if an index falls to a certain level (down) (these two are also known as 'knockouts'); '*up and in*,' where an option comes into existence (in) if an index reaches a certain level (up); and, finally, a '*down and in*,' where an option comes into being (in) if the index falls below a certain level (down) (the latter two are sometimes referred to as 'knock-ins'). Knock-outs and knock-ins are not, in fact, new products; they have been in existence since the late 1960s (see Cox and Rubinstein, 1985). They have, however, become much more popular in recent years.

As an example of a path dependent barrier, a bank may purchase an at-the-money 6-month Nikkei call struck at 16,000 with a 'down and out' knock-out on the index at 15,000 where, if the Nikkei falls below 15,000, the call will no longer be operational. To the extent that the Nikkei falls below 15,000 and rises above 16,000 during the 6-month period, the bank will no longer have the benefit of index appreciation, as the call will have been 'knocked out'. As another example, a bank may purchase an 'up and in' put on the S&P 500 at 375, where the benefit of the put only comes into effect once the value of the S&P 500 rises above 375. If there is a subsequent fall once the option has become operational, the bank will receive the benefit of the index depreciation (as long as the strike price has been breached). Naturally, if the index never reaches the appropriate barrier level, the put buyer will never receive the benefit of the S&P's depreciation. As a final example of this class of options, our bank may contract to buy an 'up and in' call on the FTSE 100 where, if the FTSE rises above

1500 (or 10 per cent more than its current level), it will benefit from index appreciation. Until that point is reached, however, the option is not in effect and the bank will not receive the benefit of what it would receive under a normal call structure.

From the standpoint of a bank buying a path dependent barrier where it loses some of its traditional economic benefits, the clear motivation for entering into such transactions is to lower the premium paid to the seller. From the standpoint of the seller of the option, though it will receive less premium income, it will assume a lower degree of risk by not having to pay appreciation or depreciation when normally required, or by having a contractual obligation eliminated entirely if a particular level is breached. Note that these barrier options may be incorporated into the equity derivative swap structures covered in the previous chapter. The comparison of a conventional call option and an 'up and out' call option is demonstrated in Figure 6.1.

Another type of path dependent option is the *lookback option*. In a lookback the buyer of the put or call will receive from the seller the greatest economic value achieved during the life of the option, regardless of the level at expiry. The buyer is able to 'look back' during the life of the transaction and select the point which yields the greatest economic gain (e.g. the lowest purchase price in the case of a call, the highest selling price in the case of a put), with the benefit of complete hindsight. A lookback therefore provides 100 per cent certainty that the best value has been obtained in a given transaction; in an American option, which is exercisable at any time until, and including, maturity a purchaser is never certain until the conclusion of the transaction whether its exercise results in the greatest gain. In a European option, where the buyer only has the benefit of exercise at maturity, the opportunity for the greatest gain occurring on one particular day is small and far less likely than either an American or a lookback. The Asian (or average strike) option, which allows the buyer to set the

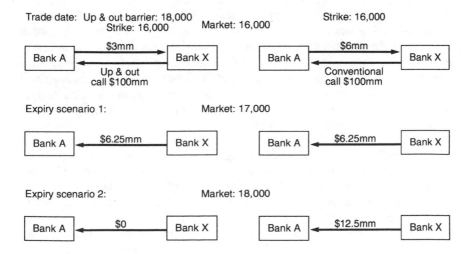

Figure 6.1 Call option comparison (cash settle), 'up and out' vs conventional

strike as as average over a given period, is potentially more valuable than an American or European option, but still does not have the power of a lookback. Naturally, the purchaser of the lookback derives a substantial gain in being able to select the best exercise price with the benefit of hindsight; as such, the premium charged by the writer will be higher than for other classes of option exercises (recent commentary suggests the premium of a lookback might be twice that of a plain vanilla option on the same underlying (see Chew, 1992b)).

As an example of this exotic option we can imagine a bank buying a $50MM 6-month lookback call on the All Ords. During the next 6 months the All Ords reaches a peak of 3250 and a low of 2700; at maturity the index ends with a value of 2900 (the average level for the last 30 days being 3000). With the lookback, the bank will be entitled to purchase the index at its lowest point of 2700. It effectively 'looks back' and determines the cheapest exercise price during the 6 month period.

Spin-offs of the lookback structure include step-lock options and 'cliquets' or rachets. Under a step-lock, an option will lock in gains at pre-specified levels, once those levels have been achieved (i.e. if the price of an index rises from 100 to the first level of 110, the guaranteed minimum return of the option will be 110, even if the *CMP* falls back from that point on; additional pre-specified levels which are breached add to the value of the option). A rachet, in contrast, will lock in any gains based on time, as opposed to price, thresholds (i.e. it will lock in the gains each quarter or semi-annual period).

Binary Options

Binary (or digital) options are options which provide discontinuous payoffs or protection. Under this type of option structure, the buyer will pay or receive one of two different flows if a particular level is reached. The most common digitals include the *all-or-nothing* and the *one touch*. An 'all-or-nothing' will provide the option purchaser a payout of 'all' or 'nothing' depending on the value of the option at expiration. If the option is in-the-money at maturity, the purchaser will receive a value equal to the notional of the contract. If it ends out-of-the-money the purchaser will receive nothing and the option seller will have no further obligation to the buyer. This type of payout is in sharp contrast to that of a conventional option, which will pay the buyer the difference between the current market and the strike times the notional of the transaction. An example of this type of path independent barrier would be one where Bank Z buys a $25MM all-or-nothing put on the FTSE 100 struck at 1600 (in a current market of 1700, implying a 6.25 per cent out-of-the-money obligation). At expiration we may assume the FTSE has fallen to 1400,˚or 12.5 per cent below the strike. In a conventional put, Bank Z would receive 12.5 per cent of $25MM, or $3.13MM. Since this is an all-or-nothing, however, Bank Z will receive the full $25MM, substantially more than the conventional option. In certain other all-or-nothing structures, the seller may agree to pay the buyer a set amount other than the notional (but again an amount unrelated to the intrinsic value of the option) if the option moves in-the-money; this type of payoff tends to be less common. Naturally, given the very high payout of such options, all-or-nothings have extremely high premiums and serious credit and risk management implications. One touch options are identical to all-or-nothings except they are exerciseable as soon as the strike is reached; evaluation need not wait until maturity.

Time Dependent Options

The most common time dependent option is the *preference* (sometimes '*chooser*') *option*, which gives the option buyer great flexibility in selecting the specific characteristics of the option within a given time frame. With a preference option, the buyer of the instrument receives from the seller the ability to customize the option during a given period of time, say 30 days (the time is negotiated between the two parties at outset, and may cover a longer span); during this time frame the buyer may elect whether the option should be a put or a call, where the put and call may each have their own distinct strike and maturity parameters; this is known as a 'complex chooser'. At the conclusion of the time frame (often referred to as the 'choice date') the option seller will enter into the transaction with the details as specified by the buyer, in exchange for the appropriate premium payment; as one might expect, by providing such flexibility, the writer will exact a handsome premium. Certain preference options have been created where the buyer is restricted to deciding whether an option will be a put or a call, with no flexibility as to maturity or strike price (i.e. those remain the same regardless of whether a put or call is selected); these are sometimes known as 'regular choosers'.

Preference options are particularly useful in times of extreme volatility when the outcome of a particular event is unknown and when it may have an impact on future prices. Rather than 'locking in' a very specific transaction which may or may not result in optimal gain or protection given a current scenario, the preference option allows deferral of key details which can be made concrete as time begins to make clearer a given situation or event.

Deferred Payment American Options

A *deferred payment American option* (or DPA), is a contract which is typically longer term in nature. Under the terms of a DPA, the buyer will enter into an American exercise option with a final maturity at time t. If the option moves in-the-money at some point during the transaction, the buyer will exercise and be entitled to the intrinsic value, as it would with any conventional option. However, rather than paying out the intrinsic value upon exercise, the option seller will simply defer payment until the original expiration of the option, denoted by time t. This means, in effect, that the option seller has use of the funds until time t, while the option buyer is left with a financial gain it cannot utilize until the original expiry date is reached. The incentive for the buyer to enter into a DPA is, of course, lower premium paid to the seller.

Outperformance/Basket Options

Outperformance and *basket options* provide the call or put purchaser with the ability to benefit from the comparative upward or downward performance between two markets, or between the better (or worse) performing of several markets against a pre-determined strike level. These instruments may be thought of as multi-asset structures, since their payoff is ultimately dependent on the indicative levels of various assets.

In the case of an outperformance option (also known as a relative performance option, or RPO), a bank may elect to receive, as an example, the difference between the appreciation of the FTSE and the S&P 500, as long as the FTSE outperforms the S&P 500. If the outperformance call is struck at-the-money and 6 months hence (the final maturity of the transaction), the FTSE has appreciated by 5.6 per cent and the S&P 500 by 2.2 per cent, the call purchaser will receive the differential 3.4 per cent (5.6 per cent – 2.2 per cent) times the notional amount of the call. Very often these transactions are payable in the specific currency of the index which outperforms the other. Naturally, it is possible for an investor to buy a put, instead of a call, indicating that it will benefit by selecting the market which performs worse in percentage terms; for instance, it may select the FTSE to fall more than the S&P, in percentage terms; if it does, it will receive the differential between the two. If it does not, the option will expire worthless. Outperformance options may also be bought and sold on the differential between individual stocks (often within the same industry), or between a certain group of stocks in one industry against a group of stocks in a second industry.

A basket option allows the purchaser to combine a series of indexes (or individual stocks) on a weighted basis, and to receive the appreciation (for a call) of that group of indexes (or stocks) over and above some strike level. For instance, if an investor is convinced that equity markets in Asia will rise over the next six months but is uncertain which one will do best (and whether, in fact, one might fall), it might purchase a basket call encompassing the Nikkei, Hang Seng and Singapore Straits Times indexes (assigning ⅓ weighting to each one, or perhaps some other weighting if it feels strongly that one of the indexes will rise by a greater amount). If the weighted value of the group of indexes is such that it exceeds the strike price, the investor will receive the difference between the two values (times the notional) as its payoff. If the group of indexes does not move up (or if one moves down sharply and brings the weighted average of the entire package below the strike) the investor will receive no payout. In addition to equity indexes, certain banks have written basket options on various Libor and currency rates. Although these structures are interesting in concept, activity in this product is still limited.

Quantos

A *quanto*, often known by the more formal name of *guaranteed exchange rate contract*, is effectively a forward foreign exchange contract incorporated into an underlying equity option or equity swap structure which allows the investor to lock in a known foreign exchange flow and eliminate currency risk. For instance, if an option holder's dollar quanto put on the German DAX is in-the-money at maturity, the quanto takes effect and converts the proceeds from the DAX in German marks into US dollars at a fixed rate specified in the contract. Since the level of the put at exercise is uncertain on trade date (e.g. the put may never move in-the-money, requiring no currency conversion), the amount of foreign exchange is uncertain at the commencement of the transaction.

Use of a quanto effectively allows an investor to lock in a known foreign exchange rate to avoid taking exchange rate risk. This is particularly useful if the investor fears devaluation or when it believes that spot rates will be lower than implied forward rates suggest. Quantos are often known as correlation products; that is, pricing of the product must incorporate not only the interest differential between the two currencies in question, but also any correlation which may exist between the currency and the underlying index. Quantos are regarded as correlation products whose payout is only modified, not solely dependent, on the correlation relationship. We shall discuss correlation in greater detail at various points in this text.

Vertical Equity (Call and Put) Spreads

Vertical equity call and put spreads are combinations of equity options which are utilized to create specific results. Although we have explored these combinations in much greater detail in Chapter 4 of this text, it is helpful to mention them briefly in the context of equity derivatives. In a call spread a bank will both buy and sell a call on an equity or equity index, with varying strike levels but the same notional and maturity date. If a bank sells a call which is struck closer to-the-money than the one it is purchasing, it will be a net receiver of premium, but will suffer greater exposure once the market moves up (although such exposure is effectively capped by the second call). As an example, Bank ABC may sell a call on the Hang Seng at 5200 (3.8 per cent out-of-the-money) and buy a call struck at 5600 (10.7 per cent out-of-the-money) (*CMP* is 5000); given the option it has purchased is almost 7 per cent further out-of-the-money than the one it has sold, it will be a net receiver of premium. If the Hang Seng moves up to 5300, the option it has sold will be in-the-money, while its own position will still be out-of-the-money. Only when the Hang Seng exceeds 5600 will it begin to profit from its long call position (though it will always be a net payer, given the short call is struck closer-to-the-money). Its net exposure in such instances will be limited to the differential between the strikes of 5200 and 5600. In addition to call spreads such as the one above, ABC may decide to reverse the position where it would be a net payer of premium in exchange for upside gains between 5200 and 5600. As the reader might imagine, put spreads represent the reverse, where the bank selling the nearer to-the-money put will be net receiver of premium and will be required to provide payout between the nearer strike and the strike on its own long put position which is further out-of-the-money. We shall not cover the risks of put and call spreads in this chapter, as we have already discussed them in a generic sense in Chapter 4.

It is worth stressing at this point that many of the options detailed above may be purchased separately by investors or companies seeking specific results, or they may be incorporated into other financing packages (such as bonds); alternatively they may be embedded into standard interest and currency rate swaps, or into the equity derivative swaps discussed in the previous chapter. Regardless of how they are brought to market, it is essential that the risk dimensions of the products be fully explored. For purposes of this text we shall examine the credit risk effects of each option on its own and, where necessary, detail any additional effects such options may have when incorporated into equity derivative swaps.

CREDIT RISK QUANTIFICATION

As the reader may suspect, the exotic options covered above are all impacted by movements in rates (whether stock prices, index prices, and so on). As a result, they are defined as market risk products and have to be risk adjusted through the risk equivalency method; this will yield an accurate measurement of the actual credit risk assumed by a bank active in such products. As in Chapter 5 the risk equivalency calculation will focus on the risk factor RF in the relevant risk equation.

The method we use to value many of these options begins with the general equations developed in Chapter 3. From that chapter, we know a bank's credit exposure in dealing with OTC options, including exotic equity options, will come when it is long, (i.e. the purchaser of the call or put). Short options will carry no risk to the bank, to the extent premium is received in a normal cash settlement time frame. For purposes of this chapter, option purchases and sales are executed with premium paid and received in an upfront fashion. The reader should always bear in mind the differences which exist when premium payments are either deferred or amortized during the life of the transaction (such as a Libor flow in a swap, as covered in Chapter 5); premium exposure must be adjusted when it is nonstandard.

As a reminder, we shall draw on the equations developed in Chapter 3 for valuing certain derivative options. These are:

$$REE = Premium + 0 \vee (NC \times [(RFc \times CMP) + (CMP - SP)]) \qquad (3.2)$$

for calls, and

$$REE = Premium + 0 \vee (NC \times [(RFc \times CMP) + (SP - CMP)]) \qquad (3.3)$$

for puts,

where RFc is a constantly adjusted risk factor,
NC is the number of contracts,
CMP is the current market price,
SP is the strike price.

When referring to a transaction defined in terms of a notional amount (N), we use:

$$REE = Premium + 0 \vee \left(N \times \left[\frac{(RFc \times CMP)}{SP} + \frac{(CMP - SP)}{SP} \right] \right) \qquad (3.4)$$

for calls, and

$$REE = Premium + 0 \vee \left(N \times \left[\frac{(RFc \times CMP)}{SP} + \frac{(SP - CMP)}{SP} \right] \right) \qquad (3.5)$$

for puts.

The examples in this chapter will, for the most part, focus on measurement by contracts as in Equations 3.2 and 3.3; readers interested in examining risk from a notional standpoint can easily adapt the examples given to the equations above.

With these basic equations in mind, we turn to a discussion of the credit risks of dealing with exotic derivative options, such as those we have described in the first part of this chapter.

Path Dependent Barrier Options

For purposes of the discussion on the credit risk of knock-ins and knock-outs it is necessary to focus on the various 'in' and 'out' combinations.

'UP AND IN' From a long position, the credit risk of an 'up and in' is twofold: premium plus the risk that the counterparty will not perform should the option come into play. That is, if the barrier is reached and the option is activated (either out-of-the-money or in-the-money), the bank purchasing the option will be faced with normal market risk. It will be looking to the option seller to perform on the option once it comes into being and, depending on whether the option is activated in- or out-of-the-money, the bank will have the risk characteristics of a typical option position. A conservative stance would suggest that the option be valued regardless of whether or not it ever comes into existence. Since a bank valuing credit risk will generally want to quantify the worst case scenario, such a method appears reasonable. A less conservative approach says that the potential market risk on the option should only be counted when, and if, it comes into existence; until such time as this occurs, only premium is at risk. The first version is, of course, precisely equal to the form in Equations 3.2 and 3.3, when the barrier is equal to the strike level (if the strike level is other than the barrier, the relevant comparison against *CMP* will remain the strike price, not the barrier).

Equations 6.1(a) and (b), for calls, show the *REE* of the two approaches mentioned above, when the barrier is equal to the strike level. As before, if the strike level is different from the barrier, the relevant calculation point will be the strike, not the barrier.

$$[when\ CMP < Barrier]$$
$$REE = Premium \qquad (6.1a)$$

$$[when\ CMP > Barrier]$$
$$REE = Premium + 0 \vee [NC \times ((RFc \times CMP) + (CMP\text{--}Barrier))] \quad (6.1b)$$

Equations 6.2(a) and (b) for puts, where the barrier is equal to the strike level:

$$[when\ CMP < Barrier]$$
$$REE = Premium \quad (6.2a)$$

$$[When\ CMP > Barrier]$$
$$REE = Premium + 0 \vee [NC \times ((RFc \times CMP) + (Barrier\text{--}CMP))] \quad (6.2b)$$

where RFc is the constantly adjusted risk factor,
NC is the number of contracts,
CMP is the current market price,
$Barrier$ is the barrier level at which the option becomes activated.
(*Barrier* will be replaced by the strike price (*SP*) if the two are not equal).

A simple example illustrates these equations. Bank C buys an 'up and in' call on the S&P 500, where the strike is set at 400 and the barrier is set at 410. The current market is 375, the maturity is 6 months and the number of contracts is 100,000. Bank C pays the call writer, Bank F, an upfront premium of $1MM for the 'up and in' call, which will only come into effect once the S&P reaches 410 (and will be in-the-money at that point). Bank C may value the risk of the transaction via Equation 6.2(b), with an initial RFc of 14 per cent, as:

$$REE = \$1MM + 0 \text{ or } [100,000 * ((0.14 * 375) + (375 - 400))]$$
$$REE = \$1MM + 0 \text{ or } [100,000 * ((52.5) + (- 25))]$$
$$REE = \$1MM + \$2.75MM$$
$$REE = \$3.75MM$$

Note that Barrier, 410, is replaced by *SP*, 400, since the two are not equal. This type of approach is clearly most conservative, in that it assumes that the barrier will be breached.

If Bank C does not wish to value the option until the barrier has been breached, it will simply allocate the $1MM premium as its credit risk. When *CMP* reaches the barrier of 410, it will immediately add additional exposure; if we assume that this occurs 4 months hence (when the *RFc* has fallen to 8 per cent), the exposure added would equal $4.28MM [100,000 * (0.08 * 410) + (410 - 400))], for a total *REE* of $5.28MM.

We must recall that if an institution wants to be particularly conservative in assigning initial risk to the above transaction, it may elect to ignore the out-of-the-money portion of the transaction and follow the method introduced by Equation 3.1, which says that:

$$REE = Premium + (RF \times (NC \times SP)) \tag{3.1}$$

Such an equation would yield *REE* on the transaction of

$$REE = \$1\text{MM} + (0.14 * (100,000 * 400))$$
$$REE = \$6.60\text{MM}$$

This is applicable not only for 'up and ins', but all the options we are discussing in this chapter.

'UP AND OUT' In this particular structure, an option will cease to exist once a particular barrier level is reached. The credit risk associated with such an instrument will, once again, initially consist of premium paid to enter into the transaction. Thereafter much is dependent on whether the barrier is ever breached. If it is not, the option will continue to exist and will have intrinsic value to the buyer, which implies required performance by the seller (which, in turn, implies credit risk exposure for the buyer). However, the maximum credit exposure in this instance is dictated not by potential market movements through the risk factor process, but by the maximum level attainable before the option is extinguished (i.e. just fractionally below the barrier level). The risk in such instances is depicted in Equations 6.3 for calls and 3.3 for puts (the put equation reverts to our original Equation 3.3 for reasons described below).
For calls:

$$REE = Premium + (NC \times (Barrier - SP)) + lesser\ of\ 0 \vee (NC \times (CMP - SP)) \tag{6.3}$$

where   *Barrier* is the barrier level at which the option is extinguished,
               CMP is the current market price,
               SP is the strike price,
               NC is the number of contracts.

Note that in an 'up and out' call, the strike price *SP* must be less than the *Barrier*, or there would be no incentive for a bank to purchase the structure. If the *Barrier* is 100 (i.e. the call is knocked out) and the *SP* is 100 (or greater), the bank will not receive an economic benefit (i.e. *CMP–SP*) because the call will have been extinguished. The call only has value to the buyer when the *CMP* is greater than the *SP* and *SP* is less than *Barrier*.

For puts, we need only refer to our original Equation 3.3. Since an 'up and out' put extinguishes when the barrier is breached by the *CMP*, this implies the put moves further out-of-the-money (implying reduced credit risk) until it is eventually eliminated. For this reason it is only necessary for us to value the normal risk on the put, as in Equation 3.3. As the put moves further in-the-money, it is moving further away from the barrier, and there is therefore no chance that it will be extinguished, more chance that it will be exercised, and increased reliance on the performance of the seller; this is quantified by the formula in Equation 3.3.

In knock-out options, if the barrier is reached, the option will be extinguished, the buyer will no longer look to the seller for performance, and the credit risk exposure will disappear. It is also reasonable to assume that premium is no longer at stake, because even if the option seller defaults after the option has been extinguished, the buyer was expecting no payment and cannot thus dispute that premium has been lost (the same cannot necessarily be said for conventional options which are out-of-the-money when default occurs).

To put the above formula in the context of an example, we may consider a 6-month 'up and out' call on the DAX, struck at 1500 in a market of 1400, with a barrier of 1650. The notional amount of the call which Bank S is buying is 10,000 contracts and, for purposes of this example, we convert to dollars at a fixed rate of DM1.5/\$ in the third step. Premium paid by Bank S to its counterparty is \$100M. The maximum risk attributable in this situation is:

$$REE = \$100M + (10{,}000 * (1650 - 1500)) + lesser\ of\ 0\ or$$
$$(10{,}000 * (1400 - 1500))$$
$$REE = \$100M + (10{,}000 * 150) + lesser\ of\ 0\ or\ (10{,}000 * (-100))$$
$$REE = \$100M + \$1MM + (-\$667M)$$
$$REE = \$433M$$

Should Bank S's DAX option move in-the-money during the life of the transaction (i.e. any value above 1500), S will suffer increasing credit exposure, up to a maximum level of 1650. The maximum dollar equivalent loss which S can suffer should default occur just prior to the barrier being breached is \$1MM, plus the initial \$100M upfront premium payment. If the barrier is breached, and then default occurs, S will sustain no loss, not even loss of premium. Note that in this equation we also subtract the out-of-the-money portion of the transaction, just as in our original Equation 3.2. It is possible, of course, to exclude the out-of-the-money portion of the equation and simply value the maximum exposure which can ever be encountered (i.e. the difference between *Barrier* and *SP*). This approach more closely parallels Equation 3.1.

'DOWN AND IN' OPTION   Under this type of transaction, an option comes into existence once a barrier is breached on the downside. The approach taken to valuing credit risk exposure in this instance will be similar to the 'up and in' option described above, where a bank may opt for a conservative view, valuing both the premium exposure and the market exposure of an option which may, or may not, come into existence; this may be adjusted for the in- or out-of-the-money portion. Alternatively, it may choose a less rigid view (valuing only the premium, and adding in the option's market exposure if the barrier is ever hit). The risk equations used in such instances will be similar to those indicated above in Equation 6.1 and 6.2, except for inverting the conditions comparing the *Barrier* and *CMP* levels. The call equations are shown as Equations 6.4(a) and (b) and the put equations as 6.5(a) and (b) below:

Equations 6.4(a) and (b) for calls:

$$[when\ CMP > Barrier]$$
$$REE = Premium \qquad\qquad (6.4a)$$

$$[when\ CMP < Barrier]$$
$$REE = Premium + 0 \vee [NC \times ((RFc \times CMP) + (CMP - Barrier))] \qquad (6.4b)$$

Equations 6.5(a) and (b) for puts, where the barrier is equal to the strike level:

$$[when\ CMP > Barrier]$$
$$REE = Premium \qquad\qquad (6.5a)$$

$$[when\ CMP < Barrier]$$
$$REE = Premium + 0 \vee [NC \times ((RFc \times CMP) + (Barrier - CMP))] \qquad (6.5b)$$

where NC is the number of contracts,
            RFc is the relevant risk factor,
            CMP is the current market price,
            Barrier is the barrier level at which the option becomes activated.

The reader should once again bear in mind that *Barrier* will be replaced by the strike price (*SP*) if the two are not equal.

If we examine a put structure on the Hang Seng consisting of 10,000 contracts struck at 4500 in a 4800 market for a premium of $200,000, with a 'down and in' barrier at 4400 and 12 months to expiry, we would note the following possible *REE* outcome (note that we use HK$7.8/$ and a 30 per cent risk factor, and that we substitute *Barrier* with strike price *SP*, since the two are unequal):

$$REE = \$200,000 + 0 \text{ or } [10,000 * ((0.30 * 4800) + (4500 - 4800))]$$
$$REE = \$200,000 + 0 \text{ or } [10,000 * ((1440) + (-300))]$$
$$REE = \$200,000 + \$1,461,000$$
$$REE = \$1,661,000$$

In today's market, our bank would value the potential risk as the combination of premium, plus potential value of the option based on historical market movements (less the portion which is currently out-of-the-money). This yields total risk of $1.661MM, which is updated on a constant basis and presumes that the 4400 barrier will be breached. If the Hang Seng falls to 4401, the option will be in-the-money but will have no value to the buyer. If the barrier is breached during the life of the trade, the option at that moment will be nearly $130,000 in-the-money. From a less 'strict' point of view, the risk exposure of the option will be the premium of $200,000, until such time as the *CMP* is less than the barrier level, if ever. A far more conservative view would not take account of the out-of-the-money component and value via Equation 3.1, with a slight adjustment: *SP* is replaced by *Barrier,* since the put will not have value until the barrier is breached; this translates into *REE* of nearly $1.9MM.

'DOWN AND OUT' OPTION   Our analysis of 'down and out' options is similar to the 'up and outs' discussed above. In particular, a 'down and out' will extinguish the option once a certain lower bound has been reached. Until such time as this is reached, the option buyer will face normal option risk, which is to say premium plus the potential market movements on the put or call itself. Once again, the limiting factor in determining maximum risk will be the barrier, after which the option ceases to exist and credit risk exposure disappears.

Equation 6.6 captures the credit risk equivalency for 'down and out' puts:

$$REE = Premium + (NC \times (SP - Barrier)) + lesser\ of\ 0 \vee (NC \times (SP - CMP)) \tag{6.6}$$

where   *Barrier* is the barrier level at which the option is extinguished,
              CMP is the current market price,
              SP is the strike price,
              NC is the number of contracts.

In the same way an 'up and out' put equation focuses on the risk attributable to a normal put option, a 'down and out' call focuses on the risk formula reflected in Equation 3.2. Once again, a 'down and out' call becomes ineffective once *CMP* falls below the barrier; as this occurs, of course, the call will be moving further out-of-the-money and will therefore carry no credit risk other than premium (because the call only has value once *CMP* is greater than *SP*, which means it is moving away from the knockout barrier). Once the barrier is reached and the call is knocked out, all credit risk disappears.

A 'down and out' put and a 'down and out' call are demonstrated in the following examples.

Bank A purchases 10,000 'down and out' puts on the Nikkei struck at 18,000 in a 19,000 market, with a 'down and out' barrier of 16,000. Premium paid is $100,000, the maturity is 9 months and the index is converted to dollars at a fixed rate of Yen 120/$, in the third step. Risk exposure attributable to this transaction at inception is:

$REE = \$100M + (10,000 * (18,000 - 16,000)) + lesser\ of\ 0\ or$
$\qquad (10,000 * (18,000 - 19,000))$
$REE = \$100M + (10,000 * 2,000) + 0\ or\ (10,000 * (-1,000))$
$REE = \$100M + \$166,667 + (-\$83,333)$
$REE = \$100M + \$83,333$
$REE = \$183,334$

If the put travels to its maximum level before knockout, 16,001, and the counterparty defaults, A will lose a total of nearly $267,000. Again, no risk factors are utilized since the determining factor of maximum market movement is not the potential movement in the Nikkei, but the lower bound on the knockout.

If Bank A had purchased a call, instead of a put, with the same trade details as above (except for a higher premium, since the option is already struck in-the-money, and assuming an initial RFc of 17.5 per cent), the *REE* would be:

$$REE = \$350,000 + 0 \text{ or } [10,000 * ((0.175 * 19,000) + (19,000 - 18,000))]$$

$$REE = \$350,000 + 0 \text{ or } [10,000 * ((3325) + (1000))]$$

$$REE = \$350,000 + \$360,400$$

$$REE = \$710,400$$

As the *CMP* moves away from the barrier of 16,000, the call moves further in-the-money. Thus, upside risk is not confined to the difference between the strike and the barrier, as in the case of the put, it is dependent on upside market movements as dictated by our ongoing risk factor *RFc*. As the *CMP* moves down to the barrier, the call moves further out-of-the-money; depending on the time left to maturity (which is reflected, as we know, in an ever declining *RFc*) the only amount at risk may be the original premium. That in turn will be equal to 0 once the 'down and out' barrier has been reached.

LOOKBACK OPTION In a lookback option, the buyer has the hindsight benefit of being able to select the value of the option which produces the greatest payoff (via the lowest purchase price or highest selling price), once the transaction is complete. This enables maximum economic gain, and as one might also suspect, maximum credit risk, at maturity. The appropriate fashion by which to approach the credit risk on a lookback is to simply value the option, whether a put or call, by the Equations reflected in 3.3 and 3.2. Since our predictive risk factor framework provides us with information on the maximum expected market movement during the life of the transaction which, in turn, translates into the maximum expected risk exposure, we can be quite certain that the figure we obtain will incorporate the value of the actual payoff at the conclusion of the option. Thus, no changes are required to the underlying risk formulae.

Despite use of the same equations, credit officers must be aware of differences between lookbacks and conventional options. In a conventional option, in order for a bank to lose the maximum amount as predicted by our *REE* framework, it must suffer a counterparty default when the option has moved to the furthest in-the-money point predicted by *RF*. Naturally, the timing of two such events is not likely to occur with frequency and, as such, a bank may sustain a loss due to counterparty default, but it is unlikely to be the maximum loss predicted by *REE*. With a lookback, however, the timing is related primarily to counterparty default at maturity, because by the nature of the transaction, that point will always reflect the maximum value of the option (i.e. at maturity the parties will look back and determine the maximum value of the option).

Thus, any credit officer considering lookbacks must be sensitive to the final maturity of the transaction, since this is where maximum risk will occur (to the extent the option moves in-the-money at any point during the life of the trade).

Binary Options

The reader will recall from above that a binary or digital option involves the payment or receipt of certain flows on a discontinuous basis (rather than the continuous payout profile characteristic of conventional options) if a certain strike is reached. From a credit risk perspective it is vital to focus on the maximum level a bank expects to receive during the life of the digital. This represents the most conservative stance, since it enables the bank to assess the maximum it expects to receive during the life of a transaction. Naturally, the bank is not certain at the outset that the greater amount will ever be at stake, but it should generally approach the transaction with a 'worst case' expectation. Let us consider the 'all-or-nothing' option. 'All-or-nothing' options, which we have described earlier in the chapter are relatively straightforward to analyse from a credit risk standpoint. Having said that, they are certainly the riskiest of the embeddos in terms of actual exposure assumed by a bank purchasing the structure. In an all-or-nothing, the payout of the option as it moves in-the-money is not reflected by $(CMP - SP)$ or $(SP - CMP)$, as is common with other options. Instead, as the name states, payout will equal either 'all', the notional value of the option (if it terminates in-the-money) or 'nothing' (if it terminates out-of-the-money; this is, of course, also true for conventional options). To the extent an all-or-nothing option's payout is established beforehand as some other amount (which may be less than the notional but, once again, unrelated to the differential between the current and strike prices), an adjustment can be made to the risk quantification process by substituting the appropriate payout level for N in the equation below.

In addition to relying on the option seller for delivery of the notional if the instrument ends with value, the option buyer is also likely to be paying a rather substantial premium for the potential benefit. As such, a bank's *REE* for the all-or-nothing is greater than 100 per cent of the notional of the transaction. Risk of these trades is captured by:

$$REE = Premium + N \qquad (6.7)$$

where N is the notional amount of the trade (or the total payout agreed in advance between buyer and seller).

If Bank Q buys a 12-month $25MM all-or-nothing call on the S&P 500 struck at 400 (in a 360 market), paying a $5MM premium, the associated *REE* per Equation 6.7 is $30MM. Intuitively this is easy to understand: if Q's counterparty defaults when the S&P index is over 400, Q will lose both its premium payment and the anticipated 'all' payment of $25MM it was expecting. These are very high risk options indeed. Note that the credit risk evaluation for 'one touch' options is identical to what we have covered for 'all-or-nothings', since the conservative stance presumes the strike will be reached during the life of the option.

For the seller of a binary option there is no credit risk, assuming satisfactory receipt of the premium. Since the seller expects no performance from the buyer once premium is in hand, it does not have credit risk issues to deal with. From a risk management standpoint the seller will have to ensure that it is appropriately hedged; this is an important task beyond the scope of this text.

Time Dependent Options

These instruments, also known as preference options, allow the option purchaser to customize details of the option during a set time period. Since a preference option by definition does not have all of its parameters set by trade date, it is impossible for a credit officer to assign a precise credit risk value to the instrument at the outset. Only when the bank determines such items as whether the option will be a put or call, will the credit officer have sufficient information to judge the risk of the transaction. At that point, it is likely that the risk assumed by the bank will be calculable through Equation 3.2 or 3.3, assuming a generally standard structure. It is only between the trade date and the time when all preference option details must be defined that the credit risk exposure cannot be quantified with great accuracy. Naturally, if the bank has some general idea of what it wants to do before defining the transaction, it can communicate such details to the credit unit which can then make an estimate based on the equations above. *REE* calculation can be refined once all parameters are definite. From the viewpoint of the option seller, there is again no risk once premium has been received.

Deferred Payment American Options

Under a DPA option we know that the buyer of the option will have to forego use of the economic gain realized through the exercise of an in-the-money option until some future date (which is the original maturity date of the option contract). In exchange for giving up the right to use the intrinsic value of the option immediately, as would normally be the case with a conventional option, the buyer pays a smaller premium to the seller. From a credit risk standpoint, we may evaluate the risk of a deferred payment put or call as we would any other conventional option, via Equations 3.2 or 3.3. The premium element we incorporate in our calculation will be smaller than it would be for a regular option, but it is still at risk. Market risk will still be present, and will be calculated through our risk factor framework. Thus, credit risk to the buyer of a DPA will approximate the risk of a conventional option.

Despite the fact that our risk calculation is the same, there is a key element regarding DPAs of which credit analysts must be aware. As in the case of the lookback option covered above, the critical time for counterparty failure in a DPA does not come when intrinsic value has reached its peak. In the case of a DPA it comes from the moment of exercise until maturity of the transaction, since that is when our bank expects to receive the payoff. While we are normally concerned with market risk moving to its maximum point at the time of default, such is not true for a DPA. In the case of a DPA, market risk can reach its maximum, at which point exercise may occur; however, default need not occur at that moment, it can occur at any time subsequent to that moment, until maturity, when the intrinsic value is to be forwarded to the buyer (note that we presume the buyer exercises at or near the peak of the market movements, when intrinsic value is maximized). Thus, while risk quantification does not change we need to be aware of the final time horizon and the fact that maximum market movements and default need not occur at the same point.

Outperformance/Basket Options

As indicated above, these options give the buyer the right to the gains based on the differential between the best performing index and the comparison index (to the extent the purchaser selected which index would outperform the other), or the gains of a group of two or more indexes. In the case of the latter, a *basket option*, our credit risk evaluation calls for a focus on the potential market movement of the entire group of indexes or rates being measured. Since the basket call option allows the purchaser to receive the gains from several indexes taken in tandem, our credit risk exposure will focus on measuring the maximum gain the entire basket will yield (note that we will only discuss calls, not puts, as calls are more prevalent in what is still a very narrow market). In a typical basket, separate components of the basket will have individual weightings; such weightings must be accounted for in the risk evaluation process.

Let us consider the following example: Bank X buys a basket call, stuck at-the-money, which will allow for gains if the group as a whole remains above the strike. The call consists of a 10 per cent weighting in the Nikkei (at 18,000), 30 per cent Hang Seng (at 6500) and 60 per cent Singapore Straits Times (at 1600). Thus, the weighted value at inception is 4710; if the call finishes above 4710 at maturity, X will have a gain. Note that to finish above 4710 it is not necessary for all 3 indexes to finish higher: one may rise sharply and two may fall moderately and the call may still end in-the-money. This is one of the advantages of a basket option. From a credit risk standpoint we know that our initial focus will be on premium paid for the call. We assume in this case that X pays $100,000 for a 12-month $20MM basket call.

The next item we focus on is market risk. In a normal option our risk factor provides us with a measure of market movements to quantify credit risk. In a basket option we also need to use risk factors, but we need to weight them according to their value within the total structure. For instance, rather than attribute a 25 per cent Nikkei risk factor for the 10 per cent Nikkei component indicated above, we will only include 2.5 per cent against the original notional amount, since that is the value which the Nikkei component adds to the basket. If our associated risk factors for the Hang Seng and Straits Times are 35 per cent and 30 per cent respectively, then our total weighted risk factor is 31 per cent (25%∗10% + 35%∗30% + 60%∗30%). Our initial *REE* is, therefore, $6.2MM, plus premium.

If we assume that during the life of the transaction X's counterparty defaults when the indexes have risen to the maximum level dictated by our risk factors, X may choose to replace the transaction. Rather than purchasing a new basket option, let us suppose that X will buy the index components separately; this helps illustrate our approach to valuing risk through a weighted risk factor scheme. To replicate the position it would purchase $2MM ($20MM ∗ 10%) Nikkei at 22,500 (18,000 ∗ 1.25), for a loss of $500,000 (e.g. it costs $2.5MM to replicate the same original notional amount, assuming fixed exchange rates); $6MM ($20MM ∗ 30%) Hang Seng at 8775 (6500 ∗ 1.35), for a loss of $2.1MM; and $12MM ($20MM ∗ 60%) Straits Times at 2080 (1600 ∗ 1.3), for a loss of $3.6MM. The total loss is $6.2MM, precisely the amount of our original calculation. Use of a weighted risk factor, which corresponds to the composition of the basket, should be clear to the reader. We may calculate our weighted risk factor by:

$$RF_w = \left(\sum_{i=1}^{n} RF_i \times W_i \right) \tag{6.8}$$

where *W* is the relevant weight in the basket.

Thereafter we may revert to our traditional option calculation method outlined in Equations 3.2 to 3.5, depending on whether we use contracts or notional. Returning to our example above, let us assume that in six months the Nikkei has risen to 19,000, the Hang Seng has fallen to 6400 and the Straits Times has risen to 1700. The weighted current market price of the basket is 4840 (1900 + 1920 + 1020). Based on Equation 3.4, our total risk (assuming our new *RFc* is 22 per cent (31% ∗ $\sqrt{0.5}$)):

REE = $100,000 + ($20MM ∗ (0.22 ∗ 4840/4710) + ((4840 − 4710)/4710))

REE = $100,000 + ($20MM ∗ (0.226 + 0.0276))

REE = $100,000 + $5.072MM

REE = $5.172MM

We see from above that, even though the Hang Seng fell, the call is still in-the-money. Total risk is, therefore, premium plus potential market risk for the remaining six months of the basket, plus the intrinsic value of the option.

The risk on the *outperformance* option may be analysed as follows: since the purchaser of the outperformance option will receive the differential between the two indexes, to the extent it selected the better of the two, its credit risk exposure will focus on premium paid as well as the widest spread between the two indexes. Based on our *REE* framework, this calls for an assumption that the index selected to outperform will move to its maximum positive point for calls or its maximum negative point for puts;

at the same time, the comparison index must move in an inverse fashion. This, by definition, will yield the widest differential between the two indexes and, therefore, the maximum payoff and maximum credit risk which may occur during the life of the trade.

An approach of this type presumes that the correlation between the two indexes is close to 0; that is, the correlation cannot be strongly positive, or any upward move in one index would imply an upward move in the second index (and therefore a narrower differential and less credit risk exposure). We shall assume the correlation between the two indexes comprising the outperformance will be close to 0 in order to proceed with a worst-case credit risk scenario. (If there is substantial evidence that the correlation is strongly positive, the risk should be adjusted to reflect that the spread differential will not reach its maximum point. If the correlation is strongly negative, we need make no changes, as the maximum/minimum points will be defined by our risk factor in any event). Our approach, then, is captured in Equations 6.9 for calls and 6.10 for puts for (notional-based transactions):

$$REE = Prem + \left(N \times \left[\left(\frac{RF_{c1} \times CMP_1}{SP_1} + \frac{CMP_1 - SP_1}{SP_1} \right) + \left(\frac{RF_{c2} \times CMP_2}{SP_2} - \frac{CMP_2 - SP_2}{SP_2} \right) \right] \right)$$

(6.9)

$$REE = Prem + \left(N \times \left[\left(\frac{RF_{c1} \times CMP_1}{SP_1} + \frac{SP_1 - CMP_1}{SP_1} \right) + \left(\frac{RF_{c2} \times CMP_2}{SP_2} - \frac{SP_2 - CMP_2}{SP_2} \right) \right] \right)$$

(6.10)

where N is the notional amount of the trade,
RF_{c1} is the risk factor associated with the first index,
CMP_1 is the current market price of the first index,
SP_1 is the strike price of the first index,
RF_{c2} is the risk factor associated with the second index,
CMP_2 is the current market price of the second index,
SP_2 is the strike price of the second index.

Note that those wanting to use uncalibrated risk factors (per our discussion in Chapter 3), may utilize the following form for calls (and the opposite for puts, which we shall not show):

$$REE = Premium + \left(N \times \left[\left(RF_{c1} + \frac{CMP_1 - SP_1}{SP_1} \right) + \left(RF_{c2} - \frac{CMP_2 - SP_2}{SP_2} \right) \right] \right)$$

Several items bear noting at this juncture. Firstly, the initial risk factor, current price and strike price terms denoted by the 1 subscripts are those attributable to the index expected to outperform. Secondly, the equation is arranged so as to assign the maximum risk movement in the first index (adjusted for in- or out-of-the-money amounts) while adding in the maximum market risk movement of the second index (again, adjusted for intrinsic value). Note that we subtract the in- or out-of-the-money portion from the second term because, as the index moves further in-the-money, it narrows, instead of widens, the differential between the two indexes; a narrowing between the index lowers payout and, therefore, the credit risk. Note that just prior to maturity, when there is no longer any possibility for market movements to affect the transaction, the *RFc*s are set at zero in our equations and we focus strictly on the risk as measured by the differentials; this will also equal the expected payout (less the premium).

Let us consider the following example: an investor buys a 12-month out-performance call between the Nikkei (*CMP* of 18,000 and *SP* of 20,000, implying a 10 per cent out-of-the-money call) and the Hang Seng (*CMP* of 5000 and *SP* of 5500, implying a 9.10 per cent out-of-the-money call) for $100,000. The investor expects the Nikkei to outperform the Hang Seng; if it does, and the initial strike on the Nikkei is breached, the investor will receive the differential between the two. The notional is a fixed $10MM (note that this is a dollar-based transaction and we ignore any currency effects – we are simply valuing the percentage difference in the spread between the two indexes against a dollar notional); the risk factors for the 12-month Nikkei and Hang Seng are 25 per cent and 30 per cent respectively. We may examine the risk of this trade at inception, in six months and at maturity. We may further assume that this is either a European call or one which the buyer does not exercise until maturity, so that we may track the *REE* of the transaction at various points in time. As a final note, it should be pointed out that this type of an outperformance is cheaper in price than a normal outperformance, since it only has value if the strike on the Nikkei is breached. Standard outperformances have value as long as the index selected to outperform does, in fact, do better than the comparison index; no strike need be reached. The formulae given in Equations 6.9 and 6.10 are useful for either structure; for the standard outperformance options strike prices SP_1 and SP_2 are simply the starting points for the measurement of index movements.

At inception:

$$REE = \$100M * (\$10MM * (((0.25 * 18{,}000)/20{,}000) + (18{,}000 - 20{,}000)/20{,}000)) + ((0.30 * 5{,}000)/5{,}500) - (5{,}000 - 5{,}500)/5{,}500)))$$

$$REE = \$100M * (\$10MM * (0.225 + (-0.10)) + (0.27 - (-0.091)))$$

$$REE = \$100M + (\$10MM * ((0.125) + (0.361)))$$

$$REE = \$100M + \$4.86MM$$

$$REE = \$4.96MM$$

Adjusted historical movements have shown that the Nikkei can move by 25 per cent in a single year, but our index begins 10 per cent out-of-the-money. Conversely, the Hang Seng can move by 30 per cent in a year. Since this index is starting 9.1 per cent out-of-the-money, we effectively add this to the maximum downward movement (we do so because if the Nikkei moves in-the-money tomorrow and the Hang Seng remains unchanged, the investor will be entitled to the differential between the two indexes, which includes the 9.1 per cent difference between the Hang Seng's SP and CMP). The maximum expected difference between the two indexes per our calibrated RFcs, 48.6 per cent, is the potential differential in a worst case scenario, adjusted for out-of-the-money components; since this represents potential payout by the option seller to the buyer, it is also the maximum anticipated risk exposure (along with premium paid).

Six months hence: the Nikkei has moved in-the-money to 21,000, while the Hang Seng has moved at-the-money, to 5500. Our new RFcs are 17.7 per cent and 21.2 per cent respectively. The mid-period *REE* is, therefore:

$$REE = \$100M * (\$10MM * (((0.177 * 21{,}000)/20{,}000) +$$
$$(21{,}000 - 20{,}000)/20{,}000)) + ((0.212 * 5{,}500)/5{,}500) -$$
$$(5{,}500 - 5{,}500)/5{,}500)))$$
$$REE = \$100M * (\$10MM * (0.186 + (0.05)) + (0.212 - (0.0)))$$
$$REE = \$100M + (\$10MM * ((0.236) + (0.212)))$$
$$REE = \$100M + \$4.48MM$$
$$REE = \$4.58MM$$

Since the Nikkei has moved in-the-money by 5 per cent and the Hang Seng is at-the-money, the differential is now 5 per cent. If the counterparty defaults today, the investor will lose, with certainty, $100,000 in premium and $500,000 of index differential, for a total of $600,000. The balance of our *REE*, $3.98MM, is included to reflect potential future market movements which might cause the differential to widen further.

Just prior to maturity: the Nikkei finishes 3000 points above the strike, at 23,000. The Hang Seng suffers a decline of 100 points in the final months and ends at 5400. On the day before maturity (when the possibility of default still exists, however remote) we calculate the following *REE* (note that per Equation 6.9 above, *RFc*s are now set at 0 since there is no longer any realistic possibility for market movements):

$$REE = \$100M * (\$10MM * ((0.0 + (23{,}000 - 20{,}000)/20{,}000)) +$$
$$(0.0 - (5{,}400 - 5{,}500)/5{,}500)))$$
$$REE = \$100M * (\$10MM * (0.0 + (0.15)) + (0.0 - (-0.0181)))$$
$$REE = \$100M + (\$10MM * ((0.15) + (0.0181)))$$
$$REE = \$100M + \$1.68MM$$
$$REE = \$1.78MM$$

At maturity the payout will, of course, equal $1.68MM, which is the differential between the two indexes (as indicated in the figure above), less the premium. We note that if the Nikkei had finished at 20,000 (at-the-money), the payout differential would

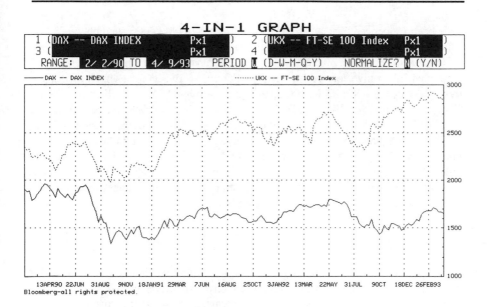

Figure 6.2(a) FTSE 100 versus DAX

Source: Bloomberg Financial Markets

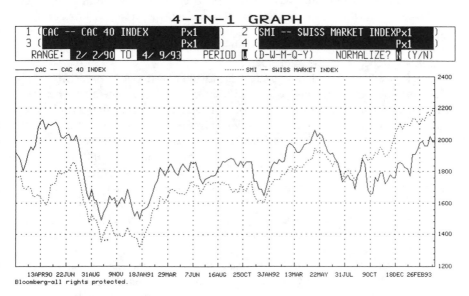

Figure 6.2(b) CAC 40 versus SMI

Source: Bloomberg Financial Markets

have been 1.8 per cent instead of 16.8 per cent. Had the Nikkei finished below 20,000 (out-of-the-money) there would have been no exercise and, therefore, no payout.

In order to see from a practical standpoint how an outperformance option might be employed by an investor, we highlight in Figure 6.2 two graphs which reflect the movement of the UK's FTSE 100 against the German DAX, as well as the French CAC 40 against the Swiss SMI. In order for us to evaluate the payoff on an outerperformance option we would, of course, select a starting point, an ending point, and determine the percentage increase or decrease in each of the indexes during the time interval between the two points (e.g. the tenor of the option). To the extent the index expected to outperform did, indeed, perform better than the comparison index, the payoff would equal the differential between the percentage changes in each of the two indexes.

Quantos

We know from above that a quanto is effectively a foreign exchange component which can be incorporated into a broader structure to convert proceeds into a desired currency at the conclusion of a transaction. The clear advantage of utilizing a quanto is that the derivatives purchaser need not be exposed to foreign exchange risk by participating in a given local market unless it deliberately chooses to do so (in which case no quanto would be employed). From a risk quantification standpoint it is relatively easy to assign a risk factor to account for the potential market movements of converting from, say, yen into dollars, or DM into sterling. Since the quanto involves setting a fixed exchange rate today, for use at some future point (maturity), the risk encountered by the purchaser is that the currency rate will move in a fashion detrimental to it, which will crystalize a loss if default occurs by the counterparty.

For instance, if Bank X has a quanto which will convert yen proceeds from the Nikkei into dollars at a fixed rate of yen 125/$ and the counterparty defaults when the yen/$ rate has moved to yen 135/$, X will sustain a loss in converting the yen proceeds into dollars at the new spot rate. In other words if X is due yen 100MM from index appreciation, which equals $800,000 based on the fixed rate specified by the quanto, conversion via the new spot of 135 will yield net proceeds of $770,000, or $30,000 less than anticipated; this presumes, of course, that the yen proceeds from the appreciation had already been credited to X's account before default. If default occurred before local currency credit took place, the loss sustained by X would be equal to the foregone index appreciation plus any premium involved plus the foreign exchange loss. Risk of a quanto, then, only adds to the total potential risk sustainable by X, it is not a replacement for other types of risk.

The clear difficulty in quantifying the risk of the quanto is the unknown amount of principal which may ultimately be converted into another currency. At trade date, in standard structures, a bank entering into a quanto is uncertain how much, if any, notional will exist to convert at maturity. If our bank purchased a call on an index and the index rose, it would have to convert the differential between the current price and the strike price, times the notional; the proceeds for conversion are clearly dependent on the intrinsic value of the call. If the index fell, no FX conversion would be required. As such, there is no precise way to quantify how much risk is assumed today, trade date, in adding a quanto element to the derivative structure.

There is, of course, a conservative fashion by which to evaluate risk assumed in such transactions. This approach would look at the maximum expected movement in the index or equity as dictated by our risk factor model. Since this is the maximum likely movement under certain scenarios we establish at the outset, we should also be comfortable that the figure yielded by such an inspection will equal the maximum which may realistically be converted back into the desired currency via the quanto (e.g. it is the maximum expected intrinsic value). This, then, would be the maximum foreign exchange market risk exposure we would encounter on the trade. Note that we are only concerned with the risk of the market movements and not the value of the entire index, because payout for standard put and call structures will focus on the intrinsic value, not the full value of the index (unless we are dealing with the an 'all or nothing' or 'one touch' option, in which case our associated *REE* will take this into account). Although this approach will overstate by a certain amount the true exposure (because it is likely we will never reach the maximum dictated by our *RF* under normal market circumstances), it can also be continually adjusted through the use of the *RFc*, as time goes by. Note that in our scenario we assume if the index in question rises (or falls), implying a gain to be converted at the fixed rate, the exchange rate has also moved to some maximum point in order to cause the maximum credit loss should default occur. If there is reason to believe that such is not the case, an adjustment would have to be made to the risk factor of the FX portion. We shall present the worst case scenario.

Our equation for capturing the relevant notional in one of the structures covered above would focus on the *REE* for that particular instrument, less any premium paid (though that is at risk, it is clearly not a part of the FX conversion process). Our risk equation, therefore, is:

$$REE_{FX} = (REE_{orig} - Premium) \times RF_{cFX} \qquad (6.11)$$

where $\qquad REE_{orig}$ is the risk equivalent exposure associated with the original trade,
$Premium$ is the premium paid in the original trade, if any,
RF_{cFX} is a constantly adjusted risk factor for *FX* market movements.

Let us consider an example to assist in highlighting the calculation. Bank XYZ purchases a 12-month put (10,000 contracts) on the FTSE 100, struck at 1600 in an 1800 market. The risk factor for a 12-month FTSE is 25 per cent, and the option contains a quanto which will convert the depreciation gains into dollars at a rate of $1.5/£.

XYZ pays the put writer an upfront premium payment (in dollars) of £250,000 (the sterling amount is shown only for simplicity). The risk in the original put is derived from Equation 3.3:

REE = £250,000 + 0 or [10,000 * ((0.25 * 1800) + (1600 − 1800))]

REE = £250,000 + [10,000 * ((£450) + (− £200))]

REE = £250,000 + (£2.5MM)

REE = £2.75MM

Note that we have not, as yet, converted the sterling REE into dollars (as we have in previous examples). Utilizing Formula 6.11 above, we assign the following to the foreign exchange risk of the quanto, assuming a 20 per cent RFc for $/£:

$$REE_{FX} = (£2.75MM - £250M) * 0.20$$
$$REE_{FX} = £2.5MM * 0.20$$
$$REE_{FX} = £500M$$

This indicates that XYZ's total risk on the entire transaction is equal to £3.25 MM (or $4.875MM at the quanto FX rate). The rationale for utilizing the above approach is, quite simply, that the bank's FTSE put has a chance of ending with a maximum anticipated value of £2.5MM when we take account of the fact that it is struck out-of-the-money and has 200 points to travel before turning in-the-money. Since £2.5MM is the maximum expected value of the put based on our risk factor framework, it is also the most XYZ realistically expects to have to convert into dollars 12 months from now. Given that our foreign exchange risk factors indicate that $/£ is likely to move no more than 20 per cent against the position, this adds a further £500M of risk to the trade, and is the portion specifically attributable to the quanto. As the REE from the original trade declines (the put moves further out-of-the-money and/or the time value of the option decreases, causing the RFc to decrease), the REE_{FX} will also fall (both as a result of the falling REE from the original trade, as well as the RFc associated with the FX position).

In a worst-case scenario, we can imagine XYZ, which needs the dollar proceeds from the FTSE index at maturity, facing default by its counterparty when the put has moved into-the-money at a CMP of 1400. Let us assume that at maturity the spot $/£ FX rate has moved to $1.35/£. Rather than receive £2MM * 1.5, or $3MM, as expected from exercising the put at 1400 with the quanto, XYZ would now have implied loss of £2MM. In addition, if it converted some alternate sterling flow (instead of the flow from its put gains) to dollars at a less preferential rate of $1.35/£ (instead of the $1.50/£ dictated by the quanto), it would only receive $2.7MM, instead of the $3MM if all had proceeded as originally planned, indicating an incremental loss of $300,000. Finally, it will also have lost its original premium.

EQUITY DERIVATIVE OPTIONS EMBEDDED IN SWAPS

Our discussion above has sought to isolate the risk exposure effects of derivative option structures. As we have already indicated equity derivatives are, by definition, instruments which can be tailor-made to fit an issuer's or investor's very specific requirements. As a result, an analyst will often encounter a multi-faceted structure, where all risk elements must be considered.

In order to evaluate the credit risk of a derivative swap with embedded option(s), it is always simplest to separate the structure into its component parts, and review the risk of each independently. Where necessary, such as in the payment of premium, adjustments can be made so as not to double count exposure.

We may consider the following as an illustrative example. Bank Y contracts with Bank Z to enter into the following transaction: Y will buy an equity derivative call swap (notional Y1.3B or $10MM) where it will pay Z 12-month Yen Libor flat each year beginning at inception, in exchange for the appreciation in the Nikkei over 26,000 (in today's market of 20,000). In order to defray the cost of the premium, Y is willing to have the call knock out at 17,000 (a 'down and out' call structure); had the knockout not been included, Y's annual premium payment would have been equal to 12-month Libor + 25 basis points. Finally, Y wants to ensure that any appreciation in yen be brought back into dollars, so the deal incorporates a quanto at yen 130/$.

We examine Y's risk to Z by isolating the components and applying the appropriate risk factors:

(1) 5 year Nikkei risk factor is 56 per cent (25 per cent adjusted historical volatility $* \sqrt{5}$)

(2) 12-month Yen Libor is currently 4 per cent; adjusted historical volatility is 10 per cent, so anticipated Libor flows over 5 years are as follows:
Trade date: 4.0 per cent
Start year 1: 4.4 per cent
Start year 2: 4.8 per cent
Start year 3: 5.3 per cent
Start year 4: 5.9 per cent

(3) 5-year yen/$ risk factor is 45 per cent (20 per cent adjusted historical volatility $* \sqrt{5}$)

Utilizing Formula 5.1 and 5.1(a), as well as some of the formulae covered in this chapter, the total risk components, therefore, are:

$REE = ((0.56 * Y1.3B) + (Y1.3B * (20,000 - 26,000/26,000)) + ((Y1.3B * 0.04) + (Y1.3B * 0.044) + (Y1.3B * 0.048) + (Y1.3B * 0.053) + (Y1.3B * 0.059))$

$REE = (Y428MM) + ((Y52MM) + (Y57MM) + (Y62MM) + (Y69MM) + (Y77MM))$

$REE = (Y428MM) + (Y317MM)$

$REE = Y745MM$

At this point, the potential risk exposure is equal to Y745MM ($5.73MM) on a notional of Y1.3B ($10MM) equivalent. Turning to the quanto portion of the trade:

$$REE_{FX} = (Y745MM - Y317MM) * 0.45$$
$$REE_{FX} = Y193MM$$

The latter component adds nearly Y193MM ($1.5MM) of risk to the transaction, bringing the total *REE* to Y938MM, or $7.2MM. Note we need make no adjustment for the 'down and out' call, because as the current market price falls toward the barrier, the value of the swap moves further out-of-the-money for Y, implying reduced exposure. Once the 17,000 barrier is breached, Y will have no exposure to Z, as it is not expecting performance on any front from its counterparty. Figure 6.3 illustrates the transaction above and highlights the credit risk Y faces.

The discussion in this chapter, and Figure 6.3 in particular, should assist in showing the reader that the credit risk equivalent of complex derivative trades can be very high indeed, even when structures begin out-of-the-money. These instruments can be long term in nature (such as the one illustrated above) and are often driven by indexes or prices which have displayed substantial historical volatility. In addition, the separate components of these trades, taken in unison, can add extra dimensions of risk to a given transaction. It is vital for any credit officer dealing with equity derivative options, or complex structures with embedded options, to isolate every specific risk which might come into play during the life of a transaction. It is especially important that all details of a given structure be thoroughly vetted. To that end we present, in Appendix III, a series of twenty questions which a credit officer may wish to employ when discussing a highly structured transaction with a derivatives marketer or trader seeking

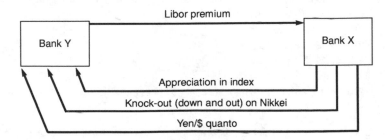

Sources of credit risk for Y (e.g. if X defaults):
    Loss of premium payment
    Loss in gains if Nikkei appreciates
    Reduced gains (or outright losses) if yen weakens

Figure 6.3   Equity derivative swap with embedded options

credit approval. As a final note, it is worth mentioning that new option-like structures are being developed and refined on a continuous basis. Care must be taken to keep abreast of these financial innovations.

Part IV

The Credit Risk of Complex Swaps

7: A Review of Swap Credit Exposure Evaluation

The calculation of swap risk exposure is one of the central discussions occurring at banks and regulatory bodies throughout the world. At present there is no universally agreed fashion by which to assign risk to swap transactions; much is dependent on the views of regulators and individual institutions. There are at least two broad approaches which must be considered: the calculation of risk exposure for regulatory purposes, and the calculation of risk for an individual institution's purposes. In some cases these may be the same, particularly if an institution falls under the purview of a certain regulator which is enforcing a particular methodology. In other instances the approaches may be different; this occurs when there is no governing regulatory guideline or when a certain institution wants to develop alternative risk calculations for credit and pricing (though not capital) reasons. We shall discuss both approaches in this chapter, with a caveat to the reader that there are many other means by which to calculate swap risk. At the end of the chapter we illustrate the results of a number of studies designed to estimate swap risk.

THE REGULATORY APPROACH TO CREDIT RISK

In 1988 the Bank for International Settlements (BIS), in its discussion of capital requirements for banking institutions in member countries, set out its current exposure method (*CEM*) and original exposure method (*OEM*) for the calculation of swap credit risk (with details communicated through the key document, *International Convergence of Capital Measurement and Capital Standards*). The *CEM* calls for swap credit risk to equal the replacement cost (or mark-to-market value) plus some future credit exposure factor, while the *OEM* focuses strictly on the future credit exposure factor and ignores the idea of a replacement, or mark-to-market, component. As is by now well known, the BIS agreement has called for banks to allocate capital in support of their activities, including interest rate and currency swaps and derivatives. The original formulae by which to allocate capital to swaps via *CEM* and *OEM* are given by:

$$Capital\ ratio = \frac{k}{(MTM + (CEM_{factor} \times N) \times RW)} \tag{7.1}$$

and

$$Capital\ ratio = \frac{k}{((OEM_{factor} \times N) \times RW)} \tag{7.2}$$

where   *Capital ratio* is an institution's target BIS ratio,
k is the capital required to support a transaction (and represents an unknown to be solved),
CEM_{factor} is the appropriate current exposure method factor (highlighted below),
OEM_{factor} is the appropriate original exposure method factor (highlighted below),
N is the notional of the swap,
RW is the risk weighting.

Credit exposure factors (what we have termed risk factors in this text) for the *CEM*, as dictated by the BIS, currently include 0.5 per cent for interest rate swaps over one year and 5 per cent for currency swaps over one year. The *OEM* factors were recently lowered and now include 0.35 per cent for interest rate swaps and 1.50 per cent for currency swaps under 1 year, 1.75 per cent and 3.75 per cent for interest and currency swaps from 1–2 years, and an additional 0.75 per cent and 2.25 per cent per year for interest and currency swaps over 2 years. The *OEM* factors are extremely high because they do not value the replacement, or mark-to-market, cost inherent in swaps once they are underway.

Banks adhering to the BIS capital requirements (i.e. banks in the Group of 10 countries, plus Switzerland and Luxembourg), plus banks in certain other countries (such as Indonesia, Singapore, who choose to adhere to these, or stricter, guidelines on a voluntary basis or through the dictates of their local regulators), allocate capital by one of the above formulae in support of their derivatives activities. UK banks follow the *CEM*; US banks use the *CEM*; Australian banks may utilize either the *CEM* or *OEM*; Canadian banks must now use the *CEM*. It should be stressed that banks which adhere to the BIS capital guidelines must utilize the factors detailed above when allocating capital in support of a given transaction; they have no choice in the matter.

However, for purposes of allocating risk against credit limits, many institutions adopt their own risk valuation methods, believing in many instances that the *CEM* and *OEM* factors are too high and are not representative of potential swap risk. When considering credit risk allocations for swaps against predetermined credit lines, any overstatement in the credit factors used for *CEM*/*OEM* calculations may well result in excessive usage of available credit limits. Others may develop their own credit risk factors because they disagree with the methodology (or parameters in the methodology framework) employed by regulators in creating the *CEM*/*OEM* conversion factors. As we shall see below, development of a methodology to value swap risk is highly subjective and is dependent on the use of parameters which may vary greatly from institution to institution.

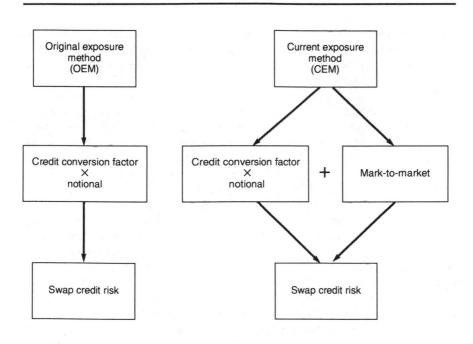

Figure 7.1   Swap credit exposure: the regulatory approach

With the substantial growth experienced in the swap market over the past five years, credit limit availability has become a serious concern for a number of institutions. As the head of capital markets at one major US institution has put it: 'Credit is now such a scarce resource that we have had customers...who have told us not to bid on a swap because they want to save their credit exposure with us for the structured deals. We've gone to customers and said the same thing' (*Risk*, 1992). This is echoed by the head of derivatives at a major European firm: 'The industry is certainly aware of the [credit availability] problem and is doing something about it. If no one did, there is no question that the major players would already be up to their limits with each other' (*Risk*, 1992). Several institutions are currently pioneering so-called 'credit derivatives' which will enable institutions effectively to swap counterparty credit availability as required. The regulatory approach to swap credit risk is summarized in Figure 7.1.

NETTING OF SWAP CREDIT EXPOSURES

The ability to net swap exposures within a given counterparty's swap portfolio is a topic of much discussion, since this would allow credit limits to be freed up. For an institution active in the swap market with a portfolio of fixed pay swaps and fixed receive swaps with a single counterparty, it is very likely that the net exposure of all trades will be far lower than the gross exposure of all trades. On a net basis, therefore, the true amount at risk in the event of default is the differential in the value between the two books. This figure may be positive or negative (though it is unlikely that an institution would allocate a negative net risk figure to the swap portfolio – it would be more likely to set the net amount at risk equal to zero).

Though a net measure may be the true risk of a portfolio of swaps, at present only the US specifically allows netting by close-out (i.e. if a counterparty defaults, all transactions governed by a master swap agreement are accelerated and netted down to a single payment in one direction of the other). This ability is provided in law by the 1989 Financial Institutions Reform, Recovery and Enforcement Act (FIRREA), as well as amendments to the US Bankruptcy Code. Although other countries are presently considering the legitimacy of netting by close-out in their own legal systems, no other changes have taken place to date. Note that the BIS, in its original 1988 document, permitted netting by novation. This form of netting, which a number of countries have adopted, allows netting to occur by amalgamating all existing transactions under one contract and rewriting the master contract every time a payment is made. This is clearly more onerous than netting by close-out, but it does provide a means of netting exposure. (It should be noted that in April 1993 the BIS released a statement indicating its willingness to accept bilateral netting of exposures, provided that the legal requirements in each local jurisdiction are met. It therefore appears that an important step toward bilateral netting has been achieved. As previously mentioned, it will fall to individual countries, and their legal systems, to consider the matter.)

If counterparties are legally able to net exposures across a portfolio of swap trades, they will utilize less of their credit limits and run less risk of a bankruptcy receiver 'cherry picking' only those contracts favourable to a defaulting counterparty.

With regard to the first point, let us assume a credit officer at Bank X establishes an *REE* swap limit of $100MM for business with Bank Y. If Bank X has a series of swap trades with Bank Y, where the two institutions have swaps on both sides of the market (i.e. some swaps are pay fixed, others are receive fixed), it is possible for the portfolio to be condensed to a single net exposure figure. If X's gross exposure to Y is $100MM but its net exposure is only $50MM (that is, the net figure owed X (including future market movements) is netted down to a value of $50MM) it would theoretically allow a further $50MM *REE* of swaps to be transacted with Y. This presumes netting is enforceable in all jurisdictions. If X and Y are both US banks there is a strong argument, based on changes in FIRREA and the Bankruptcy Code, that a further $50MM *REE* of swaps could be transacted. If, however, X and/or Y are not US banks, there is as yet no legal comfort that further swaps can and should be transacted. As such, there would be no reduction in the potential amount at risk and, therefore, no reduction in the potential usage against existing credit limits.

In addition, in a regime where netting by close-out is not allowed, there is some question as to the treatment of a full portfolio of swaps in the event of bankruptcy. It is possible that upon default a bankruptcy receiver will honour only those contracts with value to the defaulting counterparty, while dismissing those with a detrimental effect to the defaulting counterparty (which are of value to the non-defaulting counterparty). If, in our example above, Bank X's actual mark-to-market exposure on the pay fix swaps is $20MM (i.e. Y owes X a total of $20MM), but the mark-to-market on the receive fix swaps is ($30MM) (i.e. X owes Y a total of $30MM), the net payment in bankruptcy, assuming close-out, would be $10MM from X to Y. However, a bankruptcy receiver might seek to dismiss the $20MM pay fix swaps and only enforce the $30MM receive fix swaps; as such, X would be forced to pay a full $30MM to Y, instead of the $10MM it was anticipating.

THE INDIVIDUAL INSTITUTION APPROACH

While some financial institutions may be required to follow either the *CEM* or *OEM*, other swap participants may not be required to (e.g. securities firms and insurance companies need not adhere to the BIS framework), or they may prefer their own internal methodology for credit allocation and pricing reasons. In such instances, they may develop their own individual approaches to valuing swap credit risk.

There are numerous ways to value swap risk (and to develop models which estimate parameters important in the determination of swap risk). Two different approaches shall be considered in this chapter; these methods are among the most commonly utilized in the swap market today, each with its own advantages and disadvantages. We summarize these as:

(1) The mark-to-market approach
(2) The potential market exposure approach
   Historical basis
   Option basis
   Simulation basis

THE MARK-TO-MARKET APPROACH

In the case of the first method, the mark-to-market approach, an institution may seek to apply only the ongoing mark-to-market value of a swap against available credit lines. It might do so through the following formula, which is reasonably standard for marking-to-market (and which we have discussed in Chapter 5):

$$MTM = \sum_{x=1}^{p} \left(\frac{N \times (r_n - r_0)}{(1 + r_n)^x} \right)$$

(7.1)

where r_n is the new rate in period x,
r_0 is the original rate,
p is the number of years until maturity,
N is the notional of the swap.

Note that if the swap is a semiannual pay, r_n and r_0 would be divided by 2; if it is a quarterly pay, r_n and r_0 would be divided by 4. The periods to maturity would also be adjusted. We may thus expand the equation to a more generic form (as presented in Chapter 5):

$$MTM = \sum_{x=1}^{p} \left(\frac{N \times \dfrac{(r_n - r_0)}{t}}{\left(1 + \dfrac{r_n}{t}\right)^x} \right) \tag{5.8}$$

where t is the frequency of payments per year under the swap (e.g. 1 for annual pay, 2 for semi-annual pay, 4 for quarterly pay),

p is now the number of periods until maturity.

The equations above represent the economic replacement cost of the swap and may be positive (implying exposure) or negative (implying no exposure), depending on the direction of rates between inception and default. The equations effectively measure the difference between the original coupon and the new coupon (times the notional), from the time of default to the maturity of the originally contracted swap, discounted back to the present at the new rate. This represents the loss or gain in entering into a new swap in a new rate environment.

Very often the *MTM* approach is expressed in terms of a net present value (*NPV*). The *NPV* of a swap at default, for a fixed rate payer, is shown as:

$$NPV_{FixPay} = NPV_{OP} - NPV_{NP} \tag{7.2}$$

where NPV_{OP} is the *NPV* of the swap based on the originally contracted payments,

NPV_{NP} is the *NPV* of the swap based on the new replacement payments.

NPV$_{fix\ pay}$ may be positive or negative, depending on whether rates have risen or fallen from original trade date to time of default. From the standpoint of a fixed rate payer, if rates rise this figure will be negative, implying a loss. Intuitively this makes sense, because the fixed payer will have to establish a new series of fixed payments in a higher, more costly, interest rate environment. For a fixed rate receiver, we reverse the terms:

$$NPV_{FixRec} = NPV_{NP} - NPV_{OP} \tag{7.3}$$

If rates fall (i.e. NPV_{NP} is lower than NPV_{OP}), our fixed rate receiver will lose money; this is shown by a negative answer. Again, this makes sense, since the bank will have to replace the swap in an environment where fixed rates, and therefore payments to be received, are lower.

The general formula for the *NPV* of a fixed rate annuity is:

$$NPV_{fixed} = PMT \left(\frac{1 - \left(1 + \frac{r}{t}\right)^{-n}}{\frac{r}{t}} \right)$$

(7.4)

where PMT is the periodic fixed payment under the swap,
r is the relevant interest rate,
t is the frequency of payments per year under the swap,
n is the number of payments to be made until maturity.

The valuation of *NPV* of floating rates is considerably more involved, and requires the calculation of a forward-forward rate. Although valuing the *NPV* of an entire swap (i.e. fixed and floating) is vital for pricing purposes, for our text we need only focus on the *NPV* of the fixed stream (under the assumption that when we value the replacement cost of a swap, there will be another fixed rate which will guide our calculation of the actual economic replacement cost, which we have termed $NPV_{Fix\ Pay}$ or $_{Rec}$ above).

In order to calculate $NPV_{Fix\ Pay}$ or $_{Rec}$ defined above, we focus on the expected *PMT* under the original and new rates, since this is the cash flow which determines whether more or less will be paid or received. However, when we discount via the relevant interest rate r above, we utilize the new rate in existence at the time of default (since this is the only rate which is relevant at the time of default if we have already calculated the original amount *PMT* based on original rates). Intuitively the above tells us that the amount we stand to gain or lose, for a fixed pay swap, is simply the difference between what we were originally expecting to pay (NPV_{OP}) less the amount we are now going to pay (NPV_{NP}); both terms are discounted back to the present using the new rate, in order to account for the time value of money. We do the reverse for a fixed receive situation.

We may show through an example that the *MTM* Equation 5.8, and the *NPV* calculation 7.4 are, in fact, equivalent.

Let us consider the following simple example: Bank X enters into a \$100MM interest rate swap with Bank Q. It calls for X to pay a fixed rate of 10 per cent in exchange for 12-month Libor, on an annual basis. The term of the swap is 5 years. Assume that 2 years hence, when the swap still has 3 years until maturity, Q defaults. At the time of default fixed rates have risen to 12 per cent, indicating that if Bank X wants to replace the swap, it will have to enter the market and do so at a higher rate, implying a loss. Under this scenario we would expect the *MTM* to be positive, implying exposure to the counterparty and a credit loss. Under our *NPV* formula in Equation 7.2 we would expect the result to be negative, again signifying a credit loss. By Equation 5.8 we note the *MTM* value of the swap (rounded) is:

$MTM = ((\$100MM * (0.12 - 0.10)/(1 + 0.12)^{\wedge}1) + (\$100MM * (0.12 - 0.10)/$
$(1 + 0.12)^{\wedge}2) + (\$100MM * (0.12 - 0.10)/(1 + 0.12)^{\wedge}3))$

$MTM = (\$1,786,000) + (\$1,594,000) + (\$1,424,000)$
$MTM = \$4,805,000$

This is, of course, today's economic cost of replacing the original 10 per cent fixed pay swap in an environment where rates are now 12 per cent; time to maturity is now 3 years, not 5 years. As we have mentioned, if an *MTM* figure is positive it implies exposure and, therefore, potential credit loss.

By Equations 7.2 and 7.4 we note the *NPV* of the swap (both at original and new payment levels) is:

$NPV_{OP} = \$10MM * ((1 - ((1 + 0.12)^{-3}))/0.12) = \$24,025,000$
$NPV_{NP} = \$12MM * ((1 - ((1 + 0.12)^{-3}))/0.12) = \$28,830,000$
$NPV_{Fix\ Pay} = NPV_{OP} - NPV_{NP} = \$24,025,000 - \$28,830,000 = -\$4,805,000$

Not surprisingly, these two values are identical and show X losing just over $4.8MM.

In addition to the above calculations (by whichever method), the *MTM* approach generally also factors in an accrued interest receivable (*AIR*) component which may exist when the bank is a more frequent payer than receiver. If, for instance, the bank pays quarterly and receives annually, and its counterparty defaults after receiving the first three quarterly payments but before making its own larger annual payment, there is clearly added exposure. The *AIR* may be calculated as:

$$AIR = \left(\frac{r}{PayF} \times \frac{(PayF - RecF)}{RecF} \right) \times N \tag{7.5}$$

where r is the interest rate,
             PayF is the pay frequency,
             RecF is the receive frequency,
             N is the notional of the swap.

In most instances if the *AIR* is a negative number (i.e. the bank receives more frequently than it pays, implying a risk exposure benefit), it is simply set at 0, not subtracted from the total *REE* equation detailed below. The total risk equation under a mark-to-market approach is shown as:

$$REE = MTM + AIR \tag{7.6}$$

where   *MTM* is the current mark-to-market value of the swap as defined above,
             AIR is the accrued interest receivable as defined above.

These components are often grouped together under the heading of 'Actual Exposure', as we shall discuss below. The clear advantage of the *MTM* approach is that it only attributes the actual risk of a swap at any point in time and, therefore, does not overstate credit risk in any way. This means that no unnecessary usage is applied against existing credit limits, an important consideration for many institutions. It is computationally easy to derive the *MTM/AIR* on a continuing basis, and is not difficult to track if the proper systems are in place. The great flaw of the *MTM* approach is, of course, that an analyst considering a transaction at the inception of a deal will be faced with an *REE* of 0, as rates will not yet have moved. Under these circumstances the bank has no way of valuing the risk exposure inherent in the swap, which might increase over time as rates move. The *MTM* approach takes no account of potential market movements in its framework and, as such, is understating the risk that may be faced over the life of the swap. It is also difficult for an institution to set appropriate pricing and capital levels when potential movements are not factored into the equation. In practice, many banks prefer using the *MTM* approach as a component of their total risk evaluation; it is certainly an essential dimension when valuing actual risk on the books and when quantifying the exact loss at the point of default, but it does a poor job of providing an estimate of what total risk might be faced at inception and as a market begins to move.

THE POTENTIAL MARKET EXPOSURE APPROACH

The second approach, which we term the potential market exposure (*PME*) approach, more closely approximates the BIS's *CEM*; it may be calculated by employing historical, option or simulation methodology. These models employ a risk evaluation framework which values the *MTM* component discussed above, while providing a variable for the potential future market movements which might affect the value, and therefore the credit exposure, of the swap. In the same fashion that the *CEM* calls for a *MTM* valuation and a future credit exposure component, many banks employ a framework encompassing actual exposure (*AE*), and potential market, fractional, or time-to-decay, exposure. Actual terminology may well vary from bank to bank, but the concepts are generally very similar and are shown as:

$$REE = AE + PME \tag{7.7}$$

We know that the actual exposure component is reasonably standard, and includes both *MTM* and *AIR*. We thus expand our equation as follows:

$$REE = (MTM + AIR) + PME \tag{7.8}$$

The *PME* approach (by any of the three methods) is more useful than the strict *MTM* approach primarily because it provides an ex ante method by which to value future market movements, which gives an indication of the maximum amount a bank could lose if its counterparty defaults. This makes the credit decision easier as it provides an analyst with an exposure it may encounter during the life of swap; pricing and capital allocation are also much simpler and far more realistic. In addition, the *PME* approach will not result in an understating of potential risk over the life of the swap, as might occur if one simply used an *MTM* valuation.

The three disadvantages resulting from a potential market exposure framework are, first, that true credit exposure is likely to be somewhat overstated at any given point in time, and could affect the level of business an institution might transact with a given counterparty. Second, from an operational and systems standpoint such methodology is likely to be more complex, as it results in additional variables and information (e.g. *RFc*) which must be updated. Third, the *PME* approach by definition requires certain parameter inputs in order to yield a risk factor. Such inputs are highly subjective and vary from bank to bank. As such, there is no universally correct means of calculating risk factors under the *PME* approach, and great disparities may exist within the swap dealer community. Despite these disadvantages, it is generally thought that a potential market exposure framework is most useful for evaluating the credit risks inherent in swaps.

At this point we need to distinguish between the historical, option and simulation methods mentioned above. The derivation of a factor for *PME*, which is equivalent to the BIS's credit conversion factor times the notional of the swap, can be calculated in a variety of fashions. The central focus of the *PME* process is the establishment of a value for our risk factor *RF* (which is analogous to the BIS's credit conversion factor). How the *RF* is developed depends on the specific method being utilized.

Historical approach
In the historical approach, an institution may employ historical rate movements in its calculation of the potential market exposure component. Specifically, it would utilize some past history of interest or swap rate movements and, through statistical regression analysis, utilize the results to estimate where future rates might travel. Since future rates are what ultimately dictate how much our bank will lose (or gain) in the event of counterparty default, this method provides a certain amount of guidance in valuing swap credit risk. Although this is a legitimate technique for valuing swap risk, and requires knowledge of statistical techniques and modelling, we shall not spend further time on this approach. Although certain institutions utilize this methodology, many others have opted to follow either the option or simulation methods discussed below and, as such, we shall concentrate our discussion in these areas.

Option approach
The second approach to valuing swap credit risk under a *PME* framework is based largely on suggestions that swaps can be compared with options. The option approach says that a swap is akin to a series of options, where we may think of *PME* as the time

value of the option and actual (or *MTM*) exposure as the intrinsic value of the option. We know that as time goes by and maturity draws near, the *RF* of a given deal will decline; we know the same is true for the time value of an option. In addition, market movements may affect both the swap (actual or *MTM* exposure) and the option (intrinsic value). The International Swap Dealers Association (ISDA), in its 1987 Comment Letter response to the Federal Reserve/Bank of England swap risk proposal (discussed below), also made the case for viewing a pair of matched swaps as a series of at-the-money puts and calls.

Several studies have been conducted on use of option pricing methodology for swaps (including Whittaker, 1987). Utilizing the parallels between the two, Whittaker, and others, have expressed swap credit risk in terms of an option pricing model, such as the Cox, Ross and Rubinstein Binomial Option Pricing Model. Though we shall not go into a detailed discussion of the option approach, readers may reference other works on the topic (Whittaker, 1987; Smith, Smithson and Wilford, 1990).

Simulation approach

The third method under the potential market exposure framework is the simulation approach. Once again, this strategy utilizes an actual and potential market exposure concept to develop the appropriate *REE*. Where this model differs from the other approaches, however, is that the development of risk factors for the *PME* component is done through statistical simulations rather than historical examinations of data or option pricing equations. An institution may elect to model future interest rate patterns through some mathematical equation or relationship. Creating an equation which reflects a possible view of future interest rates, and incorporating the equation in a numerical procedure, can assist in providing a simulated value of future interest rates which may then be used to value a swap at certain future intervals.

Many simulation models rely on certain underlying historical information and statistical assumptions as parameter inputs (such as historical volatility of the Treasury or swap curve and the distribution of expected observations), as well as use of certain mathematical equations to help dictate the direction of future rates at statistically significant levels. In fact, the derivation of the BIS's *CEM* credit conversion factors was created utilizing simulation techniques. The Federal Reserve and the Bank of England, in a technical working paper, utilized a simulation approach to derive potential credit conversion factors for capital purposes. Their simulation called for use of a lognormal distribution, and then involved generating random samples from the distribution over the life of the swap. Based on these random samples, they were able to calculate the value of a swap at future rates and, knowing the probability distribution function, calculate appropriate confidence intervals; the end result was a series of credit conversion factors. Many other researchers have incorporated simulation techniques in their studies, and there are various excellent works which the reader may reference to obtain differing views and results on simulation (e.g. Smith, Smithson and Wilford, 1990; Ferron and Handjinicolaou, 1987; Hull, 1989; Muffett, 1986; Giberti, Mentini and Scabellone, 1993; Hunter and Stowe, 1992; (the latter in respect of simulation for derivative options)). At the end of this chapter we present sample

163

risk factors from select potential market exposure models (simulation and option-based) for the reader's reference.

The most commonly used numerical procedure for simulating the movement of random variables is the Monte Carlo technique. A Monte Carlo simulation is a procedure by which an expected value of a random variable can be estimated utilizing a repeated, and sizeable, drawing of random samples and applying such samples to some equation or relationship. For instance, if one were hoping to value an option on a stock utilizing a Monte Carlo run, the process could be achieved by simulating the path of the future stock price over a period of time by:

(a) Specifying the model of the path followed by the stock price (which would include a term representing a random drawing from a given distribution with specified mean and variance).
(b) Specifying the starting level of the stock price.
(c) Drawing a random sample and computing the resulting stock price given by the formula in step (a).
(d) Repeating the process a number of times to develop an average value of the stock price at time $t+1$.
(e) Repeating the above steps for each time interval until $t+n$, or option expiry. This will create one path of the stock price over time, until expiry. At the end of the process, one will have obtained a value for the stock price at expiry, which can then be used to value the option.

The information obtained in step (e) would represent a single realization or iteration of a Monte Carlo run. In order for this to have some meaningful contribution, it is likely that tens of thousands of iterations would be computed, with the average value of all iterations being utilized to value the option.

Interest rates may also be simulated through a similar process. A typical approach to the process would start with an assumption that rates will move randomly over time, but that the possible values can be defined in terms of a particular distribution (e.g. normal, lognormal) with certain mean and variance. Knowing the starting rate, the statistical distribution and the mathematical relationship of future movements, a random generation of an artificial future path can be created. Thousands of realizations will yield a set of interest rate values, the average of which may be taken as a representation of the future value of the rate. Utilizing these values, the replacement cost of the swap may be calculated at various points in time (perhaps every semi-annual period), with the resulting period calculations discounted back to the present. The sum of such discounted calculations will yield a risk factor which is used to calculate *PME*.

Note that in the simulation process certain methodologies focus on average replacement costs (based on average rate movements) while others opt for a maximum replacement cost (based on peak rate movements). Once again, there is no single correct answer, and much is dependent on an institution's own view of average versus maximum costs. Use of the maximum replacement cost is clearly more conservative

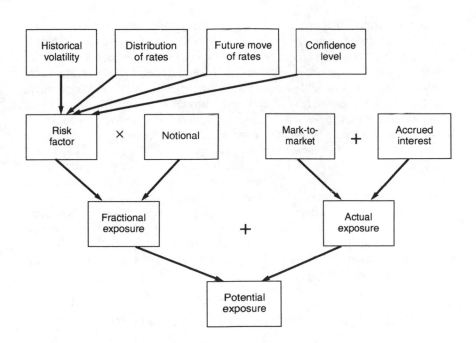

Figure 7.2   Swap credit risk, the simulation/fractional exposure approach

in that it presumes default will occur when simulated future rates have reached their maximum point.

We shall not present a specific example of a simulation approach to swap credit risk in this chapter. A more detailed example of a general method by which to value future rates, and to utilize those future rates in a replacement cost framework, is given in Appendix II. The example highlighted in the Appendix contains equations which may be used to value the path of future rates; as the reader may suspect, there are a variety of ways by which to define the path of future rates.

The simulation approach to valuing swap credit risk is shown in Figure 7.2.

SWAP RISK IN A COMPLETE FRAMEWORK

At the conclusion of the potential market exposure approach (through whichever method an institution deems most appropriate for its own purposes), we will have at our disposal some type of risk factor *RF* (which parallels the credit conversion factors from the BIS). Utilizing the *RF* in a general equation for swap risk, shown as:

$$REE = RF \times N \qquad (7.9)$$

we are in a position to assign our *REE* to a given par swap transaction. If we are considering a $50MM interest rate swap where the relevant RF is 5 per cent, the *REE* of the swap transaction is $2.5MM. We know this to be the case because swaps are market-risk products, impacted by movements in interest rates. In addition, at no time in an interest rate swap are notional amounts exchanged. As such, it is most appropriate to evaluate credit risk exposure through the risk equivalency framework. The methods above, and the general equation in 7.9, provide a means of adjusting swap exposure to its most relevant measure. Note that the same logic can be applied to currency swaps, although the initial and final exchanges of principal (especially the latter), heighten the risk considerably. The maximum risk point for a cross currency swap occurs at the end of the transaction, where in an interest rate swap it occurs ⅓ to ½ through the transaction. We shall discuss this in greater detail in Appendix II.

Basic changes to the equation above can be incorporated for different types of swap derivatives, such as swaptions, forward swaps, non-par swaps, and so on. Although these are important instruments within the product framework, we shall not deal with them in this text, as they have been covered in a previous text (for additional information see Banks, 1993).

EMPIRICAL FINDINGS ON SWAP RISK FACTORS

We have noted above a variety of ways by which swap risk factors (which are effectively percentage replacement costs) can be derived. There is no single correct way by which to value swap risk, since each institution operates under a different set of requirements, constraints and opinions. To put the above discussion in the context of actual swap risk factors, we highlight below some of the findings obtained by researchers in the development and application of their own models. These figures are presented for the reader's general information. By now it should be clear that there is no single correct solution to the problem, and the tables detailed below evidence the array of factors which can be derived depending on the particular approach and assumptions being utilized.

Federal Reserve/Bank of England

The Federal Reserve and the Bank of England were among the first to develop a methodology for creating risk factors in their 1987 technical paper entitled 'Potential Credit Exposure on Interest Rate and Foreign Exchange Rate Related Instruments'. They examined the average replacement cost of a pair of matched swaps, as well as the maximum replacement cost of a single swap utilizing a simulation procedure. The maximum replacement cost factors are shown as:

Years	1	2	3	4	5	6	7	8	9	10
RF per cent	0.5	1.5	2.8	4.3	6.0	7.8	9.6	11.5	13.4	15.3

Key assumptions: 90 per cent confidence level, lognormal distribution, 18.2 per cent volatility, 9 per cent initial interest rate.

Arak, Goodman and Rones

Arak, Goodman and Rones (1986) presented a model which simulates maximum exposure and yields the following risk factors (for a semi-annual fixed pay/floating receive swap):

Years	2	3	4	5	7	10
RF per cent	1.43	2.69	4.17	5.94	9.51	15.08

Key assumptions: upward sloping yield curve and volatilities based on active Treasuries in 1985, short term rates which follow a random path with no drift coefficient.

Whittaker

Whittaker's 1987 model, which is option-based, yielded the following risk factors (for a swap with semi-annual fixed receive/floating pay flows):

Years	1	2	3	4	5	6	7	8	9	10
RF per cent	0.23	0.56	0.86	1.18	1.50	1.81	2.11	2.45	2.77	3.09

For a matched pair of swaps, the risk factors are shown as:

Years	1	2	3	4	5	6	7	8	9	10
RF per cent	0.43	1.13	1.79	2.48	3.15	3.82	4.45	5.22	5.91	6.57

Key assumptions: Cox, Ross and Rubinstein option pricing model, lognormal distribution, 22 per cent volatility to 7 years, 23 per cent volatility beyond 7 years.

Ferron and Handjinicolaou

Ferron and Handjinicolaou (1987) (and in Schwartz and Smith, 1990) presented a lognormal simulation-based model yielding the following risk factors:

167

Years	1	3	5	7	10
RF per cent	0.12	0.76	1.49	2.18	3.13

Key assumptions: lognormal distribution, 20 per cent volatility, 9 per cent initial interest rate

Muffet

Muffet (1987) developed a simulation based model where he calculated the average replacement cost for a matched pair of 5-year fixed/floating swaps as 1 per cent; adjusted to a 90 per cent confidence level, the average replacement cost rose to 2 per cent. For a single fixed pay swap (not adjusted to a 90 per cent confidence level), the maximum (not average) replacement cost was found to be 2 per cent.

Key assumptions: lognormal distribution, 18 per cent volatility, 90 per cent confidence level, 9% initial interest rate.

Hull

Hull (1989) created a simulation based model which yielded the following risk factors (for a fixed receive/floating pay swap):

Years	2	5	10	15
RF per cent	0.30	1.20	3.20	5.50

Key assumptions: 20 per cent volatility, flat term structure and an initial interest rate of 5 per cent with zero growth and constant volatility.

Giberti, Mentini and Scabellone

Giberti, Mentini and Scabellone (1993) have presented a simulation model to calculate credit exposures for interest rate and currency swaps. Their average replacement costs for fixed rate pay/floating rate receive swaps are:

Years	1	2	3
RF per cent	1.09	1.44	1.29

Their maximum replacement costs for fixed rate pay/floating rate receive swaps are:

Years	1	2	3
RF per cent	2.52	4.79	4.33

Key assumptions: reference distribution derived from historical observations of empirical data, not from a prespecified distribution (i.e. normal, lognormal), 95 per cent confidence level.

Banks

This author has presented a simulation based model (see Appendix II or Banks, 1993, for greater detail) which yields the following maximum replacement costs for a fixed rate pay/floating rate receive swap:

Years	1	2	3	4	5	6	7	8	9	10
RF per cent	0.30	0.80	1.00	1.50	2.30	3.90	4.90	5.80	7.20	7.60

Key assumptions: 90 per cent confidence level, lognormal distribution, 16 per cent volatility, 5 per cent initial interest rate.

8: The Credit Risk of Complex Swap Structures

PRODUCT DESCRIPTION

In the previous chapter we have mentioned in overview different methods of quantifying risk in standard or 'plain vanilla' swap structures (i.e. those which involve the periodic exchange of interest or currency flows between two parties, on a par, or 'on-market' basis). While generic swap structures in the interest and currency swap market are by now commonplace, there are additional swap structures created by banks which are attracting increased, or renewed, use and attention. It is our intent in this chapter to deal with some of the more common 'next step' swap structures which credit professionals are now likely to deal with in the normal course of business. In this chapter we shall treat when-in-the-money interest rate options, compound (nested) options, power caps, inverse floater swaps, leveraged swaps, differential swaps, amortizing swaps, mortgage swaps and index principal swaps. We shall not discuss other non-standard structures such as swaptions, puttable and callable swaps, forward swaps, premium/discount swaps or zero coupon swaps, as these have been dealt with in a previous volume (see Banks, 1993).

In the first section of this chapter we shall briefly describe some of the more commonly used 'variations' on the swap product. In the second section we shall turn to a discussion of the credit risk quantification of these swap derivatives.

When-In-The-Money Interest Rate Options

Among the most common interest rate options are caps and floors (note that swaptions, yield curve options and bond options are all considered part of the interest rate option category as well). Caps and floors are barriers which, when exceeded, will provide an inflow to the purchaser and an outflow to the seller, in an amount equal to:

$$Payout_C = (CMP - SP) \times N$$

and

$$Payout_F = (SP - CMP) \times N$$

where CMP is the current price of the rate index,
SP is the strike rate of the cap or floor,
N is the notional.

for the purchaser of a cap or floor, respectively, at each periodic evaluation interval (which is generally quarterly, semi-annually, or annually). Caps and floors are designed to provide buyers with protection on the upside or downside, and to give sellers premium income for providing such protection. For instance, a cap will ensure that a buyer's floating rate liability, for example, will never exceed the amount dictated by a purchased cap: if the cap is set at 10 per cent, and floating rates move the liability's index up to 12 per cent, the buyer will still pay 12 per cent on its liability, but will receive 2 per cent from the seller, effectively capping rates at 10 per cent. A floor works in the opposite fashion, by ensuring a minimum rate will always be received; a floor would be useful in the event that an institution was concerned about declining rates receivable from a floating rate asset.

Combinations of caps and floors result in the building of collars (for example, selling a cap and buying a floor) and corridors (buying a cap, and selling a higher strike cap). These enable zero-cost, or lower-cost, strategies to be developed. Use of caps and floors is widespread by swap participants, and certain other variations have been developed. One such variation is the *when-in-the-money option*, which allows the buyer of the option to defer payment of premium until such time as the option moves in-the-money. To the extent the cap or floor does not move in-the-money during the life of the contract, there is no premium payment due the option writer. This product has the advantage, of course, of not requiring the buyer to post payment for a cap or floor which may not be called into use. For the writer, the advantage occurs in the form of potential premium: to the extent a when-in-the-money option is written, the additional flexibility it is providing the buyer will be compensated via a higher premium. However, this presumes the option moves in-the-money during the life of the deal. If it does not, the higher premium will never be received (in fact, no premium will ever be received). As one might imagine, the credit risk profile of a when-in-the-money option differs significantly from traditional interest rate options, for both buyer and seller. We shall discuss these differences in the section below.

Compound (Nested) Options

Compound, or *nested*, *options* (sometimes also known as *captions* or *floortions*) are effectively options on other options, namely caps or floors (which, as we know from above, are simply interest rate options). Though compound options have been in existence for some time (see Geske, 1979, for instance), they have been reintroduced in slightly different form in recent years, and are gaining in popularity (note that compounds are also offered on currencies, indexes and equities, in addition to interest rates). A compound option gives the purchaser the right, but not the obligation, to enter into a cap or floor agreement with the compound option seller in exchange for a premium payment. For instance, Bank X could pay Bank Y premium to enter into an option to buy a cap. Under the terms of the compound option X would have the right, at any point during the life of the compound option (assuming American exercise), to enter into a cap at a prespecified strike rate; if X exercises the compound option, Y will have to provide X with rate protection on the upside, to the extent Libor (or some other base index) moves above the strike rate. In a compound option, all relevant details regarding the underlying cap (or floor) are specified in advance, including strike level, frequency of evaluation/payment, and expiry date. Note that if X exercises the compound option to enter into the underlying cap or floor, it will then pay an additional premium to Y, as it would under normal circumstances. Should X elect not to exercise the compound option for any reason (perhaps rates have fallen and are unlikely to rise, in X's view, or perhaps X no longer requires protection on the upside since a certain event may have occurred to extinguish the need), then X will not pay Y the additional premium and Y will have no further obligation to X.

The reasons for entering into a nested option may have to do with the purchaser's uncertainty over rates or other events which may affect its asset or liability streams; buying an option on an option locks in a certain level of protection without committing the institution to a transaction it may not actually require, and it enables the institution to save on premium payments for an event which may not come into play. From the standpoint of the seller, a compound option earns premium income while still providing opportunity on two fronts for not having to pay under the cap or floor: the first front would be non-exercise by the buyer of the original option, the second would be the underlying cap or floor remaining out-of-the-money.

Power Caps

A *power cap* is a relatively recent creation. As in a standard cap, the buyer of a power cap hopes to receive some protection from the seller on the upside, when the relevant index moves above the strike level. However, instead of receiving the difference between *CMP* and *SP* (as described in the equation above), the buyer receives the difference raised to some exponent or 'power'. That is, if it is a squared power cap (or a 2 power cap), the buyer will receive $(CMP - SP)(CMP - SP)$, or $(CMP - SP)^2$; if it is a cubed power cap (or a 3 power cap), the buyer will receive $(CMP - SP)(CMP - SP)(CMP - SP)$, or $(CMP - SP)^3$. In exchange for this type of payback (which can be extremely high), the purchaser pays a substantial upfront premium to the writer. As one might imagine, the risk management implications of these instruments are substantial. For instance, instead of a normal hedge for a standard cap which would protect a writer's book from a unit move in rates, a cubed power cap means that it must now be concerned with how, for instance, a 2 per cent move translates into an 8 per cent payout, instead of a 2 per cent payout. The risk dimensions of these instruments must be carefully considered. Figure 8.1 below illustrates the payoffs of conventional, 2 power and 3 power caps once rates have exceeded the cap strike level.

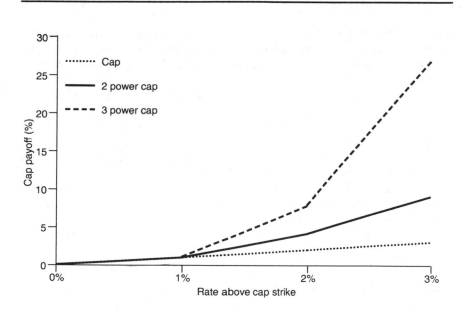

Figure 8.1   Power cap payoffs

Inverse Floater Swaps

Inverse floater swaps (sometimes known as *reverse swaps*) have been in existence for several years, and seek to take advantage of, or protect against, a steep yield curve (i.e. one where the spread between short rates and long rates may be several hundred basis points). A typical structure calls for paying or receiving a floating rate index (say Libor) versus receiving or paying a fixed rate less the same floating rate index. For instance, Bank X might receive 12-month Libor flat, and might pay 15 per cent minus 12-month Libor flat. The general form of the flows is:

$$Pay \lor rec: (\ x\% \ fixed - floating \ index\ ) \leftrightarrow Rec \lor pay : floating \ index$$

As one might expect, the above causes the inverse side's flows (e.g. *x% fixed – floating index*) to move in an 'inverse fashion' against the floating index flows. If Libor (our floating index) rises, X will receive more, based on 12-month Libor. At the same time, it will pay less, since 15 per cent minus an increasing Libor index results in a smaller payment. Inverse floater swaps may be used to leverage a specific view of Libor (or some other floating index). In our example above, X will benefit from an upward movement in rates, as calculated by Libor. However, rather than a static fixed flow on the pay side, (as would be common under a standard structure), the pay side will also benefit from the rising Libor rates, by providing X with a lower coupon

173

‚payment. Thus, the correct view allows X to 'leverage' a movement in rates. Naturally, an incorrect view of rates compounds the error. In either event, we shall see in our credit risk discussion below that a leveraging approach is useful when calculating credit risk exposure.

In addition to utilizing inverse floater swaps to take a view on a given rate, these products may also be used to hedge certain asset or liability flows which are structured in the same fashion. For instance, in recent years there have been a number of inverse floating rate notes brought to market by various issuers; a swap, such as the one described above, could act as a hedge to such a position. Government agencies, and corporations such as IBM and General Electric, have issued such instruments. In addition, there have been a number of recent warrant issues where the underlying warrant is exercisable into a note with a reverse floater component. Swaps to hedge such positions would also be useful.

Leveraged Swaps

Leveraged swaps are closely related to inverse floater swaps, except they involve far greater amounts of leverage. A typical structure might call for the inverse rate payer to contract a flow of 25 per cent – (3 * 6 month Libor) against receipt of 6-month Libor + 50 basis points. If we assume current 6-month Libor is 6 per cent, at inception, the leveraged inverse rate payer will pay 25 per cent – (3 * 6 per cent), or 7 per cent, while receiving 6.50 per cent, for a net gain of 50 b.p. From there, much is obviously dependent on the direction of 6 month Libor: if Libor rises to 7 per cent, the leveraged inverse rate payer will only pay 4 per cent, and will receive 7.50 per cent, for a net gain of 3.50 per cent. Thus, a 100 basis point upward move in Libor rates causes the inverse rate payer to save 300 basis points on its pay flow, and earn 100 basis points on its receive flow (which is what it was expecting in any event, since the receive component is not leveraged). If, in contrast, the 6-month Libor index falls to 5 per cent, the leveraged inverse rate payer will be faced with a payment of 25 per cent – (3 * 5 per cent), or 10 per cent (or 300 basis points above the starting point). At the same time, its inflow will fall to 5.5 per cent, or 100 basis points below the starting level. This results in a net payment of 4.50 per cent. Again, the effect of leverage is substantial. As indicated above, these structures are often utilized to compound the effects of a certain view on the market, or to hedge a given structured asset or liability. In our credit risk section below we shall follow a risk evaluation approach similar to the one developed for inverse floater swaps, since leveraged swaps with a floating rate component are clearly a subset of the broader inverse floater category.

Differential Swaps

Differential swaps (often referred to as '*diff' swaps*) have gained substantial popularity in recent years with institutions and investors who are attempting to capitalize on a view of foreign markets, without having to be exposed to currency risk. As we shall see below, such differential swaps are very often structured in inverse floater or leveraged form. In a typical non-leveraged differential swap, an institution may wish to receive 6-month DM Libor in exchange for paying US dollar Libor, all payable in dollars. Since the flows are payable in a single currency (e.g. dollars), the institution is taking no currency risk. Note that in a diff swap there is typically a spread subtracted from the institution's receive flow (or added to its pay flow), which reflects an interest differential between the two currencies. Under our DM/$ scenario, we would expect the DM yield curve to be above the US$ curve; in fact, it may be inverted. In recent diff swaps between DM and dollars, DM short rates (i.e. 3- to 6-month Libor) have been a full 500 basis points above dollar short rates, allowing an institution to capitalize on substantial profit opportunities (without assuming any currency risk; that risk is left to the bank, and generally represents a reasonably complex risk management exercise given the unknown amount of foreign currency potentially involved during the life of the transaction). Establishing a diff position suggests that the institution is attempting to take advantage of inaccuracies in the implied forward rates. As such, it believes the DM curve will not fall as much as the implied rates would suggest, or that the dollar curve will not rise as much as implied rates suggest. If it is correct, it will continue to earn a handsome spread.

As indicated above, another popular structure is to combine a differential swap with a leveraged and/or inverse floater structure: our bank, for instance, may wish to pay 15 per cent minus (2 times Yen Libor), in exchange for receipt of US dollar Libor – 25 basis points, all payable or receivable in dollars. Under this scenario, the bank hopes that the short end of the Yen Libor curve rises against the US$ Libor curve, since an increase in the leveraged inverse Yen index subtracts from the required payment and will mean a greater differential. At the same time, it is hoping the US$ Libor curve will also rise, since an increase in this index will also act to widen the differential. Thus, the bank is taking a broader view on global Libor movements and a narrower view on Yen/$ Libor movements.

Let us assume the following extreme scenarios: Yen Libor and US$ Libor both start at 5 per cent. During the course of the differential swap, Yen Libor rises to 6 per cent (up 100 b.p.) while US$ Libor rises to 5.5 per cent (up 50 b.p.). The differential moves from – 0.25 per cent to 2.25 per cent. In the next period, assume that Yen Libor rises a further 100 b.p., to 7 per cent, while US$ Libor rises 100 b.p. to 6.5 per cent. The differential increases from 2.25 per cent to 5.25 per cent. Finally, let us assume in the last period Yen Libor remains unchanged and US$ Libor falls by 200 b.p., to 4.5 per cent. The differential narrows back to 3.25 per cent. Thus, we see the effect of changing Libor values on the differential; given the inverse/leveraged structure, an increase in Libor curves globally will be beneficial to the bank, but a higher value or rise in the Yen Libor curve will be more advantageous.

A differential swap is often termed a correlation product, since its payout is modified by the correlation between the relevant foreign exchange and interest rates in the transaction. In fact, correlation levels and correlation risk are becoming a substantial topic among derivatives practitioners, particularly with regard to pricing. Although traders are experienced in pricing and trading the volatility of two given assets separately, there is concern on how the correlation between two markets may affect pricing. Since correlation must be priced into the derivative just as volatility is, traders are seeking accurate measures of correlation (which can take account of very substantial one day spikes in the market, such as the massive currency movements witnessed in September 1992). They are also seeking measures which predict, rather than describe, correlation. Note that correlation issues are also present in other products such as outperformance options and quantos (as we have described in Chapter 6). Outperformance options are generally described as first order correlation products (e.g. those which directly affect the payout of the option), while quantos and diffs are described as second order correlation products (e.g. those which only modify the payout of the option) (see Cookson, 1993). These are important issues, particularly with regard to pricing, trading and risk management. Though they may have an impact on credit issues, from a conservative standpoint it is helpful to presume no positive correlation exists between the various indexes comprising a given diff; this allows maximum credit risk exposure to be assigned to a transaction. We shall discuss this concept at greater length below.

Figure 8.2 highlights the construction of a differential swap, which generally involves establishing two separate fixed/floating interest rate swaps in the currencies impacting the differential.

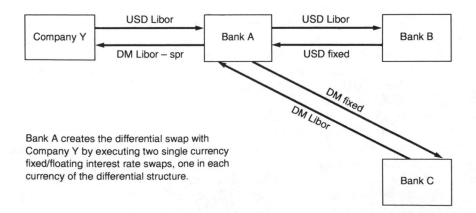

Bank A creates the differential swap with Company Y by executing two single currency fixed/floating interest rate swaps, one in each currency of the differential structure.

Figure 8.2   The creation of a differential swap

Amortizing Swaps

Amortizing swaps, which have been in use for several years, are swaps which are based on an ever changing notional principal balance. For instance, a counterparty may wish to enter into an interest rate swap where it pays fixed in exchange for floating; instead of doing so on a static notional amount, say $100MM, it may wish to do so on a balance which decreases at a certain pace. In this example, the notional principal may decline every year, for five years, by an equal amount. Thus, interest payments exchanged (or netted) on each payment date become increasingly smaller. The motivation for entering into an amortizing swap is that a counterparty may wish to swap an exact series of flows derived from some form of liability financing.

For example, an institution may have a series of lease payments to make, which are reduced on a straight line basis each year. It may want to 'lock in' the level of its payments during the course of the lease, and could do so by entering into a fixed-floating amortizing swap. Airlines are very often users of amortizing swaps, with notional principal reductions coinciding with aircraft lease schedules. In addition to leases, a counterparty may have a loan or financing which amortizes on a prearranged periodic basis which it may want to swap. It should be noted that a swap amortization schedule need not necessarily be straight line in nature. Any type of principal reduction may be considered and swapped, though an even flow of reductions tends to be most common. Other common amortizing strategies may be found in both mortgage swaps and index principal swaps, treated below.

Mortgage Swaps

Mortgage swaps are a relatively recent creation, but are drawing increased interest from a broad range of institutional investors. Mortgage swaps are, in essence, swaps which are structured to replicate the flows found in a certain pool or package of mortgage backed securities (MBS); since the structure is synthetic, it is generally true that no physical mortgage backed securities are held by the investor. However, the structure of the swap allows the investor's return to precisely equal the return derived from a specific pool of MBS.

An example of a mortgage-backed swap would be one where the investor pays a monthly floating rate (typically Libor), in exchange for a fixed rate, 'decompounded' and paid monthly. The notional principal of the swap would amortize down (just as the principal in an MBS amortizes down through principal repayments by the ultimate homeowner) at a rate which is equivalent to the amortization level of a certain FNMA (say FNMA 9s), for instance. The amortization level may be calculated (as an example) by taking the amortization rates of all FNMA 9s issued between 1990 and 1991. With these parameters the swap flows (including the declining balance) would duplicate the flows generated by holding the physical securities (without having an actual balance sheet item).

As one might imagine, there are a variety of other forms by which a mortgage swap can be created: the flows may seek not to duplicate a specific class of securities, (i.e. FNMA 9s of 2001), but a specific security, or a pool of mortgage-backed securities (such as a collateralized mortgage obligation, or CMO). In the case of a CMO swap, the investor would again pay Libor against receipt of a fixed coupon. The swap notional would amortize down on a schedule determined by the Public Securities Association (PSA) rates, tied to a monthly amortization factor. Another structure might involve the replication of a FNMA (adjustable rate mortgage (ARM)) passthrough based on the COF Index (11th District Cost of Funds). Under such a swap, the investor would pay Libor and receive COF (a floating index), on a notional amount which amortizes at a rate equal to the FNMA COF ARM passthroughs.

Index Principal Swaps

Index principal swaps (IPSs), sometimes also referred to as *index amortizing swaps* (IARs), are a recent creation. These swaps function in a fashion similar to the mortgage swaps detailed above. A typical IPS is one where the notional principal amortizes when rates fall. In a standard structure, as Libor (or some other floating index) falls, the notional principal of the swap amortizes on a set schedule (e.g. if rates fall by 50 basis points by the next measurement period, in 6 months, the notional might reduce by 20 per cent; if they fall by 100 basis points, the notional might reduce by 40 per cent, and so on). Rather than a straight step-level (i.e. 20 per cent or 40 per cent amortization based on 50 or 100 basis point movements in Libor), the actual level might be calculated through a formula so that amortization can be determined based on small changes in rates (i.e. 1 or 5 basis points). While the notional will amortize if the floating rate falls, it will not amortize if rates rise; in this case the swap will take on the characteristics of a plain vanilla transaction. In IPSs, the bank paying the floating rate is said to be the 'purchaser' of the swap; in exchange for paying the floating rate it receives a fixed rate which is typically above market. The above market rate is the bank's compensation for effectively having written a path dependent option, as discussed in Chapter 6 (i.e. if floating rates fall to a certain level, the notional pays down). The 'seller' pays the above market fixed rate and receives the floating rate. In recent deals, the above market rate paid to the 'purchaser' has been as high as 100 to 150 basis points, so the economic incentive is certainly present. This is aided by a so-called 'lockout' period during which no amortization can take place, regardless of the fall in rates; this period is typically for the first few years of a multi-year transaction.

From the standpoint of the IPS 'purchaser', stable rates are welcome. If rates fall sharply the notional of the swap will amortize down (indicating that the average life will fall) and reinvestment will have to take place at lower rates. If floating rates rise sharply, the swap will retain its full notional and final maturity aspects, and the floating rate payer will sacrifice the opportunity to invest at higher rates. Thus, the floating rate payer (or 'purchaser') will hope for stable rates. From the standpoint of the floating rate receiver (the 'seller'), either a rising or falling scenario is beneficial; a stationary scenario is not. IPSs are utilized by those seeking an asset-liability management tool, as well as by those looking to take a specific view on the volatility of interest rates.

CREDIT RISK QUANTIFICATION

The quantification of credit risk in the structures described above will focus on the general equation developed in the previous chapter, which says that:

$$REE = RF \times N \tag{7.9}$$

As we have seen, there are any number of ways by which an *RF* for swaps can be derived. Our concern in this chapter will not be on the method used to develop *RF*, but how *RF*, once developed, is employed in a broader calculation of structured swap exposure. For purposes of this chapter we shall use risk factors which are based on the approach detailed in Appendix II, which calls for a simulation of future rates utilizing a binomial model. Parameters of importance, as the reader will note from the Appendix, include the adjusted historical volatility (which we have discussed at length in Chapter 2), the starting interest rate level and the final maturity of the swap, and the binomial equation which dictates upward and downward movements. Readers are urged to consult the Appendix for additional details, or refer to: Arak, Goodman and Rones, 1986; Banks, 1993; Schwartz and Smith, 1990; and Smith, Smithson and Wilford, 1990; for other methodologies.

When In-the-Money Interest Rate Options

We have described above an interest rate option (e.g. a cap or a floor), which allows the purchaser to defer payment of premium until such time as the option moves in-the-money. If the cap or floor never has intrinsic value, the writer can expect to receive no premium. If, however, the option has intrinsic value, the writer will receive a greater amount of premium than would be forthcoming by writing a normal interest rate cap or floor. The credit risk incurred by both parties in a when-in-the-money structure is rather different than would be encountered in a standard structure.

If one assumes that the risk on a long standard interest rate cap or floor (i.e. one which our bank has purchased) can be calculated from the risk factors developed for interest rate swaps (where the cap or floor strike corresponds to the fixed interest rate from the swap risk factor grid), our risk can be shown as:

$$REE = Premium + (RF \times N) \tag{8.1}$$

where we may adjust the risk factor, *RF*, for some in- or out-of-the-money portion, if desired (just as we have in Chapter 3). We know that in a standard purchase of an interest rate option, our premium will be at risk at inception, since this is an amount which is immediately paid out to the option writer. In a when-in-the-money option, we know that premium may never be paid. If it is not paid, it means the option has no intrinsic value and, therefore, our bank will not be looking to the writer for performance.

Thus, an institution may treat the credit risk of a when-in-the-money option with varying degrees of conservatism: if it believes that the option will eventually move in-the-money (perhaps it is struck close to-the-money), it may choose to value risk as in the standard interest rate option shown in Equation 8.1. If it does not wish to value the premium until the option moves in-the-money, it may simply assign some value to the potential intrinsic value of the option over time (e.g. via $(RF * N)$) and then add premium to *REE* when it is paid; if the premium is not paid until the exercise of the option, perhaps in some net payment form, it may choose to never count the premium as risk since the protective flow it is anticipating from its option will be partially offset by the premium due the writer. These approaches may be shown as:

$$REE = (RF \times N) + Premium \vee 0 \qquad (8.2)$$

In the final form, the purchaser may choose not to assign any risk to the transaction. Although this is a very liberal approach to risk valuation, a bank may choose to follow this approach if the when-in-the-money it is purchasing is very short term and very far out-of-the-money, with no real chance of ending in-the-money; such a deep out-of-the-money option could be purchased to prevent financial loss due to an extremely sharp upward or downward movement in rates (such as those witnessed during the September 1992 European currency turmoil). Since no premium is paid upfront, as in a standard cap or floor, it might be argued that there is no real chance for credit risk exposure. Naturally this scenario changes if there is a large movement in rates. In either event it is perhaps a little naive not to assign any risk to the transaction, but we present the view for the reader's consideration.

For the seller of a standard cap or floor, there is no risk to the transaction once premium is received; since this typically happens within a five day framework, no credit risk exposure is incurred. As we know, this is standard treatment for all short option positions (except in currencies, which may still involve delivery risk). For the seller of a when-in-the-money cap or floor, the risk is clearly different: since premium is not received within five business days (unless the option moves in-the-money in that time frame), premium will be at risk. Once again, an institution writing this structure has several choices in how it wishes to value the risk. In a more conservative fashion, it may wish to value delayed receipt of premium as its risk. Once premium is received (i.e. when the cap or floor moves in-the-money), which may be several months or years in the future, risk would be set equal to zero. This is conservative in that if the option moves in-the-money, and the counterparty does not deliver the required premium, the bank writing the option will not honour its commitment under the option. Since the option will have intrinsic value to the defaulting purchaser, the writer will not deliver that value. Thus a second, less conservative, view would assign no risk to the extended settlement of the premium since non-receipt of premium would be offset by nonpayment under the option. The question at this point is whether the intrinsic value of the option more than offsets the premium. If it does not, the bank as writer would still sustain a loss, equal to the net difference between $(CMP - SP)$ – premium, for a cap, and $(SP - CMP)$ – premium, for a floor.

Compound (Nested) Options

In our discussion above we noted that a compound option is simply an option on an option. From the standpoint of the buyer of a compound option, who retains the right to exercise the compound structure into a standard cap or floor, the risk can be viewed initially as the payment of premium on the original compound option. If our bank pays $100,000 today to enter into an American-style compound option on a 7 per cent strike Libor cap, we shall lose the $100,000 if our counterparty defaults before exercise (if exercise ever occurs). On the second front, we can assume that we will only exercise when we feel that the underlying cap will add economic protection. This may occur when the strike of the underlying cap has been breached (implying that it is in-the-money), or when it is about to be breached (implying that it is very close-to-the-money). At this point we will be looking for protection (or be very close to looking for protection), so we can effectively attribute risk normally encountered on a cap or floor (which we have discussed immediately above). For instance, if we exercise the compound option into the cap, we are expecting our counterparty to perform whenever Libor is above the 7 per cent strike level. If our counterparty defaults, we shall suffer an economic loss by no longer receiving the current market price of Libor less the strike (times the notional) for each remaining period. This is, of course, simply equal to the risk encountered on a normal cap. One adjustment must be made: the premium we paid for the original compound option will no longer be relevant, as that option has been exercised and the underlying contract has been entered into. However, to enter into the new contract we will have paid some new amount of premium which is now at risk. To the extent our counterparty defaults after we have exercised the compound, our new, not our old, premium payment is at risk. For an analyst considering the risk on a compound option, therefore, the correct *REE* would focus on the standard cap or floor equation mentioned in Equation 8.1 above (adjusted for the in- or out-of-the-money portion, as required); the original premium on the compound option would be replaced by the new premium on the cap/floor, once exercise occurs. It is unlikely that a credit officer considering a transaction like this would want to ignore the potential market risk on the underlying cap/floor, as that could severely understate risk (i.e. he or she would not want to assume that the compound option will remain out-of-the-money).

For the seller of a compound option there is no risk once (a) the original premium is received and (b) exercise occurs and the second premium is received (if the original option ever moves in-the-money).

Power Caps

The credit risk on the purchase of a power cap can be substantial and must be recognized by the analyst. We know from our previous discussions of options that our risk is limited to long positions, (i.e. those where our bank pays premium in exchange for some future performance by the seller). The same is true with power caps and, as such, our discussion will focus on long power cap positions. To begin, we know that we shall initially have our premium at risk: since a power cap entails an exponential payout, the premiums associated with such options may be substantial and cannot be ignored. In addition to premium, we know that a market risk component must be considered, since failure by the power cap writer to perform on the option once it moves in-the-money will entail a loss for the buyer. In a standard cap, market risk may be evaluated by $(RF * N)$, where RF is the swap risk factor associated with a cap of a certain strike and maturity adjusted for some in- or out-of-the-money portion. Failure by the counterparty once the cap is in-the-money will result in the buyer having to replace the cap when rates are above the strike level, which represents an economic loss.

We can use this same framework for evaluating the credit risk of power caps. We need, however, to make an adjustment: since we know the payout is equal to the differential between the CMP and the SP, raised to a certain power, our market risk component must also reflect this power. Thus, our total equation takes the form:

$$REE = \text{Premium} + \frac{(RF * 100)^{x} * N}{100} \qquad (8.3)$$

where x is the relevant 'power' of the power cap

Consider the following example: Bank X buys a \$50MM cubed power cap, struck at an at-the-money rate of 8 per cent, on US\$ Libor. The maturity of the power cap is 2 years, and the evaluation period is annual (that is, Libor rates will be compared with the cap strike twice during the life of the transaction). In exchange for this cap, X pays its counterparty \$5MM. If we further assume that the risk factor for an 8 per cent, 2 year swap (or cap) is 2 per cent, the relevant REE for the power cap would be:

$$REE = \$5MM + ((0.02 * 100)^3 * \$50MM)/100$$
$$REE = \$5MM + \$4MM$$
$$REE = \$9MM$$

If rates rise to 9.5 per cent just prior to the first evaluation period, and X's counterparty defaults, the amount lost will be \$5MM in premium, plus the difference between CMP (9.5 per cent) and SP (8 per cent), cubed, times \$50MM, or \$1.69MM. There will also be a loss on the second payment; if one assumed static rates, it would equal approximately $1.54MM in present value terms. Note that use of the equivalent swap risk factor takes account of subsequent payments which might be forthcoming in the event the counterparty defaults when there are additional payments remaining (see Appendix II). Thus, the total loss would approximate $8.23MM. Under a standard cap, the premium would be lost, though it would likely be a far lower premium. In addition, the intrinsic value would be lost, which would equal 1.5 per cent times $50MM, or $750,000 plus an estimated amount for the second payment. It can be seen, then, that the amount at stake with a power cap is considerably higher. It is not accurate simply to value the maximum replacement cost, as in a standard swap or cap; it is necessary to value the maximum replacement cost, raised to the relevant power, since this represents the maximum expected economic payoff (and potential credit loss) under the power cap.

In the case of short power caps, where our bank is writer, there will be no credit risk exposure once premium has been received from the buyer. Nonetheless, as indicated above, such positions have very complex risk management issues which must be considered.

Inverse Floater Swaps

We have mentioned above, in our discussion of inverse floater swaps, that the inverse floating structure has the effect of leveraging a movement in rates: that is, an upward movement in the floating rate index will cause the payer of the inverse to pay less and receive more, while a downward movement in the index will cause the payer of the inverse to pay more and receive less. This knowledge is useful in our approach to valuing credit risk exposure. A good starting point in the entire analysis is to set the pay and receive flows equal to one another, under the assumption that if priced correctly, an institution will feel that the two components are economically equivalent at inception. To do this we say:

$$(x\% \text{ fixed} - \text{floating}) = \text{floating}$$

With simple algebra we may conclude that:

$$x\% \text{ fixed} = \text{floating} + \text{floating}$$
$$x\% \text{ fixed} = (2 * \text{floating})$$

This is, of course, equal to 2 swaps of (floating, (x % fixed/2)). This demonstrates the leveraging effect of inverse floater swaps. At this point, we might find it helpful to assign some figures to the above equations:

$$x = 15\%, \text{floating} = 12\text{-month Libor flat}$$

If we set the pay and receive components equal to each other, our inverse floater swap is:

$$(15\% - \text{12-month Libor}) = \text{12-month Libor},$$

which is equivalent to saying that a 15 per cent fixed pay swap is equal to receiving 2 times 12-month Libor flat. In order to place this in terms of our *REE* framework, we can think of this being equal to a pair of 7.5 per cent fixed pay/Libor receive swaps. Thus, if our risk factor for a 5-year, 7.5 per cent fixed pay swap is 4.3 per cent, our risk on this structure would equal 2 times 4.3 per cent, or 8.6 per cent. Intuitively, this should make sense as well, since an upward move in rates when we are paying the inverse results in a gain on the receive (implying greater credit risk exposure) and a fall on the pay (implying greater credit risk exposure). To the extent counterparty default occurs when rates have risen, our bank will have to replace the structure in a rate environment where it originally expected to receive more and pay less; its economic loss is thus greater when compared with a standard swap structure. We may capture this relationship by saying that:

$$REE = ([LF \times RF] \times N) \qquad (8.4)$$

where LF is the leverage factor,
                       RF is the risk factor,
                       N is the notional swap.

Recall that LF is calculated algebraically by setting the inverse leg equal to the floating leg, and solving for the 'number' of Libor swaps which can be 'extracted' from the original structure. The RF utilized in the equation above is simply equal to the risk factor for a standard swap with the maturity and fixed rate of a 'non-leveraged' structure. It should also be noted that, rather than leverage the risk factor, it is possible to leverage the notional (by the same LF). The *REE* impact is identical.

Leveraged Swaps

We have seen in our description above that leveraged swaps are a subset of the inverse floater swaps described above. Our credit risk analysis of these structures follows the same thinking: we can set the leveraged inverse pay flow equal to the floating receive flow and, through basic algebra, determine the appropriate leverage factor which we then apply to our standard risk factor for a swap with a 'non-leveraged' fixed rate and given maturity. If we follow the example utilized in our product description above, we note that:

$$(25\% - (3 * \text{6-month Libor})) = \text{6-month Libor}$$
$$25\% = (3 * 6 \text{ Libor}) + \text{6-month Libor}$$
$$25\% = 4 * \text{6-month Libor}$$

This is equivalent to 4 swaps where the fixed rate is 6.25 per cent, indicating that our leverage factor *LF* is 4. If we presume the final maturity on this $100MM transaction is 3 years, a standard swap risk factor might equal 1.9 per cent; per the equation developed above, our total risk on the transaction would be:

$$REE = ([4 * 0.019] * \$100MM)$$

$$REE = (0.076 * \$100MM)$$

$$REE = \$7.6MM$$

We may also state that this is equal to $400MM * 1.9 per cent, or $7.6MM. That is, we may leverage the notional amount of the swaps, instead of the risk factor. It is left for the reader to determine which approach is used, since they are algebraically equivalent. Highlighted below is a graphical representation of the flows on a leveraged inverse floater swap.

Differential Swaps

We recall from above that a differential swap is structured where a bank receives a certain floating rate from its counterparty and pays a different floating rate to its counterparty. One of the two floating rates is based on a foreign currency index (e.g. a foreign currency Libor rate), but the structure by definition means that no currency risk is being assumed. The credit risk of a differential swap, as one might suspect, is based on the spread differential which exists between two floating rate indexes at the

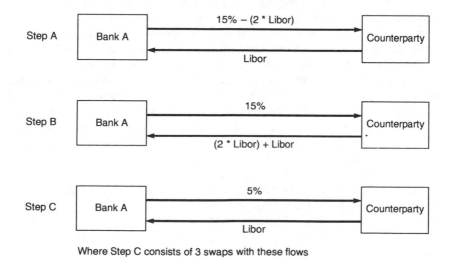

Where Step C consists of 3 swaps with these flows

Figure 8.3 Leveraged inverse floater swap

time of counterparty default. When the differential is positive (i.e. the bank receives more than it pays), there will be a credit loss; if the differential is negative (i.e. the bank pays more than it receives), there will be no credit loss.

With this as our starting point, we can imagine the following scenario: Bank A is receiving 12-month DM Libor flat (currently at 6 per cent) from Bank X, and is paying X 12-month US$ Libor (currently at 4 per cent) plus a spread. The diff transaction is 3 years in length and the payment periods are annual; the notional size is $100MM, and all flows are payable in dollars.

Our approach to the credit risk valuation of a differential swap follows the same general approach we have taken in analysing outperformance options in Chapter 6, where we also focus on the differential between two indexes, one expected to outperform the other. In a diff swap we know the amount of our credit loss will be the spread differential in existence at the time of default; our credit risk examination must therefore focus on the maximum positive and negative movement of the two curves which define the transaction (just as the credit risk examination of the outperformance option focuses on the maximum positive movement of the index expected to outperform, and the maximum negative movement of the comparison index).

In our example above, Bank A receives a flow based on the DM curve and pays a flow based on the dollar curve. Thus, the spread differential will widen as the DM curve rises and the dollar curve falls. It seems logical, therefore, to presume that the DM curve will move to a maximum point as dictated by historical volatility, while the dollar curve will move to a minimum point as dictated by historical volatility. This, by definition, will yield the maximum differential and, therefore, the maximum credit risk within the confines of our risk factor framework.

We make an assumption that the correlation between the DM Libor curve and the US Libor curve is 0, or close to 0. If there is any reason to believe that the correlation between the two is particularly strong, then it is unreasonable to presume that the DM curve will move to its maximum positive point and the US Libor curve will move to its maximum negative point; an adjustment would have to be made in such a case, by reducing the differential by an amount which reflects a strong positive correlation measure. For purposes of this chapter, however, we will assume a worst case scenario which says no correlation exists between the indexes (we need not worry about a strong negative correlation, which causes the curves to move in opposite directions, since movement would still be bounded by our historical volatility measure for each curve for a given period).

Returning to our example above, let us assume that annual historical volatility for 12-month DM Libor is 20 per cent, adjusted to a 90 per cent confidence level. 12 month Dollar Libor volatility, also adjusted for a 90 per cent confidence level, is 16 per cent. Based on our current Libors of 6 per cent and 4 per cent, respectively, this means that the maximum each index can move during the next 12 months (before our next settlement period) is:

$$\text{DM Libor: } 6\% * 20\% = 120 \text{ b.p.}$$
$$\text{US Libor: } 4\% * 16\% = 64 \text{ b.p.}$$

Thus, the DM curve shifting upward by 120 b.p. and the dollar Libor curve shifting downward by 64 b.p. implies that the differential in 12-month rates, during our next settlement period 12 months from now, may be as wide as 184 b.p. We may interpret this as a single period risk factor of 1.84 per cent, which we shall label RF_d. Since we are referring to a 3-year transaction, we need to adjust for the number of settlement periods which remain. This involves multiplying RF_d by 2, not 3, for a total RF_d of 3.68 per cent. Recall that A already has a spread differential of 200 b.p. (less the spread over Libor to X) which is based on 12 month Libor in existence today, payable in 12 months. Thus, we only have two unknown settlement periods we are estimating (e.g. at $t=1$ 12-month Libor payable in 12 months at $t=2$, and at $t=2$ 12-month Libor payable in 12 months at $t=3$), hence the multiplication by 2 instead of 3. Our total REE for the example above, then, is $3.68MM, based on a notional of $100MM.

Note that we have not subtracted off the spread payable to the counterparty; this will reduce risk, so the above is the most conservative approach to valuing credit risk. Institutions believing the approach too conservative could opt for removing the spread from the risk equation. We can condense our discussion of the above into Equations 8.5 and 8.6. Our calculation of the maximum differential is based on a maximum upward movement in the receive curve and a maximum downward movement in the pay curve. This is effectively our RF_d:

$$RF_d = Rec_{max\ up} + Pay_{max\ dn} \qquad (8.5)$$

where $Rec_{max\ up}$ is the maximum upward movement in the receive curve,
                       $Pay_{max\ dn}$ is the maximum downward movement in the pay curve.

$Rec_{max\ up}$ and $Pay_{max\ dn}$ are calculated by multiplying the current floating index by the adjusted historical volatility measure.

To calculate a total REE, we need only adjust our RF_d by the total number of settlement periods in the transaction (recalling that settlement periods are less than the final maturity, given we are estimating forward rates). This is shown as:

$$REE = (RF_d \times y) \times N \qquad (8.6)$$

where y is the number of settlement periods.

We can follow the same procedure for a semi-annual settle diff swap, remembering to focus on the adjusted historical volatility of a 6-month index and the greater number of settlement periods. As a final note it should be remembered that the above factors can be discounted to the present utilizing any discount factor an institution finds relevant; we present the unaltered risk factor for simplicity. It is interesting to note that even after discounting our result by 6 per cent to yield an RF_d of 3.20 per cent, the risk factor for this 3-year differential swap (assuming the conservative stance) is higher than that of a single currency basis swap (generally estimated at approximately $1 - 2$ per cent for a 3-year transaction), a 6 per cent 3-year fixed/floating interest rate swap (1.8 per cent by our method in Appendix II), or a dual currency coupon swap (2.5 per

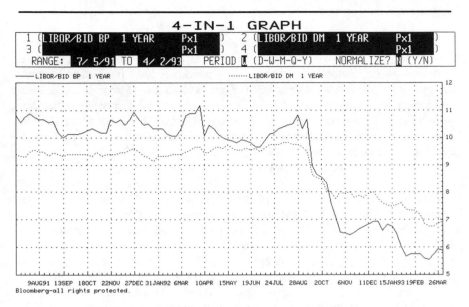

Figure 8.4   12-month sterling Libor versus 12-month DM Libor

Source: Bloomberg Financial Markets

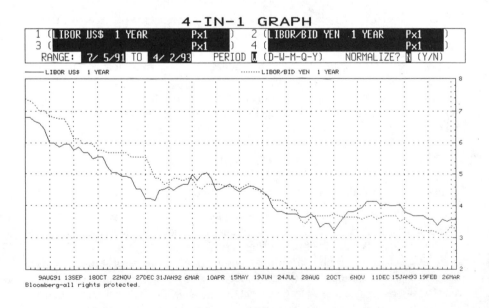

Figure 8.5   12-month yen Libor versus 12-month dollar Libor

Source: Bloomberg Financial Markets

cent assuming 2 per cent interest rate risk and 15 per cent p.a. movement in the DM/$ rate).

If our differential swap is leveraged in nature (and recall that these structures typically involve two Libor flows), we may choose to utilize the framework developed for inverse floater and leveraged swaps above. By utilizing a leverage factor *LF* in the equation we highlight in Equation 8.6, we have a means by which to assign risk to leveraged differential swaps. As with all other leveraged structures, the risk equivalent exposure will be considerably higher than that encountered on a standard diff and, as such, care must be taken when evaluating the suitability of the transaction for counterparties of lower credit quality.

We present above, for informational purposes, Figures 8.4 and 8.5 detailing the movement of various 12-month Libor rates over a period of time. Specifically, we show 12-month sterling Libor against 12-month DM Libor, and 12-month yen Libor versus 12-month dollar Libor. These graphs help to demonstrate why certain institutions employ differential swaps in their investment and risk management portfolios. By capturing the spread differentials without taking currency risk, an institution may effectively lower funding costs or enhance portfolio income. The figures provided demonstrate, however, that spreads are ever changing and that they can, on occasion, move in a fashion opposite of that intended by the investor.

Amortizing Swaps

We have mentioned above that amortizing swaps are those which have an uneven principal balance which generally (though certainly not always) declines on a straight line basis during the life of a transaction. Knowing that we are not dealing with the full notional amount for the entire duration of the swap, as we would with a typical swap, leads us to the conclusion that the risk assigned to an amortizing deal is less than that encountered in a deal with a static principal balance. There are, in fact, at least two means by which to assign risk to an amortizing deal: the average life method and the average risk method. Let us consider the two in light of the following parameters:

Bank X, our bank, is entering into a 5-year fixed/floating amortizing swap, where it will pay 10 per cent fixed on annual basis, against receipt of 12-month Libor, on a $100MM starting balance. The notional will amortize down on a straight line basis, such that principal will be reduced by $20MM each year. Our schedule of amortizing principal is, therefore:

Year	Notional
0	$100M
1	$ 80M
2	$ 60M
3	$ 40M
4	$ 20M
5	$ 0

If we utilize the average life method, we focus on a figure which gives us the average weighted value of the swap, measured in years. That is, the average maturity of the transaction is affected by the size of the notional principal. If we are referring to a straight 5-year, $100MM interest rate swap, our calculation would yield an average life of 5 years, since there is no decline in the notional principal balance. The average life can be derived by the following formula:

$$Average\ life = \frac{\sum (\ time \times amount\ prepaid\ )}{\sum amount\ prepaid} \qquad (8.7)$$

for the entire life of the swap (i.e. *time* = 0 to maturity). If we return to the cash flows above, we can calculate the average life of the swap in question:

Year	Notional	Amount Prepaid	Time*Amount Prepaid
0	$100MM	$ 0	$ 0
1	$ 80MM	$ 20MM	$ 20MM
2	$ 60MM	$ 20MM	$ 40MM
3	$ 40MM	$ 20MM	$ 60MM
4	$ 20MM	$ 20MM	$ 80MM
5	$ 0	$ 20MM	$100MM
	Sum =	$100MM	$300MM

By our formula above, we calculate the average life as 3 years ($300MM/$100MM). Utilizing this information, we may then assign a risk factor to the transaction which is based not on final maturity, but on the average life of the swap.

If we utilize the risk factors highlighted in Appendix II, we calculate the risk of a 5-year, 10 per cent fixed pay swap as $5.2MM (based on a 5.2 per cent risk factor). In contrast, a 3-year, 10 per cent fixed pay swap would yield risk of $2.7MM (based on a 2.7 per cent risk factor). Thus, our straight line amortizing swap carries considerably less risk than a standard 5-year swap, which is logical, since interest payments (and therefore potential replacement costs) are ever-declining. As a note, it should also be clear that the amortization schedule need not conform to a straight line basis or any regular or orderly decline; an average life can be calculated for any set of cash flows. To summarize, we can state that the calculation of swap risk, following the average life method, is:

$$REE = (RF_{AL} \times N) \tag{8.8}$$

where RF_{AL} is the risk factor associated with the average life of the swap, not the final maturity

A second method by which to value risk in an amortizing swap is the average risk approach. Under this scenario, an analyst would focus on the average risk of a series of swaps of declining notional amount and declining maturity. Returning to our example above, we can break the amortizing swap into a series of five separate transactions, as follows:

Swap 1: $100MM, 5 year, 10% fixed; $RF = 5.2\%$, $REE = \$5.2$MM

Swap 2: $ 80MM, 4 year, 10% fixed; $RF = 3.9\%$, $REE = \$3.1$MM

Swap 3: $ 60MM, 3 year, 10% fixed; $RF = 2.7\%$, $REE = \$1.6$MM

Swap 4: $ 40MM, 2 year, 10% fixed; $RF = 1.5\%$, $REE = \$0.6$MM

Swap 5: $ 20MM, 1 year, 10% fixed; $RF = 0.5\%$, $REE = \$0.1$MM

We know that the risk of the amortizing swap will not be the sum of the *REE* of these swaps, it will be the sum of the average of the *REE* of the swaps. That is, on average we will have in existence a transaction which is based on a series of swaps which replicate the declining notional and maturity characterizing the transaction. Our risk evaluation, therefore, focuses on the average *REE*, which we see is:

Swap 1: $REE = \$5.2$MM

Swap 2: $REE = \$3.1$MM

Swap 3: $REE = \$1.6$MM

Swap 4: $REE = \$0.6$MM

Swap 5: $REE = \$0.1$MM

Average $REE = \$10.6MM/5 = \$2.12$MM

This figure is $580,000 lower than the one calculated by the average life method (e.g the RF is 2.12 per cent vs. 2.7 per cent in the previous method). The average risk method may be summarized by the following formula:

$$REE = \frac{\sum_{t=1}^{n}(RF_t \times N_t)}{n} \qquad (8.9)$$

where RF_t is the risk factor for a given swap strip,

N_t is the notional for a given swap strip,

n is the number of swap strips comprising the amortizing swap.

To reiterate, the average risk method represents a figure which is a measure of the average credit risk of a series of swaps which, at any point in time, describe the swap at that particular instant. The average life method represents the risk of a theoretical swap where the average life is taken to be the final maturity for risk factor purposes. There is no 'right' way of valuing the credit risk in an amortizing structure; much is dependent on the preference of individual institutions.

Mortgage Swaps

Mortgage swaps are, in essence, a subset of amortizing swaps. Although a given mortgage swap may have certain distinct features which must be accounted for (particularly if non-Libor floating rate indexes are utilized, such as the 11th District Cost of Funds, which is a key long-term adjustable rate index), the standard mortgage swap structure can be examined in light of several key characteristics: fixed rate paid or received (generally monthly), final maturity of the swap and, most importantly, the amortization schedule of the swap. We have seen above the effect of a straight line amortization on the risk of a swap, which is to lower *REE* against a benchmark vanilla interest rate swap. In the same fashion, the amortizing characteristics of a mortgage swap will cause it to yield a lower *REE* figure than the plain vanilla structure.

As indicated in the product description above, most mortgage swaps which seek to duplicate specific FNMA, GNMA or FHLMC issues typically amortize on a monthly basis. This is in keeping with the monthly amortization of an actual *MBS*, or pool of *MBS*s. The accurate view of the *REE* on these transactions, then, is to determine the amortization schedule which lowers the principal balance of the swap. Once the actual declining balance of the swap is determined, an analyst may evaluate *REE* via one of the two amortizing swap methods indicated above.

It is worth noting that in a 5-year mortgage swap, with monthly amortization of principal, there will be 60 known or estimated changes to the balance. For a credit analyst attempting to calculate the risk of the swap by the average risk approach indicated above, the task would be onerous and unnecessarily precise. It would be more helpful and efficient, in fact, to utilize either the average life method, or the average risk method showing a declining balance every quarter or semi-annual period.

For mortgage swaps involving a fixed flow against Libor, the above procedures are correct. In the case of a swap involving two floating rate indexes on an amortizing principal, it is likely the analyst would choose to substitute standard fixed/floating risk factors for one which is representative of two floating rate indexes, which represents basis risk. As we have seen, basis risk factors are typically lower than standard interest rate swap factors, as movements in two floating rate indexes are more closely correlated than a fixed rate index and a floating rate index. In all cases it must be remembered that amortization of mortgage swap notionals is not an 'exact science'. Prepayment levels may well vary from those originally calculated. Nonetheless, it is unlikely that risk will be understated if the above methodology is utilized; in a worst case, there could be some slight overstatement, if amortization takes place faster than originally anticipated. However, any resulting overstatement would be modest, and should not impact credit decisions or exposure management.

Index Principal Swaps

As indicated above, index principal swaps (IPSs), may or may not amortize down during the life of a given transaction, depending on whether or not a floating index falls. If an IPS does not amortize down, the risk to the floating rate payer (the 'purchaser') will be akin to that of a vanilla swap. We may ignore the effects of the above market rate it is receiving from the 'seller'; if our bank were receiving the above market rate in exchange for providing the path-dependent option characterizing the IPS, it would not perform on its obligation (i.e. amortize the swap) if its counterparty defaulted. From the standpoint of the 'seller' it is clearly paying out an above market fixed rate and, as such, has this extra risk to account for, particularly if it pays the higher rate for several years during the 'lockout' period, only to have its counterparty default as amortization was due to begin. We may show the relevant formulae for IPS 'purchasers' and 'sellers' respectively as:

$$REE = (RFc \times N) \qquad (8.10)$$

and

$$REE = (RFc \times N) + NPV_{AM} \qquad (8.11)$$

where RFc is the risk factor,
N is the notional,
NPV_{AM} is the net present value of the above market rate paid over the life of the transaction.

Instead of counting the NPV as a lump-sum added to REE (perhaps by the method we introduce in Chapter 7), the 'seller' may adjust the RFc to show the higher above market rate it is paying.

This is clearly the most conservative stance which can be taken with regard to IPSs. We know from the amortizing swaps and mortgage swaps discussed above that any time amortization occurs, REE will be lower. Such is also the case with IPSs. Thus, if we ignore any amortization effects, we know that we will account for the worst case scenario which may occur during the life of the trade, which is simply that the full notional remains outstanding for the entire deal (e.g. that the path dependent option remains out-of-the-money).

If we wish to account for the changing value of the deal, which presumes the floating rate falls through some threshold after the lockout period, we can adjust our risk factor *RF* to reflect the new average life or average risk of the transaction. Since amortization implies a lower average life (which, as we discuss above, implies a lower risk factor), the adjustment can easily be made to the equation above (where the new *RFc* is based on fixed rate and average life, not final maturity). We may also choose to utilize the average risk method detailed in Equation 8.9.

We have presented above some of the increasingly common 'next step' swap structures which have been employed in the financial markets. There are obviously a great deal of additional swap instruments which exist; these are often simple variations on some of the structures mentioned above or, on occasion, they represent entirely new and unique structures. As one might imagine, the pace of innovation in this market is very fast, and new (or seemingly new) instruments appear with frequency. Whether a credit officer is dealing with the instruments detailed above, or one of the 'variations on the theme', care must obviously be exercised when considering and evaluating such transactions. Swap risk is long-term in nature and represents a vital and sensitive extension of credit. Not all complex swap transactions are suitable for every counterparty, particularly in unsecured form, and care must be exercised to ensure that the credit decision taken results in prudent action for bank and counterparty alike. As with all derivative products, when dealing with swap structures it is important for the credit analyst to be well aware of all aspects of the transaction so that a fair and concise evaluation of credit risk may be undertaken, and a prudent credit decision be made.

Appendices

Appendix 1: Option Valuation Methodology

We have mentioned at several points in this text how option valuation methodology is central to much of what product and credit professionals are doing with regard to derivatives. The seminal work in the area of option valuation is Black and Scholes (1973), where the two authors developed an approach to valuing European options under a certain set of assumptions, including:

(a) a world with no transaction costs or taxes;
(b) the movement of stock prices follows a continuous time stochastic process;
(c) the option is European-style on a non-dividend paying stock;
(d) there is a constant risk free rate, r, at which borrowing and lending occurs;
(e) short selling is allowable.

In addition the reader should refer to other excellent works on the topic (Cox and Rubinstein, 1985; Gibson, 1991; Hull, 1989; Merton, 1973). Many subsequent articles have sought to explain aspects of the Black–Scholes framework, or to introduce new equations or models which would allow some of the assumptions of the original model to be relaxed. For instance, the 'no dividend' restriction was dealt with by Merton in 1973; the 'continuous stock prices' by Cox and Ross in 1976; the 'European exercise only' by Roll in 1977; Geske in 1979; Whaley in 1981. We do not intend to review those models or equations in this Appendix. It is also not the intent of this Appendix to develop a detailed explanation of the mathematics of the Black–Scholes model. Instead, we highlight below a brief overview of the main points of the Black–Scholes model.

One of the key assumptions of the Black–Scholes model is that stock prices follow a stochastic process. In this case, prices follow what is known as a Geometric Brownian motion, where the returns of the stock prices are lognormally distributed (see Chapter 2 for additional detail). The stock price returns may be defined as:

$$\ln\left(\frac{S}{S_{t-1}}\right) \tag{AI.1}$$

Under the lognormal distribution the expected value of the stock at maturity of the option is:

$$E\,(S*) = Se^{\,(\mu - \frac{\sigma^2}{2})\tau} \qquad\qquad (AI.2)$$

where the price of the stock S, increases by the instantaneously compounded expected return, e to the μ, less half the variance times the maturity. Recall that this is precisely equal to our result in Equation 2.15 from Chapter 2. This is, of course, true because the natural log of the stock price has a normal distribution with an expected value of:

$$(\mu - \frac{\sigma^2}{2})\,\tau$$

(See Haley and Schall, 1979, for example.)

Black–Scholes (and other models) have shown that, because of both hedging and arbitraging, the investor will be indifferent to holding either a risk free bond or a short call/long stock position (or a long call/short stock position); since short-selling is allowed under the assumptions of the model, these two positions are precisely equal. Therefore, the option's value will not be impacted by the expected return denoted by μ above. Substituting the risk free rate, r, in the equation, the equation becomes:

$$E\,(S*) = Se^{\,-r\tau} \qquad\qquad (AI.3)$$

This is equivalent to saying the expected value of the stock $S*$, is equal to the stock price times the continuously compounded risk free rate.

It is also true, under the assumptions of the model and general arbitrage conditions, that the value of the call will be greater than, or equal to, the stock price less the discounted value of the strike price. That is:

$$C\,(S,X,\tau) \geq S - Xe^{\,-r\tau} \qquad\qquad (AI.4)$$

where S is the stock price,
                X is the strike price,
                τ is the time to maturity.

We may show this is true by comparing two portfolios: Portfolio 1 consists of a call $C(S, X,\tau)$ and a risk free bond paying a price equal to X at maturity. If we discount at a continuously compounded rate we know the current price of the bond is $Xe^{\wedge}(-r\tau)$ (e.g. a bond worth \$100 at maturity in one year is worth \$95.12 today if we discount at 5 per cent). Portfolio 2 is equal to a share of stock S. These two portfolios are, of course, consistent with our statement above which says that the investor will be indifferent to holding a risk free bond or a short call/long stock position (which is identical to holding a risk free bond/long call or long stock, as in Portfolios 1 and 2).

One of two events may occur at maturity: $S < X$, or $X < = S$. The value of Portfolio 1 when $S < X$ will be $0 + X$ (that is, the call will have no value, and our risk free bond will have a value of X). Portfolio 2 will be worth S. Therefore, the value of Portfolio 1 must be greater than the value of Portfolio 2, or else an inequality would exist (i.e. if Portfolio 1 is not greater than Portfolio 2, that is equivalent to saying that $X < S$; we have already said, however, that the price at maturity is $S < X$). If at maturity $X <= S$, the value of Portfolio 1 will be $(S - X) + X$, or S, and the value of Portfolio 2 will be S. Thus, the two portfolios will be equal, which is consistent with our original statement. Based on the above, then, we know the following condition holds true:

$$C\,(S, X, \tau) + Xe^{-r\tau} \geq S \qquad\qquad \text{(AI.5)}$$

or

$$C\,(S, X, \tau) > S - Xe^{-r\tau} \qquad\qquad \text{(AI.6)}$$

This is an integral component of the Black–Scholes equation and is used in the general form of the equation for calls:

$$C = SN\,(d_1) - Xe^{-r\tau} N\,(d_2) \qquad\qquad \text{(AI.7)}$$

where $N(d_1)$ and $N(d_2)$, defined below, represent the cumulative probability distribution function for a standardized normal variable (indicating the probability that the variable will be less than a certain amount). The $N(d)$ values can be obtained from standard tables of probability functions.

The values of d_1 and d_2 are shown as:

$$d_1 = \frac{\ln\left(\dfrac{S}{X}\right)(r + \dfrac{\sigma^2}{2})\,\tau}{\sigma\sqrt{\tau}} \qquad\qquad \text{(AI.8)}$$

and

$$d_2 = \frac{\ln\left(\dfrac{S}{X}\right) + (r - \dfrac{\sigma^2}{2})\tau}{\sigma\sqrt{\tau}} \qquad\qquad \text{(AI.9)}$$

where d_2 may also be expressed as:

$$d_2 = d_1 - \sigma\sqrt{\tau} \qquad\qquad \text{(AI.10)}$$

The variables under the equations above are defined as:

r is the risk free rate,
X is the strike price,
S is the current price,
τ is the time to maturity,
σ is the volatility.

We shall not discuss the detailed development of C, d_1 and d_2. We note simply that C is the discounted expected value of the call at maturity of the option. Through this formula, one can determine the value of a European call option on a non-dividend paying stock, under the constraints detailed above.

Knowing the above, and employing put–call parity, it is relatively easy to find that the Black–Scholes equation for puts is:

$$P = Xe^{-r\tau} N(-d_2) - SN(-d_1) \tag{AI.11}$$

Let us consider a numerical example in order to demonstrate the model. Assume we want to purchase a European call on a stock with a current price of 20 and a strike price of 22 (i.e. it is 9 per cent out-of-the-money); expiry is in 3 months (90 days). Recall that τ, time to maturity, would be adjusted to a fraction of a year if our volatility measure is annualized; in this case τ would equal 0.25 years. The risk free rate, as dictated by the US Government 3-month bill, is 4 per cent. The volatility of the stock has been observed at 20 per cent. The fair value of the call is calculated via the following:

$d_1 = (ln(20/22) + (0.04 + (0.20^2/2) * 0.25))/(0.20 * \sqrt{0.25})$
$d_1 = ((-0.0953) + (0.015))/.10$
$d_1 = -0.803$

$d_2 = -0.803 - 0.10 = -0.903$

$C = 20 * N(-0.803) - 22 * (0.99) * N(-0.903)$

Turning to statistical tables we determine the probabilities associated with $N(d_1)$ and $N(d_2)$:

$C = 20 * (1 - 0.7967) - 22 * 0.99 * (1 - 0.8238)$
$C = 4.066 - 3.837$
$C = 0.229$

Thus, one call on the stock would be worth nearly $0.23.

If we apply the same procedure to an in-the-money call (i.e. the price S is now \$24, instead of \$20, with the strike remaining at \$22), the value of the call will rise:

$$d_1 = (ln(24/22) + (0.04 + (0.20^2/2) * 0.25))/(0.20 * \sqrt{0.25})$$
$$d_1 = ((0.087) + (0.015))/0.10$$
$$d_1 = 1.020$$

$$d_2 = 1.020 - 0.10 = 0.920$$

$$C = 24 * N(1.020) - 22 * (0.99) * N(0.920)$$
$$C = 24 * 0.8461 - 22 * (0.99) * 0.8212$$
$$C = 20.306 - 17.885$$
$$C = 2.421$$

As one might expect, the value of the in-the-money call is much higher than the out-of-the-money call, at \$2.42 vs. \$0.23.

These are the results obtained by the Black–Scholes model which, despite its constraints, is widely used in the derivatives markets.

In Chapter 4 we mentioned, in brief, the terms delta, theta, lambda and gamma. These are measures which allow us to see how the price of an option reacts to changes in the stock price, time and volatility; in the case of gamma it also reveals how the delta of the option reacts to a change in the price of the stock. Utilizing the Black–Scholes model, we show the equations (though not the derivations of the equations) which capture these mathematical relationships.

Delta
It can be shown that delta (how much the option price changes for a unit change in the price of the stock) is equal to the first derivative of the option price with respect to the stock price:

$$\frac{\partial C}{\partial S} = \Delta_c = N(d_1) \tag{AI.12}$$

The quantity we obtain from $N(d_1)$ above is precisely equal to delta. We shall not explore the mathematics behind this, but we may interpret the above as saying that a short call is delta hedged by an amount of long stock equal to $N(d_1)$; conversely, a long call is delta hedged by an amount of short stock equal to $N(d_1)$. The equation for puts is:

$$\frac{\partial P}{\partial S} = \Delta_p = -N(-d_1) \tag{AI.13}$$

Returning to our in-the-money call example above, we note that the result obtained from $N(d_1)$ is equal to 0.846. This means that a portfolio would be delta hedged when a short call is offset by 0.846 shares of long stock; alternatively, a long call is hedged by shorting 0.846 shares of stock. This also means that if the stock moves up by \$1, the value of the call will move up by \$0.846.

We can apply similar explanation to the other properties. Gamma, which is the change in the delta of the option for a unit change in the stock price, is the first derivative of delta with respect to the stock price, or the second derivative of the option price with respect to the stock price. These may be shown as:

$$\frac{\partial \Delta_c}{\partial S} = \frac{\partial^2 C}{\partial S^2} = \Gamma_c = \frac{1}{S \sigma \sqrt{\tau}} N'(d_1) \qquad \text{(AI.14)}$$

where

$$N'(d_1) = \frac{1}{\sqrt{2\pi}} e^{\frac{-d_1^2}{2}} \qquad \text{(AI.15)}$$

The first derivative of $N(d_1)$ is the standard normal density function. This result is always positive, so we know that a change in the call option price (when the stock price changes by some unit amount) will be greater since the stock price is greater.

The gamma of a put is shown as:

$$\frac{\partial \Delta_p}{\partial S} = \frac{\partial^2 P}{\partial S^2} = \Gamma_p = \frac{1}{S \sigma \sqrt{\tau}} N'(d_1) \qquad \text{(AI.16)}$$

which is precisely equal to the gamma of a call. This indicates, of course, that the rate of change of the put option for a given unit change in the stock price is equal to that of a call; as with calls, the price change in the put is greater as the stock price is greater.

Returning to our example, we may calculate the gamma of the call as:

gamma = $1/(24 * (0.20 * \sqrt{0.25})) * N'(d_1)$
gamma = $0.4167 * N'(d_1)$

$N'(d_1) = 1/(2.507) * e \wedge (-0.520)$
$N'(d_1) = 0.2371$

gamma = $0.4167 * 0.2371$
gamma = 0.0988

Thus, for a \$1 increase in the stock price, the delta of the option rises by \$0.099.

Theta

Theta, which is the change in the price of an option for a change in the time to maturity, is simply the derivative of the option price with respect to the time to maturity. This is shown as:

$$-\frac{\partial C}{\partial \tau} = \Theta_c = -\frac{S\sigma}{2\sqrt{\tau}} N'(d_1) - r X e^{-r\tau} N(d_2) \qquad (AI.17)$$

where $N'(d_1)$ and $N(d_2)$ are defined above. Note the derivative of the call option price with respect to the price, if positive, yields a value greater than 0. The positive value of the derivative says that an option with a longer time to maturity, τ, has more value than an option with a shorter τ. However, we are interested, via theta, in determining how the price of the option deteriorates as time to maturity decreases (through some small interval t), hence use of a negative in the equation above.

The theta for puts is simply:

$$-\frac{\partial P}{\partial \tau} = \Theta_p = -\frac{S\sigma}{2\sqrt{\tau}} N'(d_1) + r X e^{-r\tau} N(-d_2) \qquad (AI.18)$$

In the case of an at-the-money European put, theta may not be negative; much will depend on the interaction between τ and the present value of the strike price. In our example, the theta of the call is equal to:

theta $= -((24 * 0.20)/(2 * \sqrt{0.25})) * 0.2371) - (0.04 * 22 * 0.99 * 0.8212)$
theta $= -(4.8) * 0.2371 - 0.7154$
theta $= -1.138 - 0.7154$
theta $= -1.853$

This says that if the time to maturity for the call were increased by one year, the value of the call would increase by $1.853. We may also say that the actual daily decay in the value of the call is simply equal to $1.853/365, or $0.005 (recalling that our volatility and maturity measures were on an annual basis and must be transferred to a daily basis by dividing by 365). This illustrates the effect of the time value component of the option pricing mechanism.

Lambda

In the instance of lambda (or *vega*), the change in the price of the option for a change in the volatility in the underlying stock, the derivative of the option price with respect to volatility is shown as:

$$\frac{\partial C}{\partial \sigma} = \Lambda_{cVp} = S\sqrt{\tau} N'(d_1) \qquad (AI.19)$$

203

The same equation is used for puts. If lambda is high, the option price denoted by C or P will be very sensitive to small changes in volatility. If lambda is low, C and P will be less sensitive to such changes. In our example, we can show the value of lambda as:

$$\text{lambda} = 24 * \sqrt{0.25} * 0.2371$$
$$\text{lambda} = 2.845$$

Thus, for an increase in the volatility of the underlying stock from 20 per cent to 21 per cent, the price of the call will increase by $0.028; for an increase from 20 per cent to 30 per cent, the price of the call will increase by $0.2845, and for an increase from 20 per cent to 120 per cent, the price will increase by $2.845.

This Appendix is intended only as a brief primer on Black–Scholes. Readers are strongly urged to consult other references. Eades, 1992, contains a simple, non-technical discussion; Dubofsky, 1992, contains a very concise discussion with good numerical examples; while Cox and Rubinstein, 1985, Haley and Schall, 1979, Hull, 1989, Merton, 1990, Gibson, 1991, and Cheung and Yeung, 1992, contain more complex mathematical discussions. Readers should also consult the above references for an understanding of the Binomial model developed by Cox, Ross and Rubinstein, as well as other models used in the pricing of options.

Appendix 2: A Model for Calculating Swap Risk

In Chapter 7 we outlined in general form a number of ways by which swap risk may be calculated. There is no single correct way to value the fractional or potential market exposure portion of a given swap; much is dependent on the individual views of individual institutions as well as any regulatory requirements which may exist. We present below one method of calculating swap risk; it is drawn largely from a previous work by this author (Banks, 1993, Chapter 13) and readers may wish to reference the original discussion (as well as the Appendix discussion) for additional information.

The Model

We have seen in Chapter 7 that the main components of any simulation-based potential market exposure model are (a) a method by which to simulate future interest rate movements and (b) an equation to compute the replacement cost based on simulated future rates. The combination of the two allows us to develop a risk factor for a swap with particular maturity and rate parameters; it is, effectively, our percentage measure of fractional exposure for a swap with those parameters. When we apply the *RF* to the notional of a swap, we obtain an *REE* which, on day one, is comprised solely of fractional exposure. Over time, as *RF*s decline, potential market exposure will decline (though potential exposure may increase if the swap's mark-to-market value, or actual exposure, increases). This concept is, in many respects, akin to a standard option pricing concept, where the value of the option is comprised of time value (potential market exposure) and intrinsic value (actual exposure). Our goal in this Appendix is to develop a method by which to value potential market exposure, and we begin by discussing a method of simulating future interest rates.

The Binomial Option Pricing Model developed by Cox, Ross and Rubinstein, 1979, suggests that the 'up' and 'down' movements of a stochastic variable (such as stock prices or interest rates) may be described by:

$$u = e^{\sigma\sqrt{\tau/n}} \qquad \text{(AII.1)}$$

and

$$d = e^{-\sigma\sqrt{\tau/n}} \qquad \text{(AII.2)}$$

with probabilities defined by:

$$q = \tfrac{1}{2} + \tfrac{1}{2} \left((\mu/\sigma) \sqrt{\tau/n} \right) \qquad \text{(AII.3)}$$

Note that it can be shown that the mean and variance of the binomial process converge to the mean and variance of the lognormal diffusion process described in Chapter 2 as *n* moves to infinity (see Gibson, 1991).

Rendleman and Bartter, 1980, adapted the above equations for the modelling of interest rates by incorporating several simple assumptions: namely, the growth rate of the stochastic variable (the interest rate) is constant, the volatility of the variable is constant and the market price of risk is constant. For our purposes, these assumptions are reasonable. Readers are urged to review the original work cited above. Readers may also wish to reference Hull, 1989, for a detailed explanation of the Rendleman and Bartter Model, and other equations (of varying degrees of sophistication and with varying assumptions and conditions) which may be used to model interest rate movements (e.g. the Black–Derman–Toy Model, the Vasicek Model, the Ho and Lee Model, the Cox, Ingersoll and Ross Model). The Rendleman and Bartter equations are given by:

$$u = e^{s \sqrt{\Delta t}} \qquad \text{(AII.4)}$$

and

$$d = e^{-s\sqrt{\Delta} t} \qquad \text{(AII.5)}$$

With the Rendleman and Bartter Model we focus on the upward movement of rates for fixed rate payers (which is when risk increases), and downward movement of rates for fixed rate receivers (which is also when risk increases). Adapting these equations to terms which we have covered in Chapter 2, we may state that Δt represents the time change in small intervals. In a Markov process a long interval becomes *T*, which is precisely equal to the *T* we utilize in Chapter 2 of this text (and represents a cumulative, not interval, time frame). The appropriate standard deviation measure in a stochastic Markov model is equal to *s* for samples and σ for populations. In Chapter 2 we have defined the standard deviation of rates as the historical volatility of rates *HV*, after an adjustment to the appropriate confidence level. Utilizing our own terminology, we can adjust the two equations as follows.

Upward movements:

$$u = e^{(H V \sqrt{T})} \qquad \text{(AII.6)}$$

Downward movements:

$$d = e^{(-H V \sqrt{T})} \qquad \text{(AII.7)}$$

With these equations providing information on the possible direction of future rates, we can set new rates equal to original rates times the upward (or downward) movement estimated by the equations above. For a fixed rate payer this would be:

$$r_n = r_0 \times e^{(HV\sqrt{T})} \qquad\qquad \text{(AII.8)}$$

And, for a fixed rate receiver:

$$r_n = r_0 \times e^{(-HV\sqrt{T})} \qquad\qquad \text{(AII.9)}$$

If we assume original rates today to be 10 per cent and historical volatility of interest rates to be 16 per cent (lognormally distributed and adjusted to a 90 per cent confidence level), we obtain the following results:

Time	r_0	r_n (up)	r_n (down)
0.5	10.00%	11.19%	8.93%
1.0	10.00%	11.74%	8.52%
1.5	10.00%	12.16%	8.22%
2.0	10.00%	12.54%	7.97%
2.5	10.00%	12.88%	7.76%
3.0	10.00%	13.19%	7.57%
3.5	10.00%	13.49%	7.41%
4.0	10.00%	13.77%	7.26%
4.5	10.00%	14.04%	7.12%
5.0	10.00%	14.30%	7.00%
5.5	10.00%	14.55%	6.87%
6.0	10.00%	14.80%	6.76%
6.5	10.00%	15.00%	6.65%
7.0	10.00%	15.27%	6.55%
7.5	10.00%	15.50%	6.45%
8.0	10.00%	15.72%	6.36%
8.5	10.00%	15.94%	6.27%
9.0	10..00%	16.16%	6.19%
9.5	10.00%	16.37%	6.10%
10.0	10.00%	16.58%	6.02%

We have just established the initial part of the potential market exposure framework utilizing the Rendleman and Bartter Model. There are, of course, many other means by which to model interest rates; this is but one approach an institution may consider.

Note that the above could be incorporated into a broad Monte Carlo simulation, such as discussed in Chapter 7, where a large number of realizations would yield an average value for the future path of interest rates at select points in time (in our case, semi-annually).

We now turn our attention to the replacement cost calculation. The standard replacement cost equation sums the difference between the new coupon on the swap (r_n) and the original coupon on the swap (r_0) over the number of periods remaining until maturity, discounted back by the new coupon rate (i.e. the coupon rate in existence at the time of default). This process is similar in theory to a standard mark-to-market calculation covered in Chapters 5 and 7. The equation provides an estimate of how much it will cost to replace a swap in the future (at the time of default) utilizing simulated future rates.

The use of replacement cost equation tends to be fairly standard across the industry, and may be defined as:

$$r_d = \sum_{x=1}^{p} \left(\frac{\frac{(r_n - r_0)}{t}}{\left(1 + \frac{r_n}{t}\right)^x} \right) \tag{AII.10}$$

where
r_n is the new rate in period x,
r_0 is the original rate,
p is the number of periods until maturity,
t is the frequency of payments under the swap.

The reader will recognize this as a form of Equation 5.8, our mark-to-market calculation.

We may also wish to show the above equation (which we term the calculated replacement cost) in today's terms. We do this by discounting back to today's terms using r_0:

$$r = \frac{r_d}{(1 + r_0)^q} \tag{AII.11}$$

where q is the period in which the default occurs.

We term this equation the discounted replacement cost.

The maximum result obtained by r will effectively be the risk factor *RF* for a swap with the defining parameters of final maturity and original starting rate; this may also be thought of as the maximum replacement cost we are likely to encounter during the life of the swap. This is our version of the BIS's credit conversion factor under the *CEM*.

Since we now have a framework for calculating upward and downward movements in rates and a replacement cost equation, we can complete an example which demonstrates the full development of a risk factor. Highlighted below is a five-year fixed/floating interest rate swap, with 16 per cent historical volatility, 10 per cent original rate for the fixed payer, and semiannual flow. Per the Rendleman and Bartter equations above:

Time	r_0	r_n (up)
0.5	10.00%	11.19%
1.0	10.00%	11.74%
1.5	10.00%	12.16%
2.0	10.00%	12.54%
2.5	10.00%	12.88%
3.0	10.00%	13.19%
3.5	10.00%	13.49%
4.0	10.00%	13.77%
4.5	10.00%	14.04%
5.0	10.00%	14.30%

Utilizing the simulated rates above in the calculated replacement cost equation (recalling that we compare r_n with r_0 at each semi-annual period), we obtain a discounted calculation for each semi-annual period of the 5-year swap:

Individual r_d terms (per cent)								
Number of periods remaining in swap life								
n	1	2	3	4	5	6	7	8	9
0.5	0.37	0.39	0.41	0.43	0.46	0.48	0.51	0.54	0.57
1	0.55	0.58	0.62	0.65	0.69	0.73	0.77	0.82	
1.5	0.72	0.76	0.81	0.86	0.91	0.96	1.00		
2	0.88	0.94	0.99	1.06	1.12	1.20			
2.5	1.05	1.12	1.19	1.27	1.35				
3	1.24	1.32	1.41	1.50					
3.5	1.44	1.53	1.64						
4	1.65	1.76							
4.5	1.89								
5	0.00								

Summing the individual calculated replacement cost terms above for each time period yields r_d, our total calculated replacement cost. Discounting back using r_0 yields the discounted replacement cost, r.

n	r_d (per cent)	r (per cent)
0.5	4.1	4.0
1.0	5.4	4.9
1.5	6.0	5.2
2.0	6.2	5.1
2.5	6.0	4.7
3.0	5.5	4.1
3.5	4.6	3.3
4.0	3.4	2.3
4.5	1.9	1.2
5.0	0.0	0.0

From above we note the maximum value of r is 5.2 per cent, occurring in year 1.5. This information indicates that the maximum replacement cost (and, hence, the maximum risk) we are likely to face under the above scenario is 5.2 per cent of the notional amount of the swap. We can say, therefore, that our risk factor RF for a 5-year, 10 per cent fixed pay swap is 5.2 per cent.

The reader may wonder, at this stage, why the maximum risk under this transaction occurs in year 1.5; why not in year 1 or year 4, for example? The answer to this question lies in a phenomenon known as the 'diffusion and amortization' effect. If one plots the maturity of the swap transaction on the x-axis and the replacement cost along the y-axis, we observe that the maximum risk occurs not at the beginning or end of the swap, but at some point in between. This interaction is highlighted in Figure A2.1.

The reason for the 'diffusion and amortization' effect is relatively easy to explain: simulated future rates used in the calculation of replacement cost will not have had a chance to move sufficiently in the early periods to pose the greatest economic loss (this is the 'diffusion' effect); and, insufficient payments remain to be made towards the end of the swap to pose the greatest economic loss (this is the 'amortization' effect). As a result, the greatest economic loss will occur at some point in between, when rates have had a chance to move and when there are still enough swap payments remaining to be made. Depending on the historical volatility used, the maximum replacement cost will occur ⅓ to ½ through the life of the swap. We can see in the example above that the maximum point on the 5-year swap under 16 per cent volatility conditions is reached in year 1.5, precisely ⅓ through the life of the transaction.

Once the equations above have been used to produce the series of replacement costs (discounted to today's value) it is relatively easy to create a table for risk factors (RF) to be used for easy calculation of swap risk. The procedure generally entails creating data tables with a range of fixed rates, say 5 per cent to 12 per cent, and a range of maturities, from 1 year to 10 or 15 years. We may also replicate the procedure for fixed receive swaps where our simulated rates are based on Equation A.II.9; this will yield

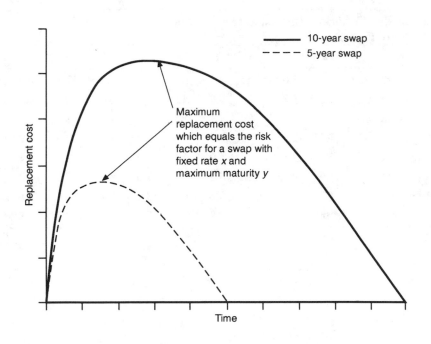

Figure AII.1   Swap replacement costs

a slightly different set of *RF*s. Such tables should encompass a normal range of likely swap rates and maturities; for each rate and each maturity, *the maximum replacement cost calculated by the method above becomes the risk factor for that maturity.* This risk factor (or replacement cost) is then multiplied by the notional to obtain *REE.* Over the course of the swap, it is entirely appropriate for the risk factors to be lowered to reflect the fractional exposure attributable to the remaining maturity.

Highlighted below are sample risk factors based on the model discussed earlier in this Appendix. The factors are based on Treasury rates with a 16 per cent historical volatility (after being adjusted to a 90 per cent confidence level, lognormal distribution). Factors are shown for fixed rates from 5 per cent to 12 per cent, and for maturities from 1 year to 10 years. This range of rates and maturities includes the most likely scenarios to be encountered by an analyst approving a transaction. As detailed earlier, the risk factor for a given swap with fixed rate x and final maturity y is simply the maximum replacement cost for a swap with those characteristics when the adjusted historical volatility is 16 per cent. For example, in applying the model presented in this Appendix, a 10-year, 10 per cent fixed rate swap will have a maximum replacement cost of 10.7 per cent, occurring in year 3. Therefore, the relevant factor to encompass the maximum point of risk is 10.7 per cent. An analyst or credit committee seeking to approve a $100MM swap with such parameters would assign an *REE* of $10.7MM to the transaction.

Sample Risk Factors for Interest Rate Swaps and Derivatives (per cent) (Fixed Payer)

Year	1	2	3	4	5	6	7	8	9	10
5 per cent	0.3	0.8	1.0	1.5	2.3	3.9	4.9	5.8	7.2	7.6
6 per cent	0.3	1.0	1.8	2.7	3.6	4.6	5.6	6.6	8.1	8.5
7 per cent	0.4	1.1	2.1	3.0	4.1	5.1	6.2	7.3	8.8	9.3
8 per cent	0.4	1.3	2.3	3.4	4.5	5.6	6.7	7.8	9.4	9.9
9 per cent	0.5	1.4	2.5	3.7	4.9	6.1	7.2	8.3	9.9	10.4
10 per cent	0.5	1.5	2.7	3.9	5.2	6.4	7.6	8.7	10.3	10.7
11 per cent	0.6	1.7	2.9	4.2	5.5	6.8	8.0	9.1	10.6	11.1
12 per cent	0.6	1.8	3.1	4.5	5.8	7.1	8.3	9.4	10.9	11.3

Appendix 3: Twenty Questions for the Derivatives Desk

Listed below are a series of twenty questions that may be put to a derivatives specialist seeking credit approval for a given transaction.

For All Structures

1. Can you explain the transaction in detail as you would to your client?

2. What is the notional amount of the transaction? Is there any amortization involved?

3. What underlying index is being utilized to determine amounts payable or receivable (e.g. interest rate, currency rate, equity index, equity price, etc.), and what are the starting levels? In the case of a currency swap, is there a full exchange of principal at inception and maturity?

4. What is the frequency of payment and receipt under the structure? Are there any payment mismatches?

5. Is there some upfront or off-market payment the bank is paying to, or receiving from, the customer? Are any of the flows or coupons constructed in an off-market fashion, or is there a leverage component?

6. What is the final maturity of the transaction?

7. Are there any options to terminate or other ways to extricate the bank from the transaction, for credit reasons? Is there a periodic mark-to-market?

8. Has the client signed, or will it sign, standard documentation governing the transaction?

9. Are there any special legal, credit, operational or risk management issues to consider?

To the Extent Derivative Structure is Contemplated:

The above questions, if necessary, plus:

10. Which side, if any, will be paying the appreciation or depreciation in the index? If the bank is payer if the index appreciates, is it expecting to be a receiver if the index depreciates (or is the payoff set at 0? i.e. is this a call swap or a call/put swap)?

11. What are the relevant starting and strike levels which will determine payoff?

12. How frequently is the current market level compared with the index level to determine payoff? Is the transaction structured as a series of forwards?

13. Has there been any unusual volatility in the underlying index recently which might cause an upward revision in risk factors?

14. Does the swap structure contain an embedded option?

15. What does the option allow the customer, or the bank, to do (i.e. knock-in, knock-out, lookback, digital, preference, outperformance, etc.)?

16. When does the option expire?

17. What is the exercise type of the option (i.e. American, European, Asian)?

18. If the bank is long the option, how is premium being paid? If it is short, how is premium being received (e.g. Libor flow, upfront payment, etc.)?

19. Is there a quanto protecting one side or the other from currency movements?

20. If an option spread transaction is involved, can the two 'legs' be split apart, or are they documented as a single transaction?

There are, naturally, other questions which can be asked, depending on the specific circumstances (i.e. if collateral is being posted, how much/what quality). This is only a sample listing, but one which should cover the main issues involved from a credit perspective, and allow a rational credit decision to be made.

Bibliography

Aldred, P. (1987) *Convertibles and Warrants* (London: Euromoney).

Antl, B. (Ed.) (1986) *Swap Finance, Volume 2* (London: Euromoney).

Arak, M., Goodman, L. and Rones, A. (1986) 'Credit lines for new instruments: swaps, over-the-counter options, forwards, and floor-ceiling agreements', *Proceedings from a Conference on Bank Structure and Competition* (Federal Reserve Bank of Chicago), May, pp.437–456.

Azarchs, T. (1992) 'Banks face manageable risks in derivative business', *Standard & Poor's Creditweek*, 9 November, pp.46–51.

Australian Financial Review (1993) Derivatives Survey, January 28.

Bacon, K. (1992) 'Risk to banks from derivatives still too high', *Asian Wall Street Journal*, 3 November, p.23.

Bank of Japan (1993) *Quarterly Bulletin*, May, **1**, No. 2.

Banks, E. (1993) *The Credit Risk of Financial Instruments* (London: Macmillan Press).

Behof, J. (1993) 'Reducing credit risk in OTC derivatives', *Federal Reserve Bank of Chicago Economic Perspective*, January–February, pp.21–31.

Beidelman, C. (Ed.) (1991) *Interest Rate Swaps* (Homewood, Illinois: Business One Irwin).

Bennett, R (1993) 'Rocket scientists produce a fresh wave of solutions', *Euromoney*, March, pp.46–54.

Bensman, M. (1992) 'Derivatives – Too damn smart...', *Global Custodian*, September, pp.132–137.

Bhala, R. (1992) *Perspectives on Risk Based Capital* (Tokyo: Toppan).

215

Black, F. and Scholes M. (1973) 'The pricing of options and corporate liabilities', *Journal of Political Economy,* May–June, pp.637–659.

Board of Governors of the Federal Reserve System and The Bank of England (1987) 'Potential Credit Exposure on Interest Rate and Foreign Exchange Related Instruments,' joint working paper, March.

Boyle, P. (1977) 'Options: A Monte Carlo approach', *Journal of Financial Economics,* **4**, pp.323–338.

Brady, S. (1992) 'Derivatives sprout bells and whistles', *Euromoney,* September, pp. 29–39.

Brady, S. (1992) 'Derivatives – Riding the US yield curve', *Euromoney,* April, pp.12–13.

Brookes, M. (1993) 'The search for a better model of volatility', *Euromoney,* March, pp.55–56.

Chase Securities (1992) 'Mundane problems, exotic solutions', *Euromoney,* August, pp.42–48.

Cheung, M. and Yeung, D.(1992) *Pricing Foreign Exchange Options* (Hong Kong: Hong Kong University Press).

Chew, L. (1992a) 'A bit of a jam', *Risk,* September, pp.82–93.

Chew, L. (1992b) 'Exotic tastes', *Risk,* October, pp.32–36.

Chew, L. (1993a) 'Quanto leap', *Risk,* April, pp.21–28.

Chew, L. (1993b) 'Good, bad and indifferent', *Risk,* June, pp.30–36.

Connolly, K. and Philips, G. (1992) *Japanese Warrant Markets* (London: Macmillan Press).

Cookson, R. (1993) 'Dangerous liaisons', *Risk,* March, pp.30–36.

Corrigan, T. (1992) 'SEC issues warning over derivatives operations', *Financial Times,* 2 December, p.22.

Corrigan, T. (1992) 'SEC and regulators deadlocked over capital requirements', *Financial Times,* 30 October, p.34.

Corrigan, T. (1992) 'Growing concern over the dangers of counterparty credit', *Financial Times*, 30 November, p.17.

Cox, J and Ross, S. (1975) 'The pricing of options for jump process', working paper (University of Pennsylvania).

Cox, J and Ross, S. (1976) 'The valuation of options for alternative stochastic processes', *Journal of Financial Economics*, **3**, pp.145–66.

Cox, J., Ross, S. and Rubinstein, M. (1979) 'Option pricing: a simplified approach', *Journal of Financial Economics*, **7**, pp.229–263.

Cox, J. and Rubinstein M. (1985) *Options Markets* (Englewood, New Jersey: Prentice Hall).

Das, S. (1991) *Swap Financing* (London: IFR Publishing).

Dubofsky, D. (1992) *Options and Financial Futures: Valuation and Uses* (New York: McGraw Hill).

Duffie, D. (1989) *Futures Markets* (Englewood, New Jersey: Prentice Hall).

Eades, S. (1992) *Options Hedging and Arbitrage* (Chicago: Probus).

The Economist (1990) 'Japan's warrant hangover', 8 September, pp.95–6.

The Economist (1992) 'Securities regulation – capital spat', 31 October, pp.80–81.

Euromoney (1990) 'Inside the global derivatives market', *Euromoney Supplement*, November.

Euromoney (1991) 'Derivatives: The markets mature', *Euromoney Supplement*, July.

Falloon, W. (1993) 'Much ado about nothing', *Risk*, February, p.72.

Fabozzi, F. and Modigliani, F. (1992) *Capital Markets – Institutions and Instruments* (Englewood, New Jersey: Prentice Hall).

Felgran, S. (1987) 'Interest rate swaps: use, risk and prices', *New England Economic Review,* November–December, pp.22–32.

Ferron, M. and Handjinicolaou, G. (1987) 'Understanding swap credit risk', *Journal of International Securities Markets,* Winter, pp.135–148.

217

Field, P. and Jaycobs, R. (Eds) (1992) *From Black–Scholes to Black Holes: New Frontiers in Options* (London: Risk).

Financial Times Survey (1992) 'Derivatives', 8 December.

Fitzgerald, M.D. (1987) *Financial Options* (London: Euromoney Publications).

Gastineau, G. (1979) *The Stock Options Manual*, 2nd ed. (New York: McGraw-Hill).

Geske, R. (1979) 'The valuation of compound options', *Journal of Financial Economics*, **7**, March, pp.63–81.

Giberti, D., Mentini, M. and Scabellone, P. (1993) 'The valuation of credit risk in swaps: methodological issues and empirical results', *Journal of Fixed Income*, March pp.24–37.

Gibson, R. (1991) *Option Valuation* (New York: McGraw-Hill).

Gramm, W. (1992) 'Plus ça change', *Risk*, October, p.88.

Group of Thirty (1993) 'Derivatives: Practices and Principles, Appendix 1: Working Papers'.

Haley, C. and Schall, L. (1979) *The Theory of Financial Decisions*, 2nd ed. (New York: McGraw-Hill).

Hansell, S. (1991) 'Risk collectors', *Institutional Investor*, September, pp.69–76.

Hansell, S. and Muehring K. (1992) 'Why derivatives rattle the regulators', *Institutional Investor*, September, pp.103–116.

Hines, W. and Montgomery, D. (1990) *Probability and Statistics in Engineering and Management Science,* 3rd ed. (New York: John Wiley & Sons).

Hull, J. (1989) *Options, Futures and Other Derivative Securities* (Englewood, New Jersey: Prentice Hall).

Hull, J. and White, A. (1987) 'The pricing of options on assets with stochastic volatilities', *Journal of Finance*, **42**, pp.281–300.

Hull, J. and White, A. (1992) 'The price of default', *Risk*, September, pp.101–103.

Hunter, W. and Stowe, D. (1992) 'Path dependent options', *Federal Reserve Board of Atlanta Economic Review,* March–April, pp.29–34.

Hunter, W. and Stowe, D. (1992) 'Path dependent options: valuation and applications', *Federal Reserve Board of Atlanta Economic Review,* July–August, pp.30–43.

Institutional Investor (1991) 'Derivatives dynamos', May, pp.111–116.

Institutional Investor Forum (1992) 'Derivatives of the future', *Supplement to Institutional Investor,* December.

International Financing Review (1992) 'IOSCO Meeting,' 31 October, p.48.

International Financing Review (1992) 'Derivative instruments' 31 October, p.90.

International Financing Review (1992) 'Management fears loss of derivatives control', 5 December, p.88.

International Financing Review (1993) 'Derivative Instruments: correlation cornered by risk', 20 February, p.94.

International Financing Review (1993) 'Derivative Instruments: fed notes highly concentrated activity in US', 26 June, p.84

Jarrow, R. and Turnbull, S. (1992) 'Credit risk: drawing the analogy', *Risk*, October, pp. 63–70.

Kaufman, H. (1992) 'Capital markets regulation: ten reasons to reform', *Euromoney*, November pp.54–57.

King, W. (1992) 'Remodeling the mortgage', *Institutional Investor Forum Supplement*, December pp.30–31.

Lee, P. (1992) 'How to exorcise your derivatives demons', *Euromoney*, September, pp.36–48.

Leong, K. (1992) 'Options: model choice', *Risk*, December, pp.60–66.

Lipin, S. (1993) 'Bankers fight to head off regulation of derivatives', *Asian Wall Street Journal*, 22 July, p.19

Luskin, D. (1987) *Index Futures and Options* (New York: John Wiley & Sons).

Makin, C. (1991) 'Hedging your derivatives doubts', *Institutional Investor*, December, pp.93–102.

Mayo, H. (1983) *Investments* (Chicago: Dryden Press).

McKenzie, S. (Ed.) (1992) Risk Management with Derivatives (London: Macmillan Press).

Merton, R. (1973) 'Theory of Rational Option Pricing', *Bell Journal of Economics and Management Science*, **4**, pp.141–83.

Merton, R. (1976) 'Option pricing when underlying stock returns are discontinuous', *Journal of Financial Economics*, March.

Merton, R. (1990) *Continuous-Time Finance*, Rev. Ed. (Cambridge, Mass: Blackwell).

Mills, R. (1977) *Statistics for Applied Economics and Business* (Tokyo: McGraw-Hill Kogakusha).

Muehring, K. (1992) 'Derivatives: who do you trust?', *Institutional Investor*, May, pp.51–55.

Muffet, M. (1986) 'Modelling credit exposure on swaps', *Proceedings of a Conference on Bank Structure and Competition*, (Federal Reserve Bank of Chicago) May, pp.473–96.

Napoli, J. (1992) 'Derivatives markets and competitiveness', *Federal Reserve Board of Chicago Economic Perspective,* July–August, pp.12–23.

Natenberg, S. (1988) *Option Volatility and Pricing Strategies* (Chicago: Probus).

Options Institute (Eds) (1990) *Options* (Homewood, Illinois: Business One Irwin).

Organization for Economic Cooperation and Development (1992) *Risk Management in Financial Services* (Paris: OECD).

Phillips, S. (1993) 'Don't panic! Don't panic!' *Risk*, January, p.68.

Picker, I. (1991) 'Son of swaps', *Institutional Investor*, February, pp.119–122.

Picker, I. (1993) 'The daffier side of derivatives', *Institutional Investor*, February, pp.102–107.

Rees, M. (1993) 'Reverse amortizing swaps gain in popularity', *Bloomberg Magazine*, July, p.21.

Rendleman and Bartter (1980) 'The Pricing of Options on Debt Securities', *Journal of Financial and Quantitative Analysis*, **15**, pp.11–24.

Risk (1992) '5 years of risk', December, pp.35–58.

Risk and Devon (1993) 'Proceedings from 'The Risk and Devon conference on equity derivatives: pricing, hedging and risk management', February, (London: Risk and Devon).

Robinson, D. (1992) 'LDC derivatives: stuck at the crossroads', *Euromoney*, October, pp.33–44.

Robinson, D. (1993) 'Equity derivatives: tailored for all tastes', *Euromoney*, February, pp.63–64.

Roll, R. (1977) 'An analytic valuation formula for unprotected American call options on stocks with known dividends', *Journal of Financial Economics*, **5**, pp.251–8.

Ross, S. (1991) *A Course in Simulation* (New York: Macmillan Publishing).

Rowley, A. (1991) 'Japanese firms return to no-frill bonds', *Far Eastern Economic Review*, 21 November, p.70.

Schwartz, R. and Smith, C. (Eds) (1990) *Handbook of Currency and Interest Rate Risk Management* (New York: New York Institute of Finance).

Schwartz, R. and Smith, C. (Eds) (1993) *Advanced Strategies in Financial Risk Management* (New York: New York Institute of Finance).

Shale, T. (1993) 'How ISDA got the message', *Euromoney*, April, pp.75–76.

Sheridan, E. (1992) 'The growing derivatives market', *Futures Industry*, December , pp.10–14.

Shinmura, T. (1993) 'Derivative trading outpaces watchdogs', *Nikkei Financial Weekly*, 8 March, p.15.

Shirreff, D. (1985) 'The fearsome growth of swaps', *Euromoney*, October, pp.247–61.

Shirreff, D. (1993) 'Making ends meet', *Risk*, February, pp.16–21.

Smith, C. (1976) 'Option pricing', *Journal of Financial Economics*, **3**, pp.3–51.

Smith, C., Smithson, C. and Wakeman, L. (1986) 'Credit risk and the scope and regulation of swaps', *Proceedings from a Conference on Bank Structure and Competition*, (Federal Reserve Bank of Chicago) May, pp.166–185.

Smith, C., Smithson, C. and Wilford, S. (1990) *Managing Financial Risk* (New York: Harper and Row).

Stark, B. (1983) *Special Situation Investing* (Homewood, Illinois: Dow-Jones Irwin).

Treanor, J. *et al.* (1992) 'Equity-linked debt: from boom to bust', *International Financing Review,* Review of the Year 1992, pp.156–159.

Waters, R. (1992) 'BIS warns banks over growth in derivatives trading', *Financial Times*, 25 November, p.19.

Waters, R. (1992) 'Search for security', *Financial Times*, 23 October, p.28.

Whaley, R. (1981) 'On the valuation of American call options on stocks with known dividends', *Journal of Financial Economics*, **9**, pp.207–12.

Whittaker, J.G. (1987) 'Pricing interest rate swaps in an options pricing framework', *Working paper RWP, 87–02* (Federal Reserve Bank of Kansas City).

Index